www.brookscole.com

www.brookscole.com is the World Wide Web site
for Thomson Brooks/Cole and is your direct source to
dozens of online resources.

At *www.brookscole.com* you can find out about supple-
ments, demonstration software, and student resources.
You can also send e-mail to many of our authors and pre-
view new publications and exciting new technologies.

www.brookscole.com
Changing the way the world learns®

MACRO SOCIAL WORK PRACTICE

A Strengths Perspective

Dennis D. Long
Xavier University

Carolyn J. Tice
University of Maryland, Baltimore County

John D. Morrison
Aurora University

THOMSON
BROOKS/COLE

Australia • Canada • Mexico • Singapore • Spain
United Kingdom • United States

Executive Editor: Lisa Gebo
Assistant Editor: Alma Dea Michelena
Editorial Assistant: Sheila Walsh
Technology Project Manager: Barry Connolly
Marketing Manager: Caroline Concilla
Marketing Assistant: Mary Ho
Advertising Project Manager: Tami Strang
Project Manager, Editorial Production: Matt
   Ballantyne

Art Director: Vernon Boes
Print/Media Buyer: Lisa Claudeanos
Permissions Editor: Chelsea Junget
Production Service: Stratford Publishing Services
Compositor: Stratford Publishing Services
Copy Editor: Judy Ashkenaz
Cover Designer: Denise Davidson
Cover Image: Copyright © Corbis
Text and Cover Printer: Webcom

Printed in Canada
1 2 3 4 5 6 7 09 08 07 06 05

For more information about our products, contact us at:
Thomson Learning Academic Resource Center
1-800-423-0563

For permission to use material from this text or
product, submit a request online at
http://www.thomsonrights.com.
Any additional questions about permissions
can be submitted by email to
thomsonrights@thomson.com.

Library of Congress Control Number: 2004116043

ISBN 0-534-64043-5

Thomson Higher Education
10 Davis Drive
Belmont, CA 94002-3098
USA

Asia (including India)
Thomson Learning
5 Shenton Way
#01-01 UIC Building
Singapore 068808

Australia/New Zealand
Thomson Learning Australia
102 Dodds Street
Southbank, Victoria 3006
Australia

Canada
Thomson Nelson
1120 Birchmount Road
Toronto, Ontario M1K 5G4
Canada

UK/Europe/Middle East/Africa
Thomson Learning
High Holborn House
50/51 Bedford Row
London WC1R 4LR
United Kingdom

Latin America
Thomson Learning
Seneca, 53
Colonia Polanco
11560 Mexico
D.F. Mexico

Spain (includes Portugal)
Thomson Paraninfo
Calle Magallanes, 25
28015 Madrid, Spain

To my companion and partner in life, Joan Holle Long
Dennis

To my favorite niece and nephew, Amy C. Tice and Brian G. Tice
Carolyn

To my wife and best friend, Maye Morrison
John

Contents

Preface

During the past decade, social work has experienced a notable increase in the number of articles and books examining the strengths perspective. Similarly, there has been a ground swell in the number of scholarly works on the subject of macro social work practice. For the most part, however, these subjects have been treated somewhat independent of each other. As the title implies, *Macro Social Work Practice: A Strengths Perspective* was written to provide social workers with a comprehensive integration of macro social work practice using ideas and concepts derived from the strengths perspective.

To date, this book is a first of its kind in social work education. In his most recent work, Dennis Saleebey has expanded his vision of the strengths perspective to include additional content and thinking on environmental context. Similarly, macro practice texts typically include some information, a chapter or two, on the relevance of the strengths perspective for practice. Until now, what has been missing is a comprehensive analysis of the implications of the strengths perspective for large-scale social change. This is the impetus for this text.

More specifically, this book was written for social work professionals aspiring to enhance and develop professional abilities and skills in macro-level change through the use of concepts and premises derived from the strengths perspective. Because the primary focus is on knowledge, values, and skills applicable to generalist social practice, *Macro Social Work Practice: A Strengths Perspective* is intended primarily for upper-level practice courses in the undergraduate curriculum and foundation coursework in practice at the graduate (MSW) level.

For the sake of students, materials are presented in an orderly, structured fashion that is both theoretical and applied in nature. At the beginning of each chapter, students can review a list of the topics to be examined. Each chapter concludes with a brief summary, a list of key terms, and a relevant case example.

Instructors will appreciate the time and attention given to the relationship between macro practice, the strengths perspective, and other related orientations (e.g., empowerment theory, problem solving, and the ecological perspective). Professors who traditionally approach macro practice from a community-organizing tradition will be excited about the primacy given to community-based practice and social advocacy. Colleagues who embrace macro practice in the form of a variety of social work roles and activities should also be pleased. For those interested in the pragmatic aspects of practice, every effort has been given to provide readers with hands-on, practical suggestions, and with skills for embracing basic tenets of a strengths perspective in macro-level intervention.

Finally, in what some may call a bold move, the notion of consumerism is embraced as a dominant feature throughout the text. In the first chapter, a rationale for embracing the consumer terminology is provided. The use of "consumer" is offered in the spirit of empowerment and is intended as an acknowledgment of the strengths and rights possessed by the people who come to our agencies and organizations for services.

ACKNOWLEDGMENTS

The authors would like to thank Lisa Gebo, Sheila Walsh, Judy Ashkenaz, Richard Welna, Peg Hubbard, and Andrea Driggs for their assistance in the production of this manuscript. Special thanks to Diane Hall for her various contributions. We would also like to thank our reviewers: Sandra J. Altshuler, Eastern Washington University; Beverly Buckles, Loma Linda University; Dennis Cogswell, Radford University; Richard L. Edwards, University of North Carolina at Chapel Hill; Charles C. Cowger, Professor Emeritus, University of Missouri–Columbia; Phillip A. Fellin, Professor Emeritus, University of Michigan–Ann Arbor; Deneece Ferrales, Our Lady of the Lake University; Carol Langer, Arizona State University West; John McNutt, University of South Carolina–Columbia; Maria Roberts-DeGennaro, San Diego State University; and Joseph Walsh, Virginia Commonwealth University.

1

Defining Macro Practice

Chapter Content Areas

Conceptualizing Macro Practice

Use of Professional Self

Consumer-Driven Nature of Macro Practice

Origins of Macro Practice

Casework, Group Work, and Community Organizing

Social Planning and Research

Political Ideology and Movements

A War on Poverty

The Family Assistance Plan

Reaganomics and the Safety Net

Wealthfare

A Contract for America

The Welfare Reform Act of 1996

A War on Terrorism

Analyzing Environmental Influences

NASW's *Code of Ethics* and Macro Practice

Empowerment and Macro Practice

Respect for Consumers

Promoting Social and Economic Justice

MACRO SOCIAL WORK PRACTICE

What is macro social work practice? You will grapple with this question not only as you read this book, but also throughout your career as a professional social worker. Indeed, practitioners and educators often differ when asked to define *macro social work practice*. If you were to ask the instructors in your program for their definition, you might be surprised at the variety of responses. Definitions would most likely vary depending on the era of the social worker's professional education, the program from which he or she graduated, and his or her practice experiences.

For many social workers educated in the 1950s, 1960s, and 1970s, the term **macro practice** probably still seems somewhat foreign. These social workers are more familiar with the notions of social casework (Perlman, 1957), environmental work (Hollis, 1972), innovation and change with organizations and communities (Rothman, Erlich, & Teresa, 1976), social welfare administration and research (Friedlander, 1976), and group work for social reform (Roberts & Northen, 1976). It would not be unusual for social workers of this era to perceive macro social work in terms of community organization, administration, research, or policy development. Indeed, much of this same language continues to be used today, as social workers have a propensity to define macro practice in terms of the roles they enact or the functions they perform.

BOX 1.1

In one of the original books written on the topic, Meenaghan, Washington, and Ryan describe macro practice as "the broad area of change/dynamic adjustment within the human service area as it relates to the human service practice specialties of planning, administering, evaluating, and organizing human service activities" (1982, p. 6). In a more recent text, Meenaghan describes macro social work practice in terms of intervening with organizations, communities, and groups of people (Meenaghan & Gibbons, 2000).

Conceptualization of macro practice, as of social work practice in general, has changed over the years and continues to evolve. From the very origins of our profession, social workers have demonstrated innovation and flexibility in defining their roles and tasks in relation to the needs and demands of those served, as Gibelman describes:

> Fluidity exists with regard to how the profession defines itself and the boundaries of what constitutes social work practice. Some of these debates about identity and status have been waged since the earliest days of the profession . . . various definitions have emerged about the purview of the profession in what can be termed an evolutionary and consensus-building process. (1999, p. 299)

Indeed, social work is a dynamic profession in that, both knowingly and also perhaps in less rational ways, its identity has been responsive to social conditions and climate. "Social work practice and education have long been influenced by development in the broader U.S. economy, particularly as they affected such issues as employment and unemployment" (Reisch & Gorin, 2001, p. 9). In addition, popular beliefs, dominant U.S. interests, cultural norms, historical events, and market or global forces have helped to shape what constitutes a social work perspective for helping professionals at any given point in time.

Throughout this book, social advocacy and **community organizing** are referenced as two particularly important methods within social work practice for creating social change. Indeed, these are macro-level approaches familiar to almost every social worker. However, the prominence of community organizing and social advocacy in this book is not intended to negate or minimize the value of other social work methods (e.g., social planning, locality development, policy development, research, and administration) in macro practice. To the contrary, a variety of approaches for use in macro social work practice are examined and endorsed in this text.

One of the more challenging aspects of being a helping professional involves the ability to question and reflect on one's conscious use of self in relation to professional ideals, the enactment of professional roles, the place of practice, and the social-cultural context of human existence. Given that macro practice is a fluid notion, make this pledge early in your professional career: *Never lose a commitment to define macro social work practice as a component driven by the will and wants—the determination—of consumers of services.*

Indeed, it is the hopes and desires of the people being served, not necessarily those of the people in positions of power and authority, that are the foremost consideration for social workers. Although it is important to work within the established mandates and norms of agencies and our profession, our primary alliance is with the consumers of social services. In any form of social change, power inherently lies in the strengths and resources of these consumers themselves, whether they are individuals, families, or groups of people (Saleebey, 1992). However we choose to define macro social work practice, respect for the consumer-driven nature of social work practice is paramount.

WHAT DOES "MACRO" MEAN?

Macro means large-scale or big. In social work, it involves the ability to see and intervene in the big picture, specifically with larger systems in the socioeconomic environment. Macro social work practice can include collaboration with consumers to strengthen and maximize opportunities for people at the organizational, community, societal, and global levels. Indeed, many social workers would argue that it is the macro level—the attention given by social workers to the big social issues of importance to consumers—that distinguishes social work from other helping professions (Glisson, 1994).

Historically, another term that has been used to describe macro social work practice is *indirect work*. Although this term is becoming less popular, the word *indirect* served for many years as a reference to social work's commitment to environmental modification and the alleviation of social problems. Whereas *direct practice* connoted face-to-face contact with clients aimed at supporting or strengthening them as individuals, *indirect practice* was the catch phrase for change efforts involving the environment and the social welfare system (Pierce, 1989, p. 167).

For many other social workers, the "macro" in "macro practice" is synonymous with community organizing. Rothman (1964, 1974, 1995) provides the

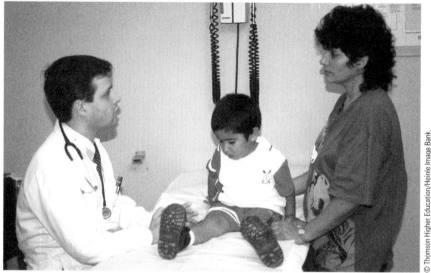

social work profession with a pointed conceptualization of large-scale change that emphasizes three basic modes: locality development, social planning, and social action. As summarized by Weil (1996), **locality development** focuses on community capacity building and the role of social workers in engaging citizens in determining and resolving community-based issues. **Social planning** refers to the use of a rational problem-solving strategy aimed at combating community problems. Social workers use their knowledge and skills in research, assessment, and program implementation as they work with clients to identify logical steps and means of addressing community problems. **Social action** references the ability of social workers and consumers of services to confront and change power relationships and the structure and function of important social institutions in communities.

As can be seen, the term *macro* has several connotations, both general and specific. In this text, preference is given to the term *macro social work practice*. Indirect practice is often viewed as a nebulous, uncelebrated term in social work (Johnson, 1999), but conceptualizing macro practice primarily in terms of community organizing is limiting. *Macro social work practice* is more specific, suggesting the importance of strengthening higher order social systems—organizations, communities, and societies.

As a contemporary illustration of macro practice, consider the frustration many people feel with health care and mental-health care in the United States. For those fortunate enough to have medical insurance, the advent of managed care has forced people to try to learn a new and often confusing terminology of co-payments, provider status, benefit levels, preferred drug lists, average lengths of stay, and diagnostic groupings (Long & Heydt, 2000). A traditional, micro social work approach would focus on helping individuals and families to navigate health care delivery systems successfully. By contrast, a macro social work approach emphasizes seeking ways in which consumers can redefine and change managed care, both locally and nationally, in order to achieve control over their lives and promote optimum access to modern medicine.

HAS MACRO PRACTICE ALWAYS BEEN A PART OF SOCIAL WORK?

The answer is yes, to varying degrees. Interest in promoting social reform and social justice to advance the well-being of people has been a major function of social work practice throughout the years. A more thorough answer, however, requires a brief overview of the historical development of macro social work practice in the United States.

Some of the first writings associated with the profession of social work provide insight into the importance of affecting larger structural issues in the lives of consumers. As a student of social work, take some time to acquaint yourself with some of the influential writers in the field—the "ghosts" of social work past. There is no substitute for reading the original words and impressions of these great authors and innovators.

Be forewarned that the following historical overview emphasizes social determinism. There is an underlying assumption about the importance of social forces (such as historical occurrences, political climate, and economic circumstances) in affecting people's desire and ability to engage in large-scale social change. Such an outlook is useful for ascertaining the various factors involved in helping to shape the methods and forms of macro social work practice over the past century.

MACRO SOCIAL WORK IN THE TWENTIETH CENTURY

The Progressive Era: Mary Richmond and Jane Addams

Mary Richmond is often described as one of the eminent founders of social work. In *Social Diagnosis* (1917), Richmond describes social work as consisting of a common body of knowledge based on collecting and understanding information, especially social evidence. Richmond was one of the first social workers to advocate for a more comprehensive method of inquiry and intervention, including a "wider view of self" (p. 368). Such an approach embraced an analysis of various forms of human relations, consideration of the social situation and surroundings, inquiries concerning social agencies, and an appreciation of economic conditions and neighborhood improvement (pp. 369–370).

While acknowledging that a majority of social workers at the turn of the twentieth century engaged in casework, aimed at "the betterment of individuals and families," Richmond clearly recognized the need for "betterment of the mass" (p. 25). But what is meant by "betterment"? The term implies strengthening, improving—making "better off." At a very early stage in the development of our profession, Richmond acknowledges, "mass betterment and individual betterment are interdependent," with the need for "social reform and social case work of necessity progressing together" (p. 25).

For Richmond, the movement from a focus on the individual to an emphasis on social concerns was directly attributable to the influence of the charity organizations. New methods emphasizing "social" diagnosis were born from campaigns by a number of social activists working to improve housing, promote child labor reform, and prevent the spread of diseases like tuberculosis. Richmond notes that in charity organizations, "some of [the] earliest leaders had grasped the idea of the sympathetic study of the individual in his [or her] social environment" (p. 32). Undoubtedly, as social activists worked to strengthen opportunities and economic means for their consumers of services, casework "had at its command more varied resources, adaptable to individual situations." As a consequence, "the diagnosis of those situations assumed [a] fresh [and broader] importance" (p. 32).

Mary Richmond is one of the best known leaders of the Charity Organization Society (COS) movement, which was grounded in convictions derived from England. Leaders of the COS often "believed that many poor people were unworthy, so that applicants for aid should be carefully investigated. Records were to be kept about each case, and a central registry was developed to ensure that no person received aid from more than one source" (Suppes & Wells, 2003, p. 87). These written records eventually became important sources of documentation for use in advocating for social change and reform. Many would argue that these early efforts to advocate for reform on the basis of documented human need constituted the beginning of community welfare planning in the United States and eventually gave rise to what we now know as the community-based United Way system.

The relationship between human need, casework, and social reform is an interesting and profound theme when we consider the emergence of macro social work practice. Richmond was astute in advancing the argument that necessity, as evidenced by human struggle, was a driving force for social reform and ultimately responsible for reshaping casework into "social" casework. If Richmond's perceptions are correct, then the movement of social work practice toward a more structural, macro orientation is directly related to consumer plight and not merely a philosophical position fashioned by progressive professionals.

Characterized by intense industrialization and massive immigration, the era from 1900 to 1920 was a decisive period for rethinking and reconstituting social services in the United States. As Mary Richmond was redefining casework, Jane Addams's Hull House became a model for the settlement movement in large urban areas across the nation. In addition to providing a wide array of goods and services in the poorest neighborhoods, settlement houses and the settlement movement "concentrated on the totality of problems in a single geographical area . . . the central focus was on the experiences, thinking, and actions of local populations that could affect broad social and economic reform" (Haynes & Holmes, 1994, p. 65).

Settlement houses were neighborhood houses or community centers. In addition to addressing the everyday needs of local residents, they often provided recreational, instructional, and community programs (Federico, 1973, p. 170). From a macro perspective, settlement houses established a place for people to meet, express ideas, share concerns, and pool their strengths. From this new, informal setting emerged leadership in identifying, specifying, and organizing to meet the issues of the day.

Indeed, the very origins of **group work** are often traced to the settlement movement. Today, many people simply see group work as synonymous with group therapy. For settlement workers, however, group meetings were not merely a medium to educate and treat people, but also a forum for exploring community-based needs. In other social work classes, you will learn more about the multiple functions and purposes of group work. Here, it is important to make a mental note that group work is a valuable method for promoting larger-scale change and an important means of promoting collective action.

It is noteworthy that although charity workers and volunteers had been hearing the struggles and misfortunes of individuals for some time, the formation of settlement houses was instrumental in identifying and advancing a united voice from consumers. At settlement houses, social workers could listen and learn directly from the mouths of people living in turmoil. This resulted in new, often group-determined ways of identifying opportunities and contemplating social change.

Given this context, it is not surprising that charity workers began to think of help as something more than face-to-face assistance to the poor for the purpose of addressing basic, everyday needs. What emerged was a penchant to seek ways to improve the neighborhood for the common good of its inhabitants. "This meant, in other words, both strengthening the community's capabilities and improving social conditions, policies, and services" (Perlman & Gurin, 1972, p. 36).

At the settlement house, people—individuals, families, volunteers, workers, community leaders, philanthropists—had a place to congregate, interact, and converse. What developed was a newfound community association—a "coming together." This constituted the birth of *community organizing*, a term that is used in social work to describe efforts to strengthen community participation and integration. Recognition of community organizing as an area of practice reflects an important conceptual shift in thinking about the delivery of social services. For social work practice, additional credence was given to structural change and to widening the scope of practice beyond treatment of the individual person and family.

In summary, within the first thirty years of the twentieth century, the origins of social casework, group work, community organizing, and planning were established in the United States. Indeed, many social workers continue to perceive themselves as caseworkers, group workers, or community organizers. Caseworkers adhere to a more individual, case-by-case focus, whereas group workers and community organizers are more closely aligned with themes of social reform.

The Expansion of Social Work in the 1930s and 1940s

Given the position that the social and environmental conditions confronting consumers have historically helped to shape social work practice, the stock market crash of 1929 and the subsequent Great Depression constitute significant social events that altered how most Americans, including social workers, viewed human need. As Garvin and Tropman (1992) suggest, "The Great Depression was a cataclysmic event in U.S. society and ushered in the era of public development" (p. 21). For those still harboring negativism toward the underprivileged and doubts about public responsibility for social conditions, the Great Depression represented a time for reconceptualization. Economic crisis and massive unemployment signaled the start of a new era for social work. Suddenly, without much warning, most citizens of the United States realized that the very fabric of our society required strengthening and enrichment to preserve both individual and common good.

Simply stated, work was not available during the Depression, regardless of an individual's motivation or will. Banks had failed; finding one's next meal was a challenge—and not just for the "other Americans." In cities, the homeless built small settlements of cardboard and tar paper shacks. In rural areas, farmers, many of whom had gone into debt to purchase land and machinery, could not make a living selling their crops. The United States was in trouble, and widespread unemployment necessitated immediate and decisive societal action.

Eventually, a federal response to this economic catastrophe came in the form of President Franklin Delano Roosevelt's New Deal. A myriad of public works and relief programs, the New Deal had as its backbone the passage of the Social Security Act of 1935. Social workers such as Harry L. Hopkins, who became a top adviser and New Deal administrator for Roosevelt, played an active role in the creation and implementation of New Deal legislation, policies, and social programming. To this day, the Social Security Act continues to fund many of the public assistance and entitlement programs that exist to help children and families.

The 1930s and 1940s were characterized by an ideological shift. Stimulated by the conditions of the Depression, "The [lingering] emphasis of the twenties upon the individual's responsibility for his or her own destiny could not hold up under the circumstances of the thirties" (Garvin & Cox, 1995, p. 86). People in the United States, now more than ever, came to realize the value of government intervention in strengthening the country's faltering socioeconomic system. Extensive and readily observable deprivation prompted citizens to view poverty as a *public issue* rather than a *private trouble* and resulted in the establishment of forms of social insurance, public assistance, and a variety of health and welfare services. This was a crucial period in the history of the United States, as intensive social planning and programming signified society as a legitimate unit of analysis for change.

The advent of World War II and deployment of troops to two battlefronts instilled solidarity in the minds of the American people and promoted a strong federal government and national leadership. First and foremost, national threat demanded a societal response. Individuals were called upon to sacrifice for the common good in many ways—via military service, work in factories, and public service, as well as through the rationing of goods. Patriotism evoked an "all for one and one for all" mentality that accentuated the goal of winning a world war and served to downplay societal divisions.

Once again, the concept of social welfare and the perception of control over human need (public versus private) were being shaped by social events and occurrences as depression and war provided the broader societal context. The New Deal and World War II years opened the gates for a flood of social legislation and federal initiatives.

It is important to note that societal need and crisis often give rise to creativity and ingenuity among people. Human strengths flourish, individually and collectively, when necessary for the greater good. Times of distress can bring out the best in people. Need is often the precursor to invention, with people finding new and ingenious ways to rally when called upon. "A severely adverse event can serve as a 'wake-up call' . . . signalling that it is time to make significant changes" (McMillen, 1999, p. 459). People often benefit from adversity because they are forced to reevaluate their beliefs about the world and human potential.

During the 1930s and 1940s, social work became a national enterprise. As a result of the proliferation of domestic programs, social workers became heavily engaged in what would now be called social planning and **social research**. Social workers, like other Americans, had acquired a newfound appreciation for strengthening a high-order social system—our society. Although *macro practice* was not yet a term in social work vocabulary, the idea of macro social work practice was certainly taking shape and being formed.

BOX 1.2

Social planning involves framing solutions. It is based on specified goals and encompasses a comprehensive plan of action for creating social change. Consumers of services can be important actors in social planning, as they constitute both *content experts*—indicating what is needed—and *skill experts*—through use of their capabilities (Miley, O'Melia, & DuBois, 2001, pp. 268–269).

The 1950s and Early 1960s

Some social historians point to the 1950s as the dormancy stage of social activism in the United States. Preceding decades had seen the federal government as an active participant in social-economic intervention. Now, with the war over, a "back-to-work" mentality held sway. It was once again seen as the responsibility of individuals and families to provide for the necessities of life.

Women played a major role in winning World War II. They were introduced to the labor force in great numbers during the 1930s and 1940s for employment in the military-industrial complex and as replacements for men serving in the military. It was during this period that many women demonstrated a newfound versatility and resourcefulness in balancing the demands of employment outside of the home with those of child rearing. But in the 1950s, with the war still a recent memory, it was time for families to reunite and redefine the nature of family—particularly in relationship to work.

From a macro perspective, "the period between the depression and the 1950's was not a good one for the women's movement. . . . The conservative swing after the war discouraged militancy among women. Even the League of Women Voters, hardly a radical organization, showed a decline in membership during this time" (Garvin & Cox, 1995, p. 88). Men had returned from overseas and reasserted their social and occupational dominance in a postwar economic system.

Meanwhile, on the political front, fueled by Senator Eugene McCarthy's attack on those he deemed to be communists or "soft on communism," the virtues of social programs were coming under heavy scrutiny. Indeed, "the 1950s saw an increasingly virulent series of attacks on public welfare and health insurance, both viewed as overtures to an un-American welfare state (Axinn & Levin, 1975, p. 235). Despite lingering unemployment, public sentiment grew in the 1950s for curtailment and reduction of the welfare rolls.

Although few would depict the 1950s as a progressive era with respect to large-scale social change, one of the most powerful court rulings in the history of the United States occurred in 1954 in the form of *Brown v. Board of Education of Topeka*. Amid a postwar sense of overall self-satisfaction, economic laissez-faire, and political conservatism emerged a decisive civil rights action from the U.S. Supreme Court. In a unanimous decision, the Court ruled that segregation of children in public schools on the basis of race, even when physical facilities and other "tangible factors" were equal, deprives the children of the minority group of equal educational opportunities (Rothenberg, 1998, p. 430). Hence, segregation in schools was struck down as a deprivation of equal protection under the Constitution as provided in the Fourteenth Amendment.

Although the 1950s and early 1960s hardly represented a radical age in American development, there was an emerging recognition of the need to create employment opportunities for the poor and upgrade the employment skills of the impoverished. At first, poverty was seen as "spotty" and regional in nature. In response, the Regional Redevelopment Act of 1961 targeted the development of new industry in areas suffering from a depletion of natural resources or a decline in the demand for traditional products (Axinn & Levin, 1975, p. 238). By the mid-1960s, however, research was demonstrating that poverty was not limited to any one geographic locale, but could be readily linked to economic and racial discrimination. "The Civil Rights Act of 1964 included a section prohibiting racial, sexual, or ethnic discrimination in employment and established an enforcement mechanism, the Equal Employment Opportunity Commission" (Axinn & Levin, 1975, p. 239).

Many historians consider the election in 1960 of John F. Kennedy as president of the United States over Richard Nixon particularly noteworthy. Although Kennedy served as president for only three years, his election signified a refocusing on the role of the national government in improving the lives of all citizens. Many of you may be familiar with the challenge President Kennedy issued in his inaugural address: '"Ask not what your country can do for you; ask what you can do for your country."

The 1960s also experienced an enormous increase in the number of people receiving public assistance, largely in the form of Aid to Families with Dependent Children (AFDC). The expansion of welfare rolls—the growing numbers of people applying for and receiving public assistance—revealed the magnitude of poverty in America and provided a gauge for measuring it. In an attempt to understand more fully the impact of social forces on joblessness, social scientists turned to the examination of racial discrimination and structural unemployment as dominant poverty-producing factors.

As the civil rights movement gained momentum and worked to strengthen the position and status of racial minorities, Michael Harrington (1962) and others educated citizens about "the other America." Harrington's portrayal of the economic misfortunes of the downtrodden helped to dispel the myth that those experiencing poverty somehow deserved their suffering.

BOX 1.3

The migration of African Americans from the South to the North in search of better employment contributed to the emergence of densely populated urban areas, particularly in cities in the northeastern United States. Unfortunately, the economic prosperity of the 1950s did not translate into economic opportunity and prosperity for all Americans. Regardless of motivation, many people, particularly African Americans, found it difficult to secure employment as a result of factors beyond their control, including their inability to acquire needed skills and credentials, the limited availability of specific kinds of jobs, and discrimination.

The Mid-1960s to Late 1970s

During the mid-1960s, the profession of social work, in a not-so-subtle way, shifted its outlook toward helping. Remember, this was a period of appreciable social change and upheaval in the United States. Citizens of all ages were questioning the role of the United States in the Vietnam War. Riots were occurring in urban ghettos, civil rights demonstrations abounded, and women were seeking liberation in new ways. Other Americans struggled with the presence of social-economic inequality, particularly amid an observable material abundance in the United States.

Indeed, the mid- to late 1960s was a time when the very ideological tenets of capitalism came under scrutiny, as many people found that simply making money for its own sake was neither sufficient for happiness nor a noble endeavor in its own right. In this climate, social welfare, too, found itself in the midst of a shift—a reconceptualization from charity to social justice (Romanyshyn, 1971). Once again, many people began to see and believe that large-scale social change was necessary to truly improve and strengthen the well-being of the underprivileged.

President Lyndon Johnson's 1964 declaration of a War on Poverty ultimately led to the creation of important societal and community efforts to bolster the nation and improve the general welfare of all its people. These initiatives included Volunteers in Service to America (VISTA), a domestic version of the Peace Corps; the Job Corps, an employment training program for school dropouts; and Head Start, a preschool educational program.

Massive expenditures on social programs inevitably prompted public and political scrutiny concerning the effectiveness of these programs and services. By the early 1970s, under President Richard M. Nixon, a more conservative, traditional approach began to reemerge, questioning community-building efforts and giving preference to a philosophy of self-help, individual responsibility, and private initiatives (Trattner, 1989, p. 305).

Although few would view the Nixon years (1968–1974) as a time of appreciable social advancement in the United States, President Nixon did in fact support—and even initiated—some interesting social policies with broad, wide-ranging implications. For example, it was during the Nixon administration that Daniel Patrick Moynihan proposed a guaranteed income for families via the Family Assistance Plan (FAP). Though never passed into law and widely criticized for the meagerness of its income allowances for the poor, the FAP represented the beginnings of a movement toward economic redistribution and a form of negative income tax. More important, the FAP signified that the role of the federal government in improving the lives of Americans had not been totally set aside, even by conservatives.

Life in the United States in the mid- to late 1970s was characterized by high inflation, rising unemployment, an aging population, and a mounting concern about overtaxation. Although many politicians (including President Jimmy Carter and Massachusetts Senator Edward Kennedy) and various labor organizations (such as the AFL-CIO) sought a workable national health care plan for Americans, little large-scale social change took place. Instead, by the late 1970s, the optimism of the mid- to late 1960s had given way to a sense of skepticism and doubt (Trattner, 1989, pp. 323–324).

The 1980s and Reaganomics

The election of Ronald Reagan as president in 1980 can best be summarized as an attack on the welfare state in United States. The mood of politics and public opinion had clearly moved toward a belief "that taxes and government programs are to blame for the deep-rooted problems in the economy" (Piven & Cloward, 1982, p. 13). Instead of advancing policies aimed at improving and strengthening social conditions as a way of eliminating poverty and injustice, human services and programs were now perceived simply as a "safety net." Government was seen as a costly intrusion into the lives of Americans that ideally would be minimized or eliminated. If social programs were to exist at all, they should be tailored to helping only those in the direst circumstances. Social services were a last resort. In this view, it was time for Americans to "pull themselves up by their own bootstraps" and not look to the government for assistance. Most of the spending cuts fell on public-service employment, public welfare programs, low-income housing, and food stamp programs.

The crux of Reagan's argument during the 1980s hinged on a belief that tax cuts and benefits for wealthy Americans would create an upward flow of income and monies that in turn would eventually "trickle down" to all Americans via a robust, healthy economy. In other words, followers of "Reaganomics" believed that as people became richer, economic opportunities (new business) and jobs would abound, even for disenfranchised citizens.

Unfortunately, Reagan's attack on the welfare state in America was particularly harsh and punitive for women and children. Abramovitz (1989, p. 362) notes, "The administration's decision to restrict AFDC eligibility, weaken work incentives, intensify work requirements, and otherwise shrink the program represented the beginning of the latest shift in the strategy for 'encouraging' AFDC mothers to work." Mandating that single mothers work, while ignoring the lack of affordable child day care services and family health benefits, was both ill conceived and often punitive to children and parents alike. The irony was that while Reagan sought ways to strengthen the economic system, most notably the pockets of the wealthy, an increasing number of poor mothers were being forced to find innovative ways to provide sustenance, supervision, and health care for their dependent children. Reaganomics constituted an unkind lesson that "wealthfare," benefits bestowed on the rich, often rests on the backs of the poor.

During the Reagan years, efforts involving macro social work practice turned to challenging the premises and misconceptions of conservative ideology and thinking. With special-interest groups, labor unions, various think tanks, and political action committees gaining power and exercising growing political and legislative influence in the United States, social workers acquired a new respect for the value of participation in the political sphere. As a result of Reagan's attack on public welfare, social workers became keenly aware of the importance of political activism. Legislative lobbying and support for the participation of consumers of social services in the political process became a focal point—one born largely of necessity.

Once again, Piven and Cloward, as well as other social workers and social work educators, were at the forefront of this movement as they initiated voter registration and political awareness campaigns with a focus on consumers of services as a source of power. There was a beginning appreciation for the idea that political action could be driven by and owned by consumers.

By the very nature of our practice, social workers often have firsthand knowledge of the stories of people in need. Disillusioned by a seemingly uncaring and underfunded system, consumers of social services often feel powerless and alienated. Consumers, questioning whether their voice or vote really counts, struggle to see the relevance of becoming politically involved. Piven, Cloward, and other social workers gave credence to the premise that when organized and informed, consumers can capture the attention and appreciation of politicians and policymakers.

The 1990s

In 1994, conservative Republicans achieved a major political victory as their party gained control of the U.S. House of Representatives. Built on the ideological foundation created in the 1980s by Ronald Reagan, and expressed in the newly written conservative rhetoric of House Speaker Newt Gingrich's "Contract for America," the mood of the country had seemingly become crystallized. Dominant beliefs included a continued emphasis on fiscal responsibility through the curtailment of government spending, a punitive outlook suggesting that only the very neediest should receive public assistance, an emphasis on traditional family structure and values, a reaffirmation of the primacy of work, and a desire for local or private control over human services (Long, 2000, pp. 64–66).

Though elected on a platform emphasizing social reform, improvement of social conditions for the poor, and the need for nationalized health care insurance, President Bill Clinton went on to sign into law one of the most restrictive pieces of social legislation in U.S. history—the Personal Responsibility and Work Opportunity Reconciliation Act of 1996. Labeled as "new federalism," this piece of legislation exacerbated the plight of the poor by reducing federal spending for low-income people by a projected $55 million over six years and further shifting social responsibility for the needy from the federal government to state, local, and private entities.

Although the 1990s were economically prosperous for many, with an unusually low unemployment rate, prosperity fell far short of reaching all Americans. Indeed, growth in the labor market involved the proliferation of low-wage service positions characterized by limited access to medical coverage, quality child care, or other family-friendly benefits.

During the 1990s, time restrictions were instituted that systematically drove consumers of public assistance from governmental rolls. Many Americans supported this move as fiscally responsible and as necessary in order to foster economic self-sufficiency by prying the poor away from dependency on the government. Unfortunately, the human consequences—both positive and negative—of forcing people in need off welfare remain largely unknown. How the poor fared through welfare reform, the real-life experiences and consequences of the legislation, clearly took a back seat to welfare reform's cost-saving benefits for the federal budget.

Many people would assert that social welfare programs and services are less needed during times of economic well-being. At face value, this argument would seem credible, but social workers know that certain segments of society (those who are only marginally employable, children, persons restricted by disabilities or by health conditions, and older adults) struggle to meet everyday needs even during prosperous times. Thus, although a strong economy provides employment to those capable of making the transition to work, "advocacy on behalf of those who cannot work is essential" (Cancian, 2001, p. 312). Additionally, "poor access to education and training, racism and other forms of discrimination, and local job market conditions are among the factors that limit employment opportunities" (Cancian, 2001, p. 312).

The 2000s

The tragedies of September 11, 2001, have most likely changed forever the American way of life and the manner in which Americans view human vulnerability. The deadly use of commercial aircraft by terrorists to destroy the World Trade Center and attack the Pentagon awakened a sleepy nation to the need for modernized security measures at airports and to the realities of twenty-first-century warfare, while the subsequent use of anthrax as a biochemical weapon confirmed that Americans could be attacked in a variety of ways.

Out of these atrocities emerged a unique and unprecedented spirit of patriotism, unity, and rekindled spirit toward giving to others in the United States. In the first two months alone following September 11, over $1 billion was donated to the American Red Cross and other associations for use in disaster relief. From catastrophe emerged an impulse toward charitable giving, born of the belief that terrorism could strike any of us at any given moment. The attacks on America during 2001 exposed the fragile nature of human existence in a graphic and televised manner.

In this way, at the dawn of the new millennium, the United States was abruptly drawn into the international scene. With little warning, Americans were introduced to a relatively new enemy: international terrorists. Economic resources, technological capabilities, and military might were quickly called upon to protect our homeland and preserve the American way of life. President George W. Bush acted promptly to reenergize the military-industrial complex in the United States to mount an unprecedented War on Terrorism.

On both a national and a global scale, the September 11 attacks demonstrate how, particularly in dire circumstances, Republicans and Democrats, allies and unlikely friends, even total strangers can be quickly called upon to bring their powers and capabilities to bear in combating a crisis. Unfortunately, when Americans began providing support and resources to the War on Terrorism or to aid victims of September 11, giving to other charitable efforts predictably suffered. Mobilizing and directing the assets and strengths of Americans, for whatever cause, serves to push other issues aside. The buildup of military forces and homeland defense diverts funding from social issues and causes. From a structural viewpoint, it is a matter of priorities and of selectively tapping into a community or society's energy and synergy.

WHAT INFLUENCES
MACRO SOCIAL WORK PRACTICE?

Several interesting observations emerge when examining the past century in relation to large-scale social change and social welfare. Foremost, the impetus and support for macro-level social work have weathered a somewhat nonlinear, to-and-fro course in U.S. history. There have been bursts of progress, when social workers and consumers of services have successfully moved forward to advance laws, policies, and programs promoting structural change for the needy. Conversely, there have been periods of stagnation, when society and social work practice have been consumed with promoting personal responsibility and individual achievement. And, although many would point to shifts in ideological winds (conservative versus liberal) as a primary influence on such fluctuations, in fact, the destiny of macro social work practice and social reform seems particularly sensitive to specific, less rational, social-economic conditions.

As examples, it is clear that war, catastrophe, economic crisis (depression, unemployment, stock market failure), demographic changes (population shifts, family composition, immigration), and international threat (war and terrorism) have the potential to affect public and professional sentiment concerning the importance of systemic, structural change in developing community and societal assets. If this assertion is accurate, then aspiring social workers would be wise to prepare for stormy seas. Yes, there will be times of smooth sailing for macro-level change. Conversely, social workers will have to endure steadfast waters dedicated to helping consumers cope and survive. Regardless of the social-historical era, it is important to remember that promoting consumer strengths and resolution of problems cannot be fully addressed "by small-scale solutions no matter how well intentioned our motivations . . . [instead] we must abandon those assumptions that constrict our policy responses so we can think and act boldly" (Reisch & Gorin, 2001, p. 16).

BOX 1.4

As an example of the impact of technological innovation, many social workers are turning to the Internet as a mechanism for promoting social change. Communication via the Internet can be an effective means of educating others about social concerns, promoting people's strengths, and coordinating social advocacy (Hick & McNutt, 2002). The Internet can be a timely source of information about various social issues and causes. It can also facilitate ongoing dialogue between colleagues and constituent groups. Information and communication are two important sources of power in relation to macro-level social change.

SOCIAL WORK'S COMMITMENT
TO MACRO PRACTICE

Commitment can take different forms at different levels. While social workers conscientiously strive each day to include macro activities in their practice, the profession as a whole is dedicated to finding ways to promote human dignity and improve social conditions. The National Association of Social Workers (NASW) and the Council on Social Work Education (CSWE) are two important professional organizations putting forward a **macro view,** both within the profession and in society as a whole. And, although social work has historically demonstrated a dedication to large-scale change, social-historical context often helps shape the forms this commitment takes. Hence, the doctrines, policies, and publications of the NASW and the CSWE serve as compasses in guiding us and keeping us focused on our professional identity.

One of the most profound documents for describing the mission of and rationale for social work is the NASW *Code of Ethics* (1996). Here, you can read the first paragraph of the preamble of the *Code of Ethics,* with key words underscored. These terms highlight the "macro" elements of practice and serve as a reminder that social work is more encompassing than our "do-good" image "of helping individuals and families to persevere."

> The primary mission of the social work profession is to enhance human well-being and help meet the basic human needs of all people, with particular attention to the needs and empowerment of people who are vulnerable, oppressed, and living in poverty. A historic and defining feature of social work is the profession's focus on individual well-being in a social context and the well-being of society. Fundamental to social work is attention to the environmental forces that create, contribute to, and address problems in living. (p. 1)

First and foremost, social workers are called upon "to enhance human well-being." This is not limited to the welfare of individuals and single families; it also involves "a social context" and "the well-being of society" in general. Social workers differ from other helping professionals in their focus on **environmental forces** and their ability to "address problems [and strengths] in living" overall. The "social" in "social work" connotes change for and with larger systems, including groups of people, organizations, communities, and society.

EMPOWERMENT AND MACRO PRACTICE

Special attention should be given to language in the NASW *Code of Ethics* pointing to "the empowerment of people." **Empowerment** is a key term for understanding and directing our efforts in terms of consumer-based "macro" change. In a general way, *empowerment* refers to the central and direct involvement of consumers in defining and determining their own struggles, strengths, and future. Social workers empower others by finding ways in which consumers of services can design and implement activities that accentuate their own unique assets in addressing needs (Delgado, 2000, p. 33).

Empowerment involves liberation. When consumers exercise the ability to plan and create social change, they gain control. Frequently, politicians and policymakers make decisions "for the sake of clients." As well intentioned as this may seem, the net effect of such a paternalistic approach runs counter to self-determination and prevents consumers from using their own capabilities to gain access to power in the social environment.

Practitioners know that when consumers take charge of the change process, a zeal for finding solutions soon follows. Indeed, the entire helping relationship becomes more collaborative: "Empowerment-based practitioners join with clients as partners and rely on clients' expertise and participation in change processes. They discern the interconnectedness between client empowerment and social change. These changes are not trivial! They redirect every phase of the practice process" (Miley, O'Melia, & DuBois, 2001, p. 88). Using an empowerment approach, consumers advocate for rights, services, and resources with assistance from social workers, rather than social workers acting on behalf of consumers.

RESPECT FOR CONSUMERS

You have probably noticed a preference in this book for the term *consumer* over *client*. Although this distinction may seem minor, it embraces the spirit of empowerment and a commitment to finding and supporting ways to advance the status of people being served. By definition, consumers are acknowledged as possessing certain rights and power. As consumers, people expect quality service and feel free to advocate for rights. By contrast, *clients* are seen as people who are being treated by professionals and are in need of professional expertise. The term *consumer* suggests that by virtue of being users of services, people are entitled to exert influence and control over their situation.

Using the term *consumer* in relation to human services has negative connotations, too. Many people, including helping professionals, associate the term *consumer* with a business orientation. In an attempt to sell goods and products, for example, marketing and advertising professionals would like us to believe that "the consumer is always right." This philosophy is put forward in order to maximize financial gain. Yet, we know that consumers are not always right. Additionally, consumers often struggle to gain control over product delivery and quality. For many people, accentuating consumer rights in the business world is seen as a strategy for boosting sales, not an earnest effort toward empowerment.

Given these limitations, the term *consumer* is given preference in this book. The quest for people to take control over their own lives, individually and collectively, lies at the heart of social work practice. The term *consumer,* at least in part, captures this spirit. It is important in human services to promote and legitimize the consumer-driven nature of social work practice whenever possible. Toward this end, *consumer* seems more desirable and more positive than *client* or *patient*.

As a social worker, you will probably be surprised to learn how commonly people in power design and implement programs and policies without even the most basic sort of consultation with the consumer. It is a condescending practice—a "we know what is best for you" approach. Control is the salient factor whenever people in positions of power make decisions for others.

SOCIAL AND ECONOMIC JUSTICE

The empowerment approach emphasizes promoting social and economic justice. Indeed, a major goal of social work practice involves helping consumers to explore and find ways to secure resources and enrich their lives. Social-economic justice also involves empowering consumers to become stakeholders in decision-making processes. Social-economic justice is an ideal condition, connoting a sense of evenhandedness or fairness where "all members have the same basic rights, protection, opportunities, obligations, and social benefits" (Barker, 1999, p. 451).

As social workers, we are particularly skillful in assessing peril, for both individuals and groups of people. In macro practice, there is a special sensitivity to **populations-at-risk,** groups of people who are vulnerable to (at risk of) oppression, discrimination, and/or exploitation. Traditionally, populations-at-risk have been defined in the United States in terms of gender, race, ethnicity, disability, sexual orientation, employability, and age. However, this is far from an exhaustive list. Many factors beyond the typical social-economic and demographic considerations can place people in various forms of jeopardy.

As just one example, are college students a potential "population-at-risk"? By virtue of your status as a college student, are you confronted with obstacles and unique forms of exploitation? Take a moment to see if you can identify a few of these hazards. Have you ever attempted to rent an apartment? Is being a college student a disadvantage or advantage? How? What about those irritating phone calls from credit card companies? Do you think that college students are targeted as inexperienced buyers prone to accumulating large debts at high interest rates?

When a strengths perspective is employed, special attention is given to identifying collective assets, capacities, and the potential for exerting change of various groups of people, particularly people deemed to be "at-risk." Unfortunately, it is very easy for helping professionals to become overwhelmed by the problems and inadequacies confronting consumers and to ignore the strengths people can bring to bear upon social situations and circumstances.

Indeed, social work's commitment to enhance well-being and promote social-economic justice reaches far beyond problem-solving strategies focusing on change with individuals and families. In subsequent chapters, a heavy emphasis is placed on the ability of social workers to encourage and advance collective action with a special eye focused on *strengths*—the abilities of people to grow, learn, and change—and *asset building*—the enrichment of resources and capabilities in organizations, communities, and society.

SUMMARY

In this first chapter, a host of concepts and terms (macro practice, consumer, strengths, empowerment, and social-economic justice, among others) have been introduced for your consideration. In subsequent chapters, these notions will be further defined, elaborated upon, and applied to practice.

You have also been given a social-historical overview of macro-level change in the United States. We have made the case that opportunities for larger-scale social change are often contingent on the social-economic-political conditions of any given time period. This is a reality that confronts all social workers in the macro components of their practice.

Finally, the concept of empowerment was briefly introduced. The chapters that follow are dedicated to a more detailed examination of the many realities associated with implementing various orientations and perspectives (e.g., problem solving, strengths orientation, empowerment, and ecological theory) in everyday social work activities.

A FEW KEY TERMS

macro practice	social action	environmental forces
community organizing	group work	empowerment
locality development	social research	populations-at-risk
social planning	macro view	

USING INFOTRAC®
COLLEGE EDITION AND INFOWRITE

InfoTrac College Edition

This chapter is dedicated to the definition and an analysis of macro social work practice. To gain a better sense of macro practice, it will be helpful to identify and read contemporary examples of macro social work practice. Complete the following exercise:

1. Go to InfoTrac College Edition.

2. Under Keyword Search, enter "macro social work practice" as a search term.

3. Find one article that describes an example of macro practice.

4. How is this article a good example of change involving larger social systems?

5. Indicate if and how the article embraces the notion of empowerment.

InfoWrite

Develop the habit of regularly questioning and critically analyzing information gleaned from various sources. For example, was the article you found published in a peer-reviewed, credible journal? The type of source is an important consideration, especially with the advent of the Internet, which has drastically increased the possibility of self-publishing. In order to refine your critical-thinking skills, do the following:

1. Go to InfoWrite.
2. Scroll to Critical Thinking.
3. Read the sections focusing on "Distinguishing Between Primary and Secondary Sources" and "Evaluating Information Sources."
4. Summarize in a paragraph the difference between primary and secondary sources.

Attempt to classify the article found in your InfoTrac College Edition exercise as either a primary or a secondary source of information. Be sure to give special attention to the notion of interpretation. Research articles and scholarly works typically follow prescribed formats and emphasize objectivity in the reporting of findings. Determine the merits of your article after critically evaluating its content and source.

CASE EXAMPLE: Inspiration from Consumers

Amy Sutton is a social worker at a regional chapter of a national organization dedicated to serving people diagnosed with multiple sclerosis. For the past ten years, she has practiced social work with people who have multiple sclerosis. For those of you unfamiliar with this disease, multiple sclerosis involves random attacks on a substance called myelin, a fatty material found in the central nervous system—the brain and spinal cord. When myelin is damaged, persons with multiple sclerosis develop scarring and often experience difficulties with balance, strength, fatigue, vision, and muscle control. Multiple sclerosis can also affect mental functioning. The progression of this disease is neither predictable nor uniform. Although people with multiple sclerosis may not be readily identifiable, they are often in pain and may experience odd sensations such as numbness. Those with more advanced forms of the disease may require assistance with walking and may experience a variety of other physical limitations.

Like many social workers, Amy is involved in a multitude of activities at her agency. She counsels consumers and provides information and referral services. Her chapter sponsors a "bike-a-thon" to raise money and broaden awareness about multiple sclerosis. Amy also organizes and facilitates group work. When consumers express an interest in a subject, Amy either serves as group leader or finds a professional leader appropriate for the topic. Group formation centers on a specific theme. In recent months, groups have explored various topics, including cognitive functioning, depression, living single, dating, and issues for the recently diagnosed.

In group work, Amy marvels at the enthusiasm and preparedness

(continued)

CASE EXAMPLE (*continued*)

of participants. She has found that people with multiple sclerosis have a passion to know. In a group exploring cognitive functioning, consumers came to sessions with the most recent research and Internet entries clutched in hand. In addition to sharing information, group members sought ways to educate employers about cognitive issues and discussed the many ramifications of disclosure in the workplace. Group members dictated the agenda and identified each week's subtopic.

Consumers are clearly in control of the format and direction of group sessions. Amy's role is analogous to that of a stage manager, as she uses her knowledge and skills to establish the setting and backdrop for group members to pursue collective interests. Meetings are consumer-driven and often focus on environmental change—for example, how can people with multiple sclerosis effectively educate family members, employers, and helping professionals to the specifics of their situation? Because multiple sclerosis can be one of those "invisible diseases," acquaintances and friends may struggle to understand what it is really like to have the disease. Conversely, once the diagnosis has been revealed, the public is often quick to pass judgment concerning the capabilities of people with multiple sclerosis.

Amy leaves most group sessions inspired and armed with new ideas born from the mouths of participants. Consumers sense empowerment as they exercise control, pursue strategies, and make decisions concerning disease management and how to relate to and educate others. Group members identify and use their capabilities to help themselves and their new comrades.

Amy Sutton also co-facilitates a consumer services committee for her region. She views this as one of her more important roles as a "macro" social worker. The consumer services committee consists of ten chapter members with multiple sclerosis and five professionals dedicated to enhancing services for people with multiple sclerosis. This particular committee meets every two or three months and reviews the various programs being offered at the agency. The primary goals of the committee are to help ensure that programs and services are appropriate and correspond to current needs—from a consumer perspective. This is a good example of how consumers can direct, control, and provide oversight for program development and implementation.

Indeed, nearly three years ago, this chapter's consumer services committee became embroiled in a delicate situation involving public relations. A national advocacy organization had commissioned a market research group to create public-service advertisements to raise public awareness about multiple sclerosis. Though well intentioned and attention getting, these commercials depicted women being suddenly attacked by barbed wire and placed in a form of physical bondage. People on Amy's consumer services committee were upset about such a portrayal of multiple sclerosis. What would young children think of it, particularly if their mother had recently been diagnosed with multiple sclerosis? Further, even for a worthy cause, is it wise or appropriate to show women being placed in bondage?

After much discussion, both within the consumer services committee and throughout the regional chapter, concerns were expressed to the national advocacy group about these advertisements. In addition, local and regional television companies were asked not to air these television spots. Once again, Amy worked to facilitate meetings and conversation, but the will of the consumers was the most important factor. Helping consumers of services to use their talents to rally around causes of importance to them can be inspirational at many levels.

THINKING CRITICALLY
ABOUT THE CASE EXAMPLE

1. People often associate group work with therapy. Yet Amy's groups clearly focus on macro-level, environmental change. Given the limited information provided in this case example, identify and contemplate two potential topics for group discussion (for example, in the areas of employment or delivery of services) that involve changes in larger social systems.

2. Creating a consumer services committee, like the one described in this case example, establishes a mechanism for eliciting input from consumers. Write a one-paragraph mission statement for such a committee, describing the committee's general purpose and function. How do you believe your document would compare to a statement written by consumers of services? In practice, what would be an optimal approach for drafting, writing, and formalizing a mission statement for a consumer services committee?

3. In this case example, entering into an association with a private market research group to promote public education about multiple sclerosis appeared to be problematic. Often, however, good results can be derived from difficult situations. Cast the reaction of consumers and others to the controversial commercials in a positive light.

REFLECTION EXERCISES

1. Ask a social work practitioner for her or his definition of "macro social work practice." Encourage this person to give you some examples of activities he or she performs that involve macro practice. Finally, ask what percentage of his or her work week is devoted to macro-practice activities. Discuss your results with classmates and contemplate how many hours per week you hope to be engaged in macro social work practice. How does macro social work practice fit into your idea of a professional social worker?

2. On your next visit to a social service agency, take special notice of the terminology surrounding delivery of services. Are the people participating in services called consumers, clients, patients, or some other name? If the term consumer is not being used, consider introducing it as a part of everyday practice. What is the reaction of others? Does the notion of consumerism have any relevance at the agency? If so, how? Do staff and administrators have any sense of what consumers really want to be called?

3. Attend an agency-based group meeting and focus your attention on consumer participation. How much, if any, of the group's dialogue is directed toward efforts for larger-scale (social) change in organizations, in the community, or at the societal level? Who seems to be in control of the group's agenda, and for what reasons? How could the group be more consumer-driven?

4. As a student, you are also a consumer. What kinds of counseling and intervention programs are provided at your university? Investigate how many social workers are employed in these programs? What opportunities exist for student representation on boards, councils, and other governing bodies of university entities, including those at your counseling center(s). Identify the ways in which your university encourages a student (consumer) voice and empowers students in the life of your school.

SUGGESTED READINGS

Jacobson, W. B. (2001). Beyond therapy: Bringing social work back to human services reform. *Social Work, 46*(1), 51–61.

Meenaghan, T. M., & Gibbons, W. E. (2000). *Generalist practice in larger settings.* Chicago: Lyceum Books.

Piven, F. F., & Cloward, R. A. (1971). *Regulating the poor: The functions of public welfare.* New York: Vantage Press.

Richmond, M. E. (1917). *Social diagnosis.* New York: Russell Sage Foundation.

REFERENCES

Abramovitz, M. (1989). *Regulating the lives of women: Social welfare policy from colonial times to the present.* Boston: South End Press.

Axinn, J., & Levin, H. (1975). *Welfare: A history of the American response to need.* New York: Dodd, Mead.

Barker, R. L. (1999). *The social work dictionary* (4th ed.). Washington, DC: NASW Press.

Cancian, M. (2001). Rhetoric and reality of work-based welfare reform. *Social Work, 46,* 309–314.

Delgado, M. (2001). *Community social work practice in an urban context: The potential of a capacity-enhanced perspective.* New York: Oxford University Press.

Federico, R. C. (1973). *The social welfare institution.* Lexington, MA: D. C. Heath.

Friedlander, W. A. (1976). *Concepts and methods of social work.* Englewood Cliffs, NJ: Prentice Hall.

Garvin, C. D., & Cox, F. M. (1995). A history of community organizing since the civil war with special reference to oppressed communities. In J. Rothman, J. Erlich, & J. Tropman (Eds.), *Strategies of community intervention.* Itasca, IL: F. E. Peacock Publishers.

Garvin, C. D., & Tropman, J. E. (1992). *Social work in contemporary society.* Englewood Cliffs, NJ: Prentice Hall.

Gibelman, M. (1999). The search for identity: Defining social work—past, present and future. *Social Work, 44,* 298–310.

Glisson, C. A. (1994). Should social work take greater leadership in research on total systems of service? Yes. In W. Hudson & P. Nurius (Eds.), *Controversial issues in social work research.* Boston: Allyn & Bacon.

Harrington, M. (1962). *The other America: Poverty in the United States.* New York: Penguin Books.

Haynes, K. S., & Holmes, K. A. (1994). *Invitation to social work.* New York: Longman.

Hick, S. F., & McNutt, J. G. (2002). *Advocacy, activism, and the Internet.* Chicago: Lyceum Books.

Hollis, F. (1972). *Casework: A psychosocial therapy.* New York: Random House.

Johnson, Y. M. (1999). Indirect work: Social work's uncelebrated strength. *Social Work, 44,* 323–334.

Long, D. D. (2000). Welfare reform: A social work perspective for assessing success. *Journal of Sociology and Social Welfare, 27,* 61–78.

Long, D. D., & Heydt, M. J. (2000). Qualitative analysis of a BSW field placement with a hospital-owned physician practice in a skilled nursing facility. *Health and Social Work, 25,* 210–218.

McMillen, J. C. (1999). Better for it: How people benefit from adversity. *Social Work, 44,* 455–468.

Meenaghan, T. M., & Gibbons, W. E. (2000). *Generalist practice in larger settings.* Chicago: Lyceum Books, Inc.

Meenaghan, T. M., Washington, R. O., & Ryan, R. M. (1982). *Macro practice in the human services.* New York: Free Press.

Miley, K. K., O'Melia, M., & DuBois, B. (2001). *Generalist social work practice: An empowering approach.* Boston: Allyn & Bacon.

National Association of Social Workers. (1996). *Code of ethics.* Washington, DC: NASW Press.

Perlman, H. H. (1957). *Social casework: A problem-solving process.* Chicago: University of Chicago Press.

Perlman, R., & Gurin, A. (1972). *Community organization and planning.* New York: Wiley.

Pierce, D. (1989). *Social work and society: An introduction.* New York: Longman.

Piven, F. F., & Cloward, R. A. (1982). *The new class war: Reagan's attack on the welfare state and its consequences.* New York: Pantheon Books.

Reisch, M., & Gorin, S. H. (2001). Nature of work and future of the social work profession. *Social Work, 46,* 9–19.

Richmond, M. E. (1917). *Social diagnosis.* New York: Russell Sage Foundation.

Roberts, R. W., & Northen, H. (1976). *Theories of social work with groups.* New York: Columbia University Press.

Romanyshyn, J. M. (1971). *Social welfare: Charity to justice.* New York: Random House.

Rothenberg, P. S. (1998). *Race, class, and gender in the United States: An integrated study.* New York: St. Martin's Press.

Rothman, J. (1964). An analysis of goals and roles in community organization practice. *Social Work, 9,* 24–31.

Rothman, J. (1974). *Planning and organizing for social change: Action principles from social science research.* New York: Columbia University Press.

Rothman, J. (1995). Approaches to community intervention. In J. Rothman, J. Erlich, & J. Tropman (Eds.), *Strategies of community intervention.* Itasca, IL: F. E. Peacock Publishers.

Rothman, J., Erlich, J. L., & Teresa, J. G. (1976). *Promoting innovation and change in organizations and communities.* New York: Wiley.

Saleebey, D. (1992). *The strengths perspective in social work practice.* New York: Longman.

Suppes, M. A., & Wells, C. C. (2003). *The social work experience: An introduction to social work and social welfare.* Boston: McGraw-Hill.

Trattner, W. I. (1989). *From poor law to welfare state: A history of social welfare in America.* New York: Free Press.

Weil, M. (1996). Model development in community practice: An historical perspective. *Journal of Community Practice, 3,* 5–67.

2

Adopting a
Strengths Perspective
in Macro Practice

Chapter Content Areas

Problem-Centered Practice

Problem Assessment

Presenting Problem

Private Problem

Public Problem

Common Human Needs

Conceptualizing the Strengths
Perspective

Ecological Theory

Strengths Assessment

Empowerment

Macro Practice

Traditional Communities

Person-in-the-Environment

Transactions

Formal, Informal, and Societal
Systems

Values

In the course of their work, social workers may experience a tension caused by conflicting theoretical approaches, paradigms, and models. On the one hand, there is a history of social work knowledge grounded in an under-standing of the complexities and problems associated with the bio-psycho-social environment (Rodwell, 1987; Franklin & Jordan, 1992; Gutheil, 1992; Cowger, 1994; Graybeal, 2001). However, there is also an increasing focus on the strengths perspective, an approach to practice that recognizes that people do better when they are helped to identify, recognize, and utilize their unique characteristics, capabilities, and strengths to create solutions to life conditions even when none seem possible (Weick, Sullivan, & Kisthardt, 1989; Saleebey, 1992, 1996).

Following the discussion of macro social work practice in Chapter 1, this is a good place to consider a **strengths perspective** for social work. Before launching into this topic, it is important to consider the influence of a problem orientation on the social work profession. For many social workers, problem-centered intervention is the cornerstone of macro practice. The **problem-centered focus** involves a series of processes intended to address an entanglement of social problems or conditions. More specifically, this orientation focuses on the problem or what underpins the problem, examining the cause of the problem by collecting evidence or data, assessing the data, reformulating the problem (e.g., via a specific problem definition, label, or diagnosis), setting goals, developing an intervention that addresses the problem(s), and evaluating outcomes.

This chapter examines the problem-centered approach, defines the strengths perspective, and integrates the latter with macro social work practice. Shifting from a problem-centered approach to a strengths perspective will present a challenge, calling on social workers to consider not only the unique strengths in individuals but also those in communities, organizations, and larger social systems.

WHAT IS THE
PROBLEM-CENTERED APPROACH?

Macro practice is often developed in response to social problems. For example, a community recognizes a growing problem with truancy in its middle and high schools. A school social worker facilitates a collaborative partnership between concerned parents, teens who have been truant and others who have not, elected officials, area clergy members, and teachers. The result is a multi-dimensional response. The group's collaboration results in extending morning free play in the gymnasium, providing program alternatives (e.g., work experiences and community service), and offering peer advising.

Unfortunately, the relationship between social problems and macro practice interventions is not always simple, and not all social problems generate macro-practice interventions. Sometimes social workers label a condition or situation as a problem to be corrected or as a source of future problems. A social problem, in this sense, is a condition that affects the quality of life for large groups or is of concern to economically or socially powerful people.

Take a moment to consider a condition that has a negative impact on a group of people. Perhaps it is the situation faced by older people who can no longer manage and maintain their homes in your community. Or perhaps you know people from another country, for whom English is not their first language; consequently, their educational, recreational, and employment opportunities are limited. Consider what needs to happen in these situations to gain the attention of decision makers. What could be some possible macro interventions to address these situations? Why is it likely that the situations might be ignored by the people in power—for instance, elected community officials?

It is important to keep in mind that problem definition is often shaped by a set of societal and personal values that reflect the preference of those in a decision-making capacity. Thus, a condition is labeled as a problem partly on the basis of analysis and partly based on the beliefs and values of people in powerful positions. For example, the high cost of prescribed drugs may be a significant problem for people with chronic health conditions and limited access to health insurance, but these high costs may not be of any concern to drug companies or to attending physicians.

To further illustrate the problem-centered approach, read the following situation and note the information that appears most important or significant to you. Even though you may desire additional information, think of what immediately comes to mind in terms of how would you start working in this situation.

> A board member from a rural AIDS task force expresses her anxiety about writing a grant for a community education program. Although the agency's board of directors has approved the grant submission, she fears that the rural community, with its geographic isolation, high poverty rates, conservative political officials, and fundamentalist religious views, is not prepared for AIDS education in the local high school. Nevertheless, the board member also knows that the number of people affected by HIV/AIDS is increasing dramatically in the tri-county region.

The social work material in this situation is very limited, but for the most part it takes only a few pieces of information to stimulate thinking about what is wrong, what are the community issues, and what may be the area's failings. A list of problems or deficits and beginning assumptions is being constructed. For the most part, the emerging picture is one of problems and program barriers. It is the problems that are emphasized as most significant, rather than the possible positive attributes of the rural community. Indeed, in many ways social workers often rewrite or translate the story told to us by consumers or communities into professional language, a language largely consisting of problems and deficits to which some form of intervention can be applied (Blundo, 2001).

The preoccupation with problems and human deficits, with what is broken or has failed in communities, has dominated the attention of social work assessment and practice. In current practice, a problem-centered orientation is related to the medical/pathology/scientific paradigm that underlies the traditional social work theories, practice models, and educational materials found in our social work curricula. Many factors enter into the social worker's problem assessment. Although the format changes from one agency or work setting to another, the problem assessment process follows a similar procedure in all of these settings. It looks like this:

Identification and Statement of the Problem The majority of social problems can be constructed as the interlocking relationship between three parts: (1) existence of a social condition or situation, (2) people's evaluation of the situation or condition as problematic, and (3) the reasons advanced to support the evaluation (Pincus & Minahon, 1973, pp. 103–104).

For example, consider a single mother who has three children under eight years of age and a high absentee rate at the chemical factory where she works. The factory manager is concerned with the pattern of missed work. The mother needs reliable child care, especially when school is closed or dismissed early. The children long to be with their mother and enjoy playing with one another. A social worker, employed in the Employee Assistance Program at the factory, is contacted regarding the mother's work absences. The social worker at the elementary school notices that the children are often tardy in arriving at school. The challenge is to examine the three components of the problem and identify the *presenting problem*—the reason that brings the consumer to the social worker (Pincus & Minahon, 1973, p. 106).

The presenting problem should be considered from a dual perspective: as a private situation and as a public issue. A private situation or condition is one that has a direct impact on an individual's quality of life or life opportunities— for example, failing health or limited work skills. The social worker must be aware that private situations are often created or exacerbated by public issues. For example, a person's failing health (a private situation) may be directly related to limited access to health care (a public issue). Thus, problem definition often links micro social work practice with the need for macro interventions.

Analysis of the Dynamic of the Social Institution At this stage, the social worker expands the problem statement to include the relevant social systems that define the situation. For example, in the presenting problem of a fifteen-year-old girl's unplanned pregnancy, the systems related to the problem include the girl's family, the father of the child, the father's family, and the school, to mention just a few.

This broad picture attempts to capture all of the individuals and systems affected by the defined presenting problem. Analyzing or mapping the problem in this way assesses the dynamics of a problematic social situation. To accomplish this, the social worker must apply current theories and social work concepts to explain and explore individual behavior, system responses, and societal responses.

Establishing Goals and Targets The social worker, together with the consumer, must establish goals for the defined problem situation. The goals must be both relevant to the consumer and feasible given the available resources and the systems involved.

Determining Tasks and Strategies The reason for the problem assessment is to design strategies that affect a course of action toward change. The cost of various strategies and the anticipated outcomes must be evaluated in order for the social worker and the consumer to decide what to do in what sequence. The social worker must exercise judgment in making decisions and work collaboratively to achieve desired goals.

Stabilizing the Change Effort Systems theory tells us that changing one aspect of a person's life or situation will have both anticipated and unanticipated consequences for other elements of the situation. Evaluation of the impact of change strategies is essential and directs the next steps in the problem-solving process.

Problem assessment serves as the traditional blueprint for planned change with consumer systems of all sizes. In the problem assessment process, the social worker is continually reassessing the nature of the problem to ensure the appropriateness of interventions. Thus, it is the problem that drives the majority of social work interventions across various consumer systems.

The premise of this problem-centered practice is derived from a medical/ pathology framework. It is the incapacity of the consumer(s) that is being addressed, not only in terms of the underlying cause of the problem but also in the ability of people to create change. As described in Chapter 1, the work of organizations such as the Charity Organization Society (COS) and of workers like Mary Richmond was directing the friendly visitors away from seeing poverty and human difficulties as mere moral failings in need of moral uplift and toward a view of human suffering as something that could be rationally understood. Mary Richmond, who was greatly influenced by the community medical practice efforts being made at John Hopkins University Hospital in Baltimore, Maryland, specifically formulated the start of much of our present-day social work language and thinking. The "study, diagnosis, and treatment" model used in the emerging science of medicine was adapted to the practice of social work.

Over the next decades, these concepts became the basis of practice and the benchmark of good practice within the developing schools of social work. Thus began the diligent practice of lengthy process recordings and intake summaries focused on obtaining a broad spectrum of information, believed to be necessary in constructing a diagnosis of the problem similar to that of an underlying medical condition.

These developments established a course for the social work profession. Specifically, social work embraced the medical/scientific method of data collection, analysis, and diagnosis. This prescribed a focus on the problem or underlying causes to be discovered by means of "objective" observation and inquiry. It demanded the incorporation of and reliance on theories of behavior and emotions to provide a means of understanding the consumer's problem.

As illustrated in Table 2.1, a result of these problem-oriented assumptions was the enormous amount of information that social workers are encouraged to gather today. Most of the practice texts used today in schools of social work contain pages of assessment forms, inventories, and grids that have been created to assist social workers in gathering an abundant amount of information. Mary Richmond's translation of the medical pathology model of practice is still the primary process used and taught today in social work practice.

During this early developmental period, social work practitioners and scholars began to embrace psychiatry and the emerging scientific inquiry into personality development, in particular psychoanalytic thinking and practices,

Table 2.1 Traditional Assessment Format

Typical Content Areas	Traditional Information
Presenting problem	Detailed description of problem(s)
	List of symptoms
	Mental status
	Coping strategies
Problem history	Onset of duration
	Course of development
	Interactional sequences
	Previous treatment history
Personal history	Developmental milestones
	Medical history
	Physical, emotional, sexual abuse
	Diet, exercise
Substance abuse history	Patterns of use: onset, frequency, quantity
	Drugs/habits of choice: alcohol, drugs, caffeine, nicotine, gambling
	Consequences: physical, social, psychological
Family history	Age and health of parents, siblings
	Description of relationships
	Cultural and ethnic influences
	History of illness, mental illness
Employment and education	Educational history
	Employment history
	Achievements, patterns, and problems
Summary and treatment recommendations	Summary and prioritization of concerns
	Diagnosis: DSM-IV, PIE
	Recommended treatment strategies

SOURCE: "Strengths-Based Social Work Assessment: Transforming the Dominant Paradigm," by C. Graybeal, *Families in Society: The Journal of Contemporary Human Services*, 82(2001), 235. Reprinted with permission from Families in Society (*www.familiesinsociety.org*), published by the Alliance for Children and Families.

along with the methods and practice procedures of medicine. The emerging knowledge base for future generations of social workers would be focused on the internal mental life of their clients. This internal mental life of clients would be at the heart of social casework. Social work was developing as a profession with a specific common mode or practice, to be called "social casework," and a body of knowledge and practice principles to support that work.

As noted earlier, this model prescribed a focus on discovering the underlying causes of the problem by means of "objective" observation and inquiry— using theories of behavior and emotions to understand the client's problem. It was the scientific knowledge possessed by the social work expert that was seen as necessary to decipher what had gone wrong or had failed, in order to address the problems.

SHIFTING TO THE STRENGTHS
PERSPECTIVE

Careful definition and explication of the problem are designed to create a base of knowledge to use in assessing the appropriateness of social work interventions. Although social work has a bias toward theoretical structures that define and label problems, the profession has not ignored the importance of individual and environmental strengths. Bertha Reynolds (1951) suggested that even before asking a client, "What problem brings you here today?," the social worker should first ask, "You have lived thus far, how have you done it?" (p. 125).

What are *strengths*? To begin this discussion, let's do an exercise to see how it feels to be described by your deficits and your strengths. This exercise can be done with a friend or alone.

First, using pathology or problem-based descriptive terms or words, describe yourself in seventy-five words or less—for example: *I suffer from long periods of feeling blue or down. Some call me depressed. When I am down, I don't clean up the house and I don't take good care of my hair or clothing. I often miss appointments on purpose and make up excuses. My eating habits become extreme. I either binge or go for long periods of time without food. Sometimes I drink an excessive amount of beer.*

Now, using strengths-based descriptive terms or words,

describe yourself in seventy-five words or less—for example: *I am a loyal friend who is kind and thoughtful. I really take good care of my family, especially my mother, who lives alone. I am independent, logical, and even enjoy a wonderful career. Even when busy with work, I manage to go to the gym three or four times a week. I am active in a neighborhood association and several social service organizations. My two Scotties give me much joy.* (Adapted from Van Berg & Grealish, 1997)

How did each style of introduction feel to you? If you were a consumer, which would you prefer as a starting point in a relationship designed to make major changes in your life? The exercise helps us to consider what it is like to be defined by our deficits, and it also sheds light on some common aspects of strengths. According to Saleebey (1997, pp. 51–52), some assets do commonly appear in strengths:

- People learn about their strengths and their world as they cope with the chaos and challenges of daily living.

- Strengths are the unique characteristics, traits, and virtues of people and communities. These attributes can become resources and a source of motivation.

- People's talents—for example, playing an instrument, writing, or home repair—can be tools to assist individuals and groups in attaining their goals.

- Cultural traditions and personal stories can provide inspiration, pride, and motivation to individuals in their communities.

The language of strengths gives us a vocabulary of hope and appreciation rather than one of disdain for the people with whom we work. Towle's (1965) *Common Human Needs* is a logical companion piece to the strengths perspective because it, too, recasts problems into a positive framework of common human needs. According to Towle:

> We fail to comprehend the interrelatedness of man's needs and the fact that frequently basic dependency needs must be met first in order that he may utilize opportunities for independence. Accordingly, funds are appropriated for school lunches and school clinics less willingly than for schoolbooks. (1965, p. 5)

In the tradition of Towle, social work intervention is a tool for helping people meet their basic needs, including food, shelter, clothing, education, and community participation (Tice & Perkins, 2002). Given this point, "people with similar needs differ widely in the barriers they face in getting their needs met" (Chapin, 1995, p. 509). Placing the emphasis on human needs presents social workers with practice considerations:

- When common needs are highlighted as the basic criteria, people do not have to be described as deficient to justify receiving benefits and having their needs met.
- The social work values of self-determination and respect for worth and dignity are operationalized by focusing on human needs.
- Recognizing common human needs supports the conceptual core of the strengths perspective, whereby social workers collaborate with people as opposed to exerting the power of expert knowledge or of institutions.
- Human needs involve communities as a resource that offers opportunities for growth and development (Chapin, 1995; Saleebey, 1992; Tice & Perkins, 1996, 2002; Towle, 1965).

More recent writers, including Shulman (1979), Germain and Gitterman (1980), and Hepworth and Larsen (1990) have stressed the importance of expanding assessments to include a focus on strengths and of including the consumer as an active participant in the change process. Saleebey (1992) advanced the assessment of strengths by articulating a strengths perspective for social work practice. According to Saleebey, the strengths perspective is represented by a collection of ideas and techniques rather than a theory or a paradigm. It seeks to develop abilities and capabilities in consumers and "assumes that consumers already have a number of competencies and resources that may improve their situations" (Saleebey, 1992, p. 15).

Table 2.2 defines the principles of the strengths perspective, as compared to problem solving, and provides a lens for examining social work practice. A theme emerges from the principles. Specifically, the strengths perspective

Table 2.2 Principles of the Strengths Perspective Compared to Problem Solving

Principle	Relationship to Social Work Practice	Problem-Solving Corollary
1. Every individual, group, family, and community has strengths.	▪ Encourages respect for the stories of clients and communities.	▪ The situation and the person in the environment are assessed.
2. Challenges may be threatening, but they may also be sources of opportunity.	▪ Clients are viewed as resilient and resourceful. ▪ Meeting life's challenges helps one discover capabilities and self-esteem.	▪ Problems are identified and prioritized.
3. The aspirations of individuals, groups, and communities must be taken seriously.	▪ A diagnosis, an assessment, or a program plan does not define the parameters of possibilities for clients. ▪ Individuals and communities have the capacity for restoration.	▪ Realistic goals and an intervention plan are developed.
4. Clients are served best through collaboration.	▪ The role of "expert" or "professional" may not provide the best vantage point from which to appreciate client strengths.	▪ Professionals facilitate a problem-solving process.
5. Every environment is full of resources.	▪ Communities are oases of opportunities. ▪ Informal systems of individuals, families, and groups amplify community resilience.	▪ Available resources are utilized.

SOURCE: From Saleebey, Dennis (Ed.), *Strengths perspective in social work practice,* 3/e. Published by Allyn & Bacon, Boston, MA. Copyright © 1998 by Pearson Education. Adapted by permission of the publisher.

demands a different way of seeing consumers, their environment, and their current situations. Social workers who approach consumers through a strengths perspective in practice can expect changes in the character of their work and in the nature of their relationship with consumers.

The strengths perspective is not yet a theory, although developments in that direction are underway (Rapp, 1996). Tice and Perkins (1996) contributed to the developing theoretical framework by specifying the ecological theory as a basis of knowledge for the strengths model. Carel Germain's "ecological perspective," first introduced in the 1979 and elaborated subsequently (Germain, 1985, 1991) attempts to advance social work theory with an analogy from biological ecology. Germain drew some ideas directly from ecology—most notably the concepts of environment, adaptation, and adaptedness—and uses others as suggested analogies. However, the concepts Germain cites as central to the

Table 2.3 Applying the Strengths Model to Ecological Concepts

Term	Ecological Concept	Strengths Model
Social environment	Conditions, circumstances, and interactions of people	Involves the community and interpersonal relationships as resources that are supportive of growth and development.
Person-in-environment	People's dynamic interactions with systems	Provides a sense of continuous membership and connectedness.
Transactions	Positive and negative communications with others in their environment	Fosters dialogue and collaboration to strengthen formal and informal support systems.
Energy	The natural power generated by interaction between people and their environments	Results in reciprocity that creates new patterns and resources.
Interface	Specific points at which an individual interacts with the environment	Recognizes that intervention begins in individualized realities.
Coping	Adaptation in response to a problematic situation	Highlights the innate ability of people to change and be self-motivated.
Interdependence	Mutual reliance of people on one another and their environment	Occurs in relationships based on reciprocity, a common purpose, and recognition of the community as a resource.

SOURCE: Adapted with permission from *Mental health and aging: Building on the strengths of older people*, by C. J. Tice & K. Perkins (Pacific Grove, CA: Brooks/Cole, 1996), p. 17.

ecological perspective appear to come mainly from the social sciences. The twin notions of *stress* and *coping* come principally from psychology, as do the concepts of *life course, human relatedness, competence, self-direction,* and *self-esteem* (Germain, 1991).

There are several reasons for selecting the ecological theory as a cornerstone of the strengths model. As illustrated in Table 2.3, the social environment component of the ecological theory involves the conditions and interpersonal interactions that permit people to survive and thrive in hostile circumstances. The concept of **social environments** includes people's homes, communities, and financial resources, as well as the laws and expectations that govern social behaviors. The ecological theory encourages active participation of people in their communities that reflects the "individuality of people and presents opportunities for personnel growth, mutual support, and an array of relationships" (Tice & Perkins, 1996, p. 16). Finally, ecological theory supports the value of transactions as a forum to build on the strengths of informal and formal support systems.

Table 2.4 A Strengths Assessment

Typical Content Areas	Traditional Information	Additional Information
Presenting problem	Detailed description of problem(s)	Emphasis on client's language
	List of symptoms	Exceptions to problem
	Mental status	Exploration of resources
	Coping strategies	Emphasis on client's solution
		Miracle question
Problem history	Onset and duration	Exceptions: When was the problem not happening, or happening differently?
	Course of development	
	Interactional sequences	
	Previous treatment history	Include "future history"—vision of when problem is solved.
Personal history	Developmental milestones	Physical, psychological, social, spiritual, environmental assets
	Medical history	"How did you do that?"
	Physical, emotional, sexual abuse	"How have you managed to overcome your adversities?"
	Diet, exercise	"What have you learned that you would want others to know?"
Substance abuse history	Patterns of use: onset, frequency, quantity	"How does using help?"
	Drugs/habits of choice: alcohol, drugs, caffeine, nicotine, gambling	Periods of using less (difference)
		Periods of abstinence (exceptions)
	Consequences: physical, social, psychological	Person and family rituals: What has endured despite use/abuse?
Family history	Age and health of parents, siblings	Family rituals (mealtimes/holidays)
	Description of relationships	Role models—nuclear and extended
	Cultural and ethnic influences	Strategies for enduring
		Important family stories
	History of illness, mental illness	
Employment and education	Educational history	List of skills and interests
	Employment history	Homemaking, parenting skills
	Achievements, patterns, and problems	Community involvement
		Spiritual and church involvement

Typical Content Areas	Traditional Information	Additional Information
Summary and treatment recommendations	Summary and prioritization of concerns	Expanded narrative—reduce focus on diagnosis and problems
	Diagnosis: DSM-IV, PIE	
	Recommended treatment strategies	Summary of resources, options, possibilities, exceptions, and solutions
		Recommendations to other professionals for how to use strengths in work with client

SOURCE: "Strengths-Based Social Work Assessment: Transforming the Dominant Paradigm," by C. Graybeal, *Families in Society: The Journal of Contemporary Human Services, 82*(2001), 238. Reprinted with permission from Families in Society (*www.familiesinsociety.org*), published by the Alliance for Children and Families.

Integral to ecological theory and the developing strengths model is a commitment to providing services in collaboration with consumers, confronting ineffective service systems, and strengthening existing social structures (e.g., organizations and communities). The notion that services and assessments are collaborative ventures supports the social work value of self-determination and nurtures the relationship between the social worker and the consumer. According to Tice and Perkins (1996), collaborative assessment occurs when (1) engagement is viewed as a distinct activity that constitutes the initial step in developing a relationship, (2) the relationship between the social worker and the consumer is recognized as essential to the helping process, (3) dialogue focuses on the consumer's accomplishments and potential, (4) consumers' directives and desires are addressed and not judged, and (5) mutual trust is discussed, acted upon, and felt by both the consumer and the social worker (p. 24).

Compare the problem assessment format described in Table 2.1 with the one found in Table 2.4. The additional information gathered in the latter format reflects the realization that consumers are the experts on their own lives. In essence, the social worker transforms the content of the assessment by the way it is written, through the questions asked of consumers, and by the inclusion of responses that come from a place of hope and possibility.

Empowerment is integral to the strengths assessment. Defined as the process of assisting people, families, and communities to discover and expend the resources and tools within and around them, empowerment requires that human service resources be tailored to individuals in such a way that those receiving help have the opportunity to experience the personal power that leads to change (Holmes, 1992; Rapport, 1990). A product of the 1980s and 1990s, Solomon's (1976) *Black Empowerment: Social Work in Oppressed Communities,* a classic in the policies and practice of empowerment, concludes that the aims of empowerment are to do the following:

- Support consumers in finding solutions to their own problems.
- Recognize the knowledge and skills that social workers can offer consumers.

- Consider social workers and consumers as partners in solving problems.
- Consider the power structure as complex and open to influence (Payne, 1997, pp. 277–278).

The basic objective of empowerment is social justice—giving people greater security and political and social equality—through mutual support and shared learning that moves incrementally from micro- to macro-level goals (Rees, 1991). Considering the following example:

CASE EXAMPLE

Rosa Gonzales is a social worker with a Family Services Center, a multiservice agency for families. During a session with Chung Li, an immigrant from Vietnam, Rosa learns that the Li family has been denied library membership because the family members are not citizens. Mrs. Li is concerned because she is working with her children on language acquisition, and the library is a major resource for books and films as well as an array of literacy programs.

After some investigation, Rosa realizes that the Li family is not the only immigrant family denied library membership. In time, Rosa and Mrs. Li organize a few families through the Family Services Center who agree to invite the county librarian to a meeting to discuss their needs. The librarian takes the concerns of the families to the library's board of directors for discussion. Eventually, the board revises the membership qualifications to include community membership.

How did the individual wants of Mrs. Li incrementally change to a macro focus of the community? What are the political and social issues embedded in the situation? Finally, what are some of the strengths Mrs. Li displayed? As illustrated by Mrs. Li, concepts of empowerment include control over one's life, confidence in the ability to act on one's own behalf, and access to choices and independence from others in making life decisions (Gutierrez, 1995). The following describe other important features of empowering practice:

1. All people and their communities have skills, capabilities, and the ability to change.
2. People have the right to be heard and to control their lives in the communities where they reside.
3. The problems of people and communities always reflect some issues related to oppression and discrimination.
4. Collective action is powerful, and social work practice should build on this.
5. Social workers must facilitate challenges to oppression that lead to empowerment (Payne, 1997, p. 281).

A strengths assessment nurtures empowerment by supporting the wants and needs of consumers with social work interventions that are designed through collaborative partnerships, based on soliciting and relying on consumer participation, and focused on understanding people within their own frame of reference. In essence, the strengths perspective, including the strengths assessment, recognizes the power of consumers, encourages consumers to use that power, and supports the collaboration of social workers with consumers to organize change across levels of practice. With this in mind, our attention turns to macro social work practice.

INTEGRATING THE STRENGTHS PERSPECTIVE WITH MACRO PRACTICE

At one time, the majority of social work programs included courses in community organization, development, and practice. Over the last few decades, however, the profession of social work has gradually shifted interest from community development and community organization as particular areas of practice, education, and inquiry to a more clinical focus.

A decision was made to write this book with an emphasis on **community-based practice,** because it is our communities that provide us with a network of care, support, membership, and celebration. The focus is primarily on traditional communities—cities, towns, and villages (Schriver, 1998). Warren (1978) concludes that traditional communities serve a number of vital functions, including socialization, mutual support, and social control through the enforcement of community norms. Whether urban or rural, traditional communities share similar traits, such as the inclusion of residences, recreation facilities, social service agencies, and businesses. Consequently, social interactions occur through work, play, worship, and other activities.

Take a moment to think about a community with which you are familiar, perhaps the community where you were raised or the one in which your university is located. Now consider the following questions:

1. Is the community located in a rural or urban setting? Describe the buildings of your community. Do you walk, ride public transportation, or use a private car to attend school, see a movie, or visit with a friend or family member?

2. What are some of the recreational opportunities in your community? Do the activities support people across the life cycle? For example, are there activities for young children, such as T-ball or soccer teams? What about organized events or facilities for older people? Describe opportunities for intergenerational activities?

3. Describe some of the social service agencies located in the community. List the churches, synagogues, temples, meeting houses, and mosques where people from your community worship.

4. Who has power in your community? Who is responsible for enforcing the laws and regulations of the community?

The dual professional role of working *in* and *with* the community offers social workers multiple opportunities to initiate macro change (Kirst-Ashman & Hull, 2001). For some of us, this means working at the polls on election day or supporting a candidate who will further social work goals. Some social workers are active in politically focused organizations such as Amnesty International. Others petition for revisions in laws, policies, or procedures aimed at fundamental social change.

One of the many advantages of social work education is that it develops a skill set for working with individuals and groups that is equally appropriate for community-based interventions. For example, communication skills can be used to listen and respond to one person or a mass gathering of people. Writing skills are necessary for preparing social histories and service documentation such as progress notes after an individual counseling session with a consumer; these skills are equally essential for harnessing the media, mounting writing campaigns, and creating educational materials. Advocacy skills, including assertiveness and negotiation, can be used to improve the quality of life for one person or an entire community.

In the course of work with individuals, families, groups, and organizations, social workers encounter community problems and opportunities for change. But the idea of intervening in the community or at the societal level may seem overwhelming, especially if you need to go beyond your specific job description. Further, unlike micro and mezzo social work (which involves practice with groups), macro change involves a variety of people and systems, so you will need extensive support from your colleagues, consumers, and other influential people if your intervention is to succeed. Specht and Courtney (1994) emphasize the role of macro social work practice in the change process as follows:

Social work's mission should be to build a meaning, a purpose, and a sense of obligation for the community. It is only by creating a community that we establish a basis for commitment, obligation, and social support. We must build communities that are excited about their child-care systems, that find it exhilarating to care for the mentally ill and the frail aged, and make demands upon people to behave, to contribute, and to care for one another. (p. 27)

How can the strengths perspective support your planned change process? To answer this question, it will be necessary to examine the foundation of knowledge and the value base of the strengths perceptive in the context of the macro practice. From the outset, you will notice the unifying effect that the strengths perspective has on micro, mezzo, and macro practice (Bronfenbrenner, 1979; Magnusson & Allen, 1983). The strengths perspective recognizes the interactions of each level of practice and the subsequent interconnection process that links strengths with a sense of empowerment (Compton & Galaway, 1994; Tice & Perkins, 1996).

The Foundation of Knowledge

According to Germain (1979), knowledge about people and their environment is a cornerstone of social work practice. Thus, with a person-in-the-environment focus, the strengths perspective uses ecology theory to conceptualize macro practice. As defined in Table 2.4, macro practice involves addressing environmental problems and human needs where the field of concern is the social and physical environments, including national and international political and economic structures. The power of bureaucratic organizations, their system of status definition, and their socialization of people into unhelpful attitudes can obstruct consumers' adaptation to their communities.

Social systems are also important aspects of communities, and we depend on social systems in our social work practice. Most systems are defined as one of the following:

- *Formal systems:* Professional organizations, unions, and service clubs represent formal systems. Each of these systems provides members with support based on membership criteria and obligations.

- *Informal systems:* These are systems that develop naturally in communities—family members, friends, and neighbors. Informal systems provide people with various types of support, including emotional, spiritual, and financial.

- *Societal systems:* These are service agencies, hospitals, institutions, and other organizations that provide people and communities with assistance (Pincus & Minahon, 1973).

To highlight the importance of systems in our lives, take a moment or two to do the following exercise:

Consider your informal system of support, and write a paragraph that captures the strength of that system. List an occasion or two when you went to your informal support system for assistance. How do the members of your informal system interact with the community where you live?

Ecological theory suggests that we can best understand systems by doing exactly what you just did in this short exercise on informal systems, focusing on the transactions that occur between different systems. In macro practice from a strengths perspective, social workers address the problems and strengths of interactions between systems by (1) assessing the strengths of communities; (2) enhancing and building new connections between people, resources, systems, and communities; (3) helping people to use their capabilities and strengths to solve community-based issues; and (4) solidifying change through political tactics, policy initiatives, establishment of an agency, and evaluation of the change effort (Brueggemann, 1996).

Like micro practice, macro practice from the strengths perspective begins with a strengths assessment. Kretzmann and McKnight (1993) suggest that communities have resources and assets that are often overlooked or underutilized. They conclude that communities have desperate needs and that:

> In response to this desperate situation well-intended people are seeking solutions by taking one of two divergent paths. The first, which begins by focusing on a community's needs, deficiencies and problems, is still the more traveled, and commands the vast majority of our financial and human resources. By comparison with the second path, which insists on beginning with a clear commitment to discovering a community's capacities and assets, and which is the direction [we] recommend, the first and foremost path is more like an eight-lane superhighway. (p. 1)

This is especially the case in communities in which people have learned to live under difficult situations. Community assets should be accounted for and mapped as a basis for working with and from within a community by compiling an inventory of specific resources in the community, organizing the resources according to partnerships and collaborative relationships, and targeting strong reciprocal relationships to enhance relationships that need support and attention.

Three principles define the macro-practice strengths assessment (Saleebey, 1997). Using community as a unit of analysis, the assessment starts with what resources are present in the community, not what is missing. The emphasis on strengths directs attention to community assets, possibilities, and potentials. Second, engagement in the community is necessary for the social worker to conduct internally focused community development. Engagement requires a period of observation and culminates in an understanding of the history, unique experiences, and complexities of the community (Landon, 1999). During this time frame, social workers use the principle of *professional use of self* to form relationships with others in the community (Kirst-Ashman & Hull, 1999). Finally, the entire process is driven by relationships—relationships between social workers and consumers, consumers and the various systems of support, consumers and the community, and social workers and communities.

Macro practice that embraces a strengths perspective builds a critical mass of support at the grassroots level. As one community partners with another and then another, the power structure can be challenged to support human well-being and individual and collective efficacy.

The Value Base

The knowledge base of macro social work practice from a strengths perspective is supported by values or judgments—a **value base.** Values are beliefs about what is good or desirable and what is not. Social workers employ macro interventions in organizations and communities, the environment, laws, and policies; these efforts affect what we can and should do. Table 2.5 applies the core values of social work, as defined by the National Association of Social Workers, to critical elements of macro practice.

Macro social work practice does not mean forcing people and their communities to change. Rather, self-determination, another value of social work, suggests that, when appropriate, social workers and consumers should build on the unique strengths of communities while pursuing three avenues of inquiry:

1. Consider how values may restrict progress toward the objectives desired by the community.
2. Consider possible alternatives and their consequences for achieving the objectives.
3. Consider the rights and needs of others residing in the community (Compton & Galaway, 1994, p. 111).

Confidentiality, an integral value of social work, requires that social workers and consumers negotiate who will share what information and how the macro intervention will proceed. From a strengths perspective, confidentiality is a resource that must be offered, but it should not be used as "a justification for failure to act, a justification for shielding consumers from responsibility for their own behavior, or a justification for failure to assist consumers in building support systems and mutual support groups" (Compton & Galaway, 1994, p. 163).

Another value related to those defined in Table 2.5 is social advocacy. Individual advocacy refers to activities on behalf of an *individual* that often address the accessibility, availability, and adequacy of services. By contrast, social advocacy, more directly related to macro practice, involves addressing issues that affect *groups* of people. In either form, advocacy involves resistance and subsequent efforts to change the status quo (Kirst-Ashman & Hull, 1999). The strengths perspective of macro practice embraces advocacy as a method of mediating the inevitable conflict between people and institutions and of expanding community support systems.

Table 2.5 Social Work Values and the Strengths Perspective

Value	Relationship to the Strengths Perspective
1. *Service:* Providing service and resources and helping people to reach their potential	Individuals and communities have the capacity to grow and change. Help people change and control the structures affecting them.
2. *Social justice:* Commitment to a society in which all people have the same rights, opportunities, and benefits	Define and respond to human needs on society's behalf, ensuring that resources are effectively used. Socioeconomic structures cause problems.
3. *Dignity and worth of the person:* Belief that each person is to be valued and treated with dignity	Take individual, family, and community visions and hopes seriously. Enable personal change and control.
4. *Importance of human relationships:* Valuing the connection between social work and consumers as essential to creating and maintaining a helping relationship	Share knowledge with consumers, empowering them to act on their own behalf.
5. *Integrity:* Commitment to honesty and trustworthiness	Social work should create structures for client cooperation to advocate for their own needs.
6. *Competence:* Commitment to the necessary knowledge and skill to work effectively with consumers	Social work considers the consumer to be the expert. Social workers engage in lifelong learning.

THE STRENGTHS PERSPECTIVE AND EMPOWERMENT THEORY

A considerable portion of this chapter has been dedicated to an analysis of the relationship between the strengths perspective, traditional problem-solving processes, and the ecological orientation. Indeed, when compared to traditional approaches, the strengths perspective offers a unique and refreshing outlook for social workers engaged in macro-level change in community-based practice.

At this point, it is also important to understand the relationship between the strengths perspective and empowerment theory. Although these orientations have similarities and tend to complement each other, they offer distinct contributions to macro social work practice.

Fundamentally, empowerment theory focuses on the ability of people to gain control and power over their lives. As suggested earlier, it involves identifying and building upon both personal and social dimensions of power so that people, organizations, and communities can acquire power in order to affect change. In such, empowerment offers both a conceptual outlook for macro practice and a process to help direct social workers in their work (Miley, O'Melia, & DuBois, 2001, p. 87). An important dimension of acquiring power involves identifying and utilizing strengths and resources. This is true regardless of the system level—individual, family, group, organization, community, or society. Of course, utilization of resources and strengths lies at the core of the strengths orientation.

Similarly, when social workers apply a strengths perspective and move away from a preoccupation with problems, there is a greater appreciation of the resilience, resourcefulness, and strengths found in various social systems. For example, when working with communities, there is a realization that communities have "internal assets and capabilities that can be developed and used in increasing the human and social capital of the community" (Saleebey, 2002, p. 241). The net result of any such awareness involves empowerment, as people recognize their potential in effecting change and taking control over their lives.

SUMMARY

This chapter introduced specific themes that will run throughout the remainder of the book: the belief in the strengths perspective for macro practice, the benefit of a strengths assessment, and the need to empower community members to change systems to meet common human needs. The problem-centered approach was examined as the historical base of social work practice and as a model of intervention that defines people and their communities by meticulously assessing pathologies and deficits. Next, the principles, knowledge base, and values associated with the strengths perspective were considered. Several elements of this perspective were identified, including various systems of support and transactions. This chapter concluded with a comparison of the strengths perspective with empowerment theory. Throughout the chapter, exercises and vignettes were provided in an effort to highlight the practical relevance of materials.

In the remainder of the book, attention will be given to the conditions, skills, technologies, and perspectives that influence macro social intervention from a strengths perspective.

A FEW KEY TERMS

strengths perspective	empowerment	social systems
problem-centered focus	community-based practice	value base
social environments		

USING INFOTRAC®

COLLEGE EDITION AND INFOWRITE

InfoTrac College Edition

Empowerment is a key term used through this chapter. Complete the following exercise to enhance your understanding of empowerment and its connection to practice from a strengths perspective:

1. Go to InfoTrac College Edition.

2. Search under both Subject Guide and Keyword Search.

3. Find one article on empowerment from each of the search fields.

4. Read both articles.

5. Contrast and compare the use of the term *empowerment*.

InfoWrite

To integrate the concept of empowerment more fully into your social work practice, gather your notes on the articles related to empowerment and do the following:

1. Go to InfoWrite.

2. Scroll to Modes of Exposition.

3. Find the heading "Definition."

4. Read the information under "Types of Definition."

CASE EXAMPLE: The Strengths of Consumers in Program Development

You are employed as a social worker in a rural social agency in the foothills of the Appalachian region. Along with the consumers of services, you and other colleagues have identified a significant number of people with persistent mental illness who would benefit from a drop-in center that would provide socialization and recreational opportunities as well as education and support on legal issues, parenting, housing discrimination, and employment. Consumers have become excited about the prospect of such a center and have initiated a set of planning meetings.

In the past few days, several relatively influential people learned about the plan to petition for the center and responded with outrage. They claimed the center would have a negative impact on real estate prices and would drain an already limited funding stream for social services. The administration at your agency has become concerned about the consequences of the proposed center for fund-raising efforts.

What does a strengths perspective offer to this type of situation? What kinds of opportunities exist for consumers, especially those who are vulnerable and disadvantaged? Regardless of what decision is made about proceeding with the center, why is it important that the strengths of consumers be considered and allowed to emerge?

Based on your readings, consider how the term *empowerment* reflects social values and government responsibility for issues. Take some time to write your own definition of empowerment for social work practice. Be prepared to describe how your personal definition of empowerment reflects your values and broader responsibility for social action.

THINKING CRITICALLY
ABOUT THE CASE EXAMPLE

1. What might current research indicate concerning the effectiveness of drop-in centers in providing services and programs for people with persistent mental illness?

2. Many people believe that the presence of human service centers "runs down" real estate values. Is this based on information, opinion, social facts, or bias?

3. Watch for newspaper or magazine articles depicting persons with mental illnesses. Do these articles describe the strengths of consumers of services? Strive to recognize and identify any deceptive practices in the reporting of human service delivery in the mass media.

REFLECTION EXERCISES

1. Consider your own personal and professional strengths. How do these strengths support your work with consumers, communities, and other social workers?

2. Describe the relationship between the strengths of individuals and those of communities. Consider how a particular strength of an individual might influence a community and vice versa.

3. Define at least three ways in which the strengths perspective links micro, mezzo, and macro practice in such a way that social workers can have a positive impact on the life satisfaction of consumers and communities.

SUGGESTED READINGS

Greene, A. D., & Latting, J. K. (2004). Whistle-blowing as a form of advocacy: Guidelines for the practitioner and organization. *Social Work, 49*(2), 219–239.

Lamson, P. (1976). *Roger Baldwin, Founder of the American Civil Liberties Union: A Portrait.* Boston: Houghton Mifflin.

Lee, J. A. B. (1994). Community and political empowerment practice. In J. A. B. Lee (Ed.), *The empowerment approach to social work practice.* New York: Columbia University Press.

Ryan, W. (1971). *Blaming the victim.* New York: Vintage.

REFERENCES

Blundo, R. (2001). Learning strengths-based practice: Challenging our personal and professional frames. *Families in Society: The Journal of Contemporary Human Services, 82,* 296–304.

Bronfenbrenner, V. (1979). *The ecology of human development.* Cambridge, MA: Harvard University Press.

Brueggemann, W. G. (1996). *The practice of macro social work.* Chicago: Nelson-Hall.

Chapin, R. K. (1995). Social policy development: The strengths perspective. *Social Work, 40,* 506–514.

Compton, B. A., & Galaway, B. (1994). *Social work process.* Pacific Grove, CA: Brooks/Cole.

Cowger, C. (1994). Assessing client strengths: Clinical assessment for client empowerment. *Social Work, 39,* 262–268.

Franklin, C., & Jordan, C. (1992). Teaching students to perform assessment. *Journal of Social Work Education, 28,* 222–241.

Germain, C. (1979). *Social work practice: People and environments.* New York: Columbia University Press.

———. (1985). The place of community work within an ecological approach to social work practice. In S. H. Taylor & R. W. Roberts (Eds.), *Theory and practice of community social work.* New York: Columbia University Press.

———. (1991). *Human behavior in the social environment.* New York: Columbia University Press.

Germain, C., & Gitterman, A. (1980). *The life model of social work practice.* New York: Columbia University Press.

Graybeal, C. (2001). Strengths-based social work assessment: Transforming the dominant paradigm. *Families in Society: The Journal of Contemporary Human Services, 82,* 233–242.

Gutheil, I. (1992). Considering the physical environment: An essential component of good practice. *Social Work, 37,* 391–396.

Gutierrez, L. M. (1995). Understanding the empowerment process: Does consciousness make a difference? *Social Work Research, 19*(4): 220–237.

Hepworth, D., & Larsen, J. A. (1990). *Direct social work practice: Theory and skills* (3rd ed.). Pacific Grove, CA: Brooks/Cole.

Holmes, G. E. (1992). Social work research and the empowerment paradigm. In D. Saleebey (Ed.), *The strength perspective on social work practice.* New York: Longman.

Kirst-Ashman, K. K., & Hull, G. (1999). *Understanding generalist practice.* Chicago: Nelson-Hall.

———. (2001). *Macro skills workbook: A generalist approach.* Pacific Grove, CA: Brooks/Cole.

Kretzmann, J. P., & McKnight, J. L. (1993). *Building communities from the inside out: Toward finding and mobilizing a community's assets.* Evanston, IL: Northwestern University Center for Urban Affairs and Policy Research.

Landon, P. (1999). *Generalist social work practice.* Dubuque, IA: Eddie Bowers.

Magnusson, D., & Allen, V. L. (1983). *Human development: An interactional perspective.* New York: Academic Press.

Miley, K. K., O'Melia, M., & DuBois, B. (2001). *Generalist social work practice: An empowering approach.* Boston: Allyn & Bacon.

Payne, M. (1997). *Modern social work theory* (J. Campling, consulting ed.). Chicago: Lyceum Books.

Perlman, H. (1957). *Social casework: A problem-solving process.* Chicago: University of Chicago Press.

Pincus, A., & Minahon, A. (1973). *Social work practice: Model and method.* Itasca, IL: F. E. Peacock.

Rapp, C. A. (1996). *The strengths model: Case management with people suffering* _from severe and persistent mental illness._ Unpublished manuscript, University of Kansas at Lawrence.

Rapport, J. (1990). In praise of the paradox: A social policy of empowerment over prevention. _American Journal of Community Psychology, 9,_ 1–25.

Rees, S. (1991). _Achieving power._ Sydney: Allen & Unwin.

Reynolds, B. (1951). _Social work and social living: Explorations in philosophy and practice._ Silver Springs, MD: National Association of Social Workers.

Rodwell, M. (1987). Naturalistic inquiry: An alternative model for social work assessment. _Social Service Review, 61,_ 231–246.

Saleebey, D. (1992). _The strength perspective in social work practice._ New York: Longman.

Saleebey, D. (1996). The strengths perspective in social work practice: Extensions and cautions. _Social Work, 41,_ 296–305.

Saleebey, D. (1997). _The strength perspective in social work practice._ New York: Longman.

Saleebey, D. (2002). _The strength perspective on social work practice._ Boston: Allyn & Bacon.

Schriver, J. M. (1998). _Human behavior in the social environment._ Boston: Allyn & Bacon.

Shulman, L. (1979). _The skills of helping individuals and groups._ Itasca, IL: F. E. Peacock.

Solomon, B. (1976). _Black empowerment: Social work in oppressed communities._ New York: Columbia University Press.

Specht, H., & Courtney, M. E. (1994). _Unfaithful angels: How social work has abandoned its mission._ New York: Free Press.

Tice, C. J., & Perkins, K. (1996). _Mental health issues: Building on the strengths of older adults._ Pacific Grove, CA: Brooks/Cole.

———. (2002). _The faces of social policy: A strengths perspective._ Pacific Grove, CA: Brooks/Cole.

Towle, C. (1965). _Common human needs_ (rev. ed.). Silver Springs, MD: National Association of Social Workers.

Van Berg, J., & Grealish, E. M. (1997). Finding family strengths. A multiple-choice test. _The Community Circle of Caring Journal, 1,_ 8–16.

Warren, R. (1978). _The community in America_ (3rd ed.). Chicago: Rand McNally.

Weick, A., Sullivan, W., & Kisthardt, W. (1989). A strengths perspective for social work practice. _Social Work, 34,_ 350–354.

3

Considerations
for the Practitioner

Chapter Content Areas

Beyond Problem Solving

Professional Outlook

Importance of Strengths
Orientation

Organizational Culture

Decentralized Decision Making

Organizational Climate

Promoting Consumerism

Macro-Practice Roles and Role
Salience

Strengths Orientation Applied
to Macro Practice

Role of the Consumer

Consumers as Stakeholders

Power and Control

Strengths Perspective in Macro
Practice

Diversity and Cultural Values as
Strengths

TURNING ATTENTION TO THE
STRENGTHS AND THE POWER OF PEOPLE

As described in Chapter 2, social workers have been traditionally viewed as
problem solvers—professionals dedicated to helping people conquer individual troubles and solve social problems. Indeed, many people enter this profession with aspirations to help others find solutions for everyday difficulties.
Touched by the plight of the downtrodden and the ills of the world, social
workers often feel a calling toward helping people to identify needs and pursue
healthy, do-able remedies for problems. The "work" of social work has a rich
history in assorted problem-solving processes—helping, assisting, counseling,
and intervening.

As previously mentioned, social work education has also been based in problem solving. This has been true for working with individuals and families as well as larger systems. For decades, social workers have been trained, educated, and socialized to the virtues of relationship building, assessment, problem definition, goal setting, intervention plans, resources, evaluation, termination, and aftercare. A primary purpose of social work education throughout the years has been to "enhance the problem-solving and coping capacities of people" (Pincus & Minahan, 1983, p. 9).

Similarly, social service organizations were founded on the principle of helping people to cope with or seek personal resolutions to problems. In the classic *Social Casework: A Problem-Solving Process*, Perlman (1957) narrowly defines the function of the social service agency as a means "to help individuals with the particular social handicaps which hamper good personal or family living and with the problems created by faulty person-to-person, person-to-group, and person-to-situation relationships" (p. 4).

Given this backdrop, it becomes evident how over the years *problem solving* has constituted *the* conceptual approach for intervening in people's lives. Although client self-determination has always been at the core of problem solving, it was not until the early 1990s that appreciable attention was given to considering and more thoroughly cultivating the individual and collective strengths, power, and will of the people being served.

Getting past the logic of problem solving toward a more comprehensive view of the social environment, encompassing people's abilities and capacities, is a difficult but crucial task for effective social work practice. This is especially true with respect to macro-level social work practice. Educators and practitioners continue to struggle with forming and developing strategies to promote and enhance the capabilities of organizations, communities, and society. After years of strife to cure organizational and community woes, social workers face a challenge in creating and promoting principles for building the capacities of larger social systems.

To complicate matters, the challenge in embracing a strengths orientation in social work practice is not merely an issue of theoretical import. It is multidimensional, involving the structure of and expectations associated with one's practice, as well as organizational climate, policy, and practices.

EXPANDING ONE'S PROFESSIONAL OUTLOOK

For years, social workers have been trained to scan and assess the impact of various social systems as an integral function in intervention. With the emergence of macro practice, prominence and credence were given to the influence of larger systems—organizations, communities, and society as a whole. Indeed, the crux of contemporary generalist practice involves the ability to assess, intervene, and work with consumers of various system sizes.

Although there is no single accepted definition of generalist social work practice, the idea of multiple levels and methods of intervention is commonly accepted (Landon, 1995, p. 1105). Systems of all sizes are viewed as potential consumers and candidates (targets) for strengthening. Theoretical orientations for analysis and use in creating change may relate specifically to a particular system size, or they may cut across system levels.

With the advent of Saleebey's (1992) book, tenets and principles of a strengths orientation became linked to social work practice—principally, to the strengths of individuals, families, and small groups. Subsequently, the strengths perspective has been extended to include community development, neighborhood empowerment, and the broader environmental context (Saleebey, 2002). For many practitioners, this has been an important, yet tenuous, leap in logic. Such a change in thinking involves a strong commitment and a concerted effort to include and thoroughly examine the assets and capabilities of both micro and macro systems in the social environment.

As an illustration, Akerlund and Cheung (2000) examine research describing gay and lesbian issues among African Americans, Latinos, and Asian Americans. Not surprisingly, several common themes emerge across racial and ethnic groups with regard to identity development. Minority gays and lesbians routinely confront discrimination, oppression, rejection, and the expectation that they will choose between cultures. However, Akerlund and Cheung (2000) also suggest that current research in this substantive domain is inadequate in its examination of various sources of strengths for minority gay and lesbian identity development (p. 291). For instance, there are indications that support for minority gays and lesbians exists and can be nurtured from extended family, religious institutions, merchant groups, social clubs, and the presence of positive role models. Unfortunately, "the literature does not provide much information on how minority gay men and lesbians utilize their strengths and resources" (p. 291).

Akerlund and Cheung's article is a pointed example of how social workers continue to strive to attain a fuller appreciation and better understanding of the various sources of strength and power of people at multiple levels in the social environment. Social work practitioners often attest to the inherent potential of one's place of employment, neighborhood values, voluntary associations, service agencies, and media organizations (e.g., newspapers, radio, television, and the Internet) in promoting change. Identifying, describing, and utilizing various ways in which participation in the social environment can serve to lift up our consumers and advance opportunities for them involves a fresh, enlightened mind-set for macro practice—in stark contrast to the barrier-based premises of problem solving.

ORGANIZATIONAL CULTURE

The practice of social work, regardless of venue, is influenced by organizational culture. Although an abstract term, **organizational culture** refers to established patterns occurring within a particular organization "even if they are not explicitly stated . . . a sense of group identity that permeates decision making and communication within the organization" (Netting, Kettner, & McMurtry, 1993, p. 146). It is organizational culture, as specified by a mission, ideology, language, and practices, that helps shape both the outlook and the behaviors of social workers in human service organizations.

Symbolic interactionism suggests that reality is largely determined by social interaction (Mead, 1934). It "is concerned primarily with the subjective meanings that individuals attach to their own and others' actions" (Olsen, 1978, p. 102). From this perspective, symbols and language become the building blocks of organizational culture. When people effectively "communicate meanings of their actions to each other and work out shared interpretations," a shared organizational culture emerges and provides participants with "interpretations of social life, role expectations, common definitions of situations and social norms" (Olsen, 1978, p. 107).

Accordingly, if a strengths perspective is to be taken seriously in an organizational context, then leaders, professionals, and consumers must embrace both an appropriate outlook and its associated terminology. This involves a shift in both logic and language. It calls for professionals to abandon the "I am here to help you" mentality in favor of seeking ways to better and more fully equip and empower consumers.

An organizational climate for promoting the strengths of consumers is predicated on identifying and finding ways to make use of consumers' various talents, abilities, and passions. This requires that helping professionals be nonjudgmental and promote self-determination as consumers are given encouragement, knowledge, and skills to enable them to act upon and use their unique abilities in pursuing hopes and dreams.

Unfortunately, there is no easy recipe for affecting organizational culture. Changes in organizational culture can occur for many different reasons, some planned and others unintentional. Impetus for change can include new leadership (e.g., a new director), the onset of a new program or project with new staff, and demands from external funding sources (Brody & Nair, 1997). Technology, locus of control in decision making, and the vision of an organization can also serve as powerful stimulants for creating or changing organizational culture. Indeed, "Dynamic human services organizations demonstrate a willingness to match, as closely as possible, consumer needs and expectations. . . . [M]odel centers deliver a mix of services suited to neighborhood needs and citizens of all socioeconomic levels, provide extended hours, and serve as gathering places for neighborhood residents" (Poole & Colby, 2002, p. 147).

Creating or developing an organizational culture that values the strengths of consumers will most likely require a system of **decentralized decision making.** Poole and Colby (2002) describe such agencies as ascribing to a "bottom-up" philosophy—decentralized, less hierarchical, creative, willing to take risks, and highly responsive to the expectations and strengths of consumers (p. 147). Here, consumer leaders and leadership groups or boards assume legitimate roles in formulating and dictating the agency's vision, programming, policies, and rules.

BOX 3.1 Four Rs of Building an Organizational Culture for Promoting Strengths

- *Relationships:* As a result of their training and education, colleagues may be skeptical and reluctant to implement a strengths orientation. Change is often difficult, particularly if organizational behaviors have become comfortable. Use your relationships with agency leaders and co-workers to bear witness to the strengths of consumers and capacities in your organization, the community, and the larger society. Encourage agency personnel toward "envisioning, creating, and sustaining appropriate community[society]-based opportunities" and toward seeking out supportive relationships (Walker, 2002, p. 2).
- *Repeat the message:* Organizational culture does not change overnight. This is an instance when repetition is good. You will need to find ways to have leaders hear the virtues of a strengths orientation from multiple sources. Persistence and fortitude are keys in shaping organizational culture.
- *Remember:* Consumers lie at the heart of organizational change.

Consumers constitute power and can attest to their own ability to create opportunity. Consumer boards and representatives allow leaders to think about information in new and insightful ways. Equip consumers so that they can affect organizational culture in a meaningful manner.

- *Role awareness:* This is an opportunity for social workers and consumers to work together in an effort to educate and advocate for macro-level change. Many times, our own social service agency is an important target for change. Creating an organizational culture that uses the strengths of consumers constitutes advocacy and education. It is an opportunity for colleagues to see and feel the energy and value of consumer participation. Make sure that your practice is defined in terms of advocating for and educating others to the advantages of adopting a strengths perspective in social service organizations.

© Thomson Higher Education/Heinle Image Bank.

AN APPROPRIATE
ORGANIZATIONAL CLIMATE

What constitutes a fitting **organizational climate** for implementing a strengths perspective? What is an appropriate atmosphere for a social service agency with respect to values and commitment?

Most social workers would agree that any human service organization should aspire to respect the dignity of consumers. Additionally, social workers should be nonjudgmental, respect diversity, and promote client self-determination. These are deep-rooted principles of the social work profession.

From a strengths perspective, it would be helpful for social service organizations to be sensitive and attentive to some additional features. For example, the social climate of an organization should encourage and motivate consumers, individually and collectively, to pursue their talents and passions. It is important that consumers feel free to follow their dreams and gravitate toward their abilities in an unencumbered fashion.

For this to occur, consumers need time to brainstorm and contemplate their hopes, desires, and possible courses of action. To encourage this, social service agencies need to be creative, to steer clear of the logic of "processing" consumers, predicated on billable hours and external mandates for brief intervention. Instead, a tone of collaboration, sharing, and participatory decision making needs to be created and endorsed. Consider how consumers can be brought to the planning table. Best practices would be oriented toward the use of open forums, retreats, workshops, and conferences as means of promoting consumer participation.

A primary function of the social service agency is to promote consumerism in its broadest sense. The intent is not just to find ways to raise the voices of consumers, "but rather it involves the creation of a learning community in which all members have voice and privilege . . . creating a dialogue with others . . . moving from a hierarchical model of fixing to a connecting model of sharing together" (Weiman, Dosland-Hasenmiller, & O'Melia, 2002, p. 173). It is in this type of organizational and community environment that the strengths of consumers are allowed to flourish, shine, and advance social change.

MACRO-PRACTICE ROLES

Social work has a rich tradition of defining one's practice in the context of roles. Roles can be defined as sets of expectations or behaviors; indeed, social workers often describe themselves as caseworkers, community organizers, advocates, group workers, administrators, and therapists. As social workers, we typically assume more than one of these types of practice roles, as dictated by agency demands, consumers, worker interest, and job description.

Before accepting a social work position, try to ascertain the amount of time and effort you will be devoting to various social work roles. As a prospective employee, it is easy to become consumed with issues of compensation and benefits. Yet, a meaningful assessment of role salience—the importance given to particular practice roles—will provide a sense of where and how you will be spending most of your working hours. It is crucial that social workers seek employment that matches both their areas of interest and their professional expertise.

With respect to macro practice, a wide range of possible **macro-practice roles** are available for the social worker. Whereas Meenaghan, Washington, and Ryan (1982) initially described macro practice in terms of the roles of social planner, administrator, evaluator, and community organizer, a host of macro practice roles have emerged over the years for creating large-scale social change. Though not an exhaustive list, the following represents a brief description, containing expectations and activities, of some of the most common macro-practice roles.

Social planner: Planners engage in a rational process of creating social change. This can involve many different kinds of activities, including program and policy development aimed at improving and strengthening organizations, communities, and various aspects of society. As external forces act upon delivery of service, social planners (individuals and groups of people) embrace consumers and other interested parties to design and implement strategies for reducing obstacles and advancing opportunities.

Administrator or organization leader: Successful leaders work with consumers and various constituencies to establish a vision for progress and to promote healthy and effective organizational operation. Responsibilities are typically in the areas of budgeting, supervision, mission, objectives, labor management, resource development, and organizational policy/program development.

Evaluator: Evaluators are those involved in quality assurance. Many agencies employ social workers to evaluate program effectiveness—how well programs are meeting their goals and objectives—using criteria mandated by various funding sources. Consumers are valuable stakeholders for determining organizational and program goals and providing feedback as to whether program goals are being successfully met. Progressive social workers are careful to nurture consumer participation throughout the evaluation process.

Community organizer: The community organizer is a stalwart role in social work practice. Through the use of neighborhood gatherings, community meetings, group work, and various forms of networking in the community, social workers interact with consumers and relevant leaders and decision makers to find ways to strengthen the community. In this process, consumers take ownership and gain power over their lives as they seek and secure new community-based opportunities and resources.

Educator: Social workers are educators, as they possess information, knowledge, and skills that are useful to others. However, education is not a one-way enterprise; it is multidirectional. Social workers also learn from consumers. And, possibly most important, consumers are adept at learning from one another. When social workers act as educators, they not only disseminate information but also structure activities so that learning can take place in a multitude of ways.

Advocate: An advocate backs or supports others. Social workers serve as advocates when they advance or champion the causes of consumers. This can happen with respect to social legislation, policy change, or program development, and can take a variety of forms. At times, the social worker is a role model for consumers to emulate. At other times, the social worker is a resource person to enable consumers to better voice and rally for the strengthening of their position(s) with others. Advocacy is done at the bequest and under the direction of consumers, not the reverse.

Policy analyst: The formation and development of policies for strengthening the position of and creating opportunities for consumers is an ongoing function for many social workers. Staying abreast of policy initiatives in one's area of practice can be very demanding. Hence, collaboration between professionals and consumers helps ensure a timely and broad-based analysis of relevant policies. It is important to remember that consumers hold a high stake in policies that affect their lives. Consumers are often very motivated to use technology and old-fashioned networking to track and influence policy development.

Political activist: Some social workers become politicians in an effort to champion social causes. More typically, social workers use their knowledge and skills to monitor, lobby, and influence lawmakers. This includes involvement in political action committees and political campaigns. Social workers collaborate and build coalitions with consumers and political leaders in an effort to create and advance social and economic opportunities for consumers.

Facilitator: Social workers are experts at setting the stage for social change. Consumers benefit when a professional stimulates discussion, prepares needed materials, and provides a backdrop for planning. The primary goal, of course, is to solicit new and creative ideas from consumers in creating change. Once the ball gets rolling, the facilitator helps consumers to use their strengths to take ownership.

Team or group leader: Teamwork involves the ability to get people to work together. Inherent is a quest to organize people (consumers, professionals, and/or other interested parties) into a coordinated, cooperative whole. As a team or group leader, the social worker uses relationship, communication, and organizational skills to assist consumers in examining and setting courses of social action. The goal of empowering groups of people to use their abilities to "get on the same page," set do-able priorities, and build a cohesive group or team are very important components of macro practice.

Program developer: Social programs are developed to provide services and resources to strengthen the position of consumers. It is a responsibility of the social worker to ensure the primacy of consumers and other ordinary citizens in the program development process. This can be actualized through the effective use of consumer planning councils, groups, and leadership teams. It is probable that some consumers will possess the very talents and abilities that can facilitate and propel the creation or development of a program.

Researcher: Research is a powerful tool for documenting capabilities and potentials as well as populations-at-risk. Social workers commonly find themselves in the midst of research projects assessing group, organizational, community, and societal strengths and needs. Consumers can contribute significantly to the research process by helping to determine the research questions and through the refinement of various research methodologies. Social research rarely takes place in a vacuum. Hence, the interests and insights of consumers constitute valuable input and a unique perspective for the researcher.

Grant/proposal writer: Grants are financial awards given to organizations by foundations or charitable trusts. Social workers write proposals to secure funding for specific projects and programs. Typically, a foundation identifies specific purposes for its grants based on the interests and desires of the benefactor. To be successful, grant proposals must fulfill the stipulations or requirements of the funding source. Consumer participation and ownership of this process is important for two reasons. First, consumer interest should be the impetus for seeking funding. Second, the passion and understanding of consumers is a vital element in making any proposal live and reflect reality. Strengths-based social workers use consumers and their writing and editing skills in writing grant proposals.

Fund raiser: Acquisition of needed resources is a common theme in all of the social services. Activities can include professional solicitation, dinners, raffles, bike-a-thons, media campaigns, and product sales (e.g., cookies, quilts). The idea, impetus, and person-hours for these endeavors should be consumer-based. For a social worker, it is rewarding to experience the pride, sense of accomplishment, and spirit of comradeship exhibited when consumers work together to secure funding to strengthen their cause. It is an opportunity for consumers to connect with one another and with the social service organization in a special, personal way. Beyond financial gain, fund raising pulls people together and allows for meaningful social interaction between consumers, helping professionals, and the general public.

Board/committee member: One of the more important roles for a macro social worker is to serve as a member of a planning or governing board. Membership by social workers on such boards and committees provides a source of professional expertise. In additional, social workers can use their knowledge and skills to align themselves with consumer representatives to promote the perspectives of various consumer groups. Be forewarned, boards and committee often have overrepresentation by astute business-people and philanthropists, who are cultivated by development officers in a strategic effort to nurture prospective donors. Careful collaboration between social workers and consumers can help assure that program and policy decisions are more fully consumer driven.

At face value, the expectations and behaviors described in the aforementioned macro practice roles would seem to have little in common. Each role merely represents a unique way to effect change in larger systems (organizations, communities, and society) in the realm of social work practice. To complicate matters, organizational constraints surrounding "billable" hours of service often effectively restrict the time available for a social worker to actively engage in any of these roles.

Be careful not to fall into the trap of pushing participation in macro-practice roles toward "after hours" or other personal time. Although this might appear to be a necessary evil, given the state of a particular social service agency, relegating macro practice to unpaid overtime ultimately reduces it to a secondary or ancillary function.

Using a strengths perspective, several principles can be identified to guide the enactment of each of the previously identified macro-practice roles. When contemplating participation in various macro-practice roles, these principles, shown in Table 3.1, can be used as a tool to help shape your activities and behaviors. Each of these principles involves recognition of the existing strengths of consumers and their unique abilities to make a difference.

TABLE 3.1 Principles of Strengths Orientation in Macro Practice

First principle:	*Seek and nurture the direct involvement of consumers.*
Sample activities:	Establish consumer teams, groups, and/or councils, and organize meetings to allow the strengths of consumers to come forward. Take steps to ensure that the stories and virtues (visions, resources, sources of support, and abilities) of consumers are heard and respected. This sets the stage for consumer participation.
Example:	For an administrator, the mission and goals of the agency need to reflect the interests and passions of consumers and encourage consumers to seek opportunities. This can only occur when the goals and dreams of consumers are paramount in the establishment and development of organizational mission and philosophy.
Second principle:	*Encourage consumers to acquire control.*
Sample activities:	Motivate and equip consumers to assume leadership roles. It is not enough for consumers to be participants in macro-level change. Provide information, education, and training so that consumers can be in charge of social change efforts. This might involve promoting an understanding or enhancement of computer capabilities, writing and/or verbal skills, financial management, the ability to run meetings, or savvy for strategic planning.
Example:	As an advocate, you should be preparing consumers to voice issues and facilitate structural change. Consumers should be encouraged to run meetings, organize events, and make contact with decision makers and politicians. Although your knowledge and skills concerning advocacy are very important, the consumer group should seek opportunities to take charge of efforts, using consumer talents and capabilities. Advocacy is most effective when decision makers hear the passion of consumers and know that consumers are willing to claim ownership over initiatives aimed at creating change.
Third principle:	*Be creative in identifying the strengths of consumers.*
Sample activities:	It is important to "ask questions about survival, support, positive times, interests, dreams, goals, and pride" (Saleebey, 2002, p. 217). Community meetings and neighborhood forums can easily turn into counterproductive gripe sessions. Conversely, when appropriately prompted, groups of people often take great pride in identifying and sharing with others their dreams and aspirations. Use your talents and skills in relationship building, communication, and the coordination of activities to call upon the strengths of others. Exert and allow for creativity and spontaneity in the quest of identifying the hopes and goals of consumers.
Example:	Social workers often assume the role of educator, but consumers can also be effective teachers. It is not unusual for consumer groups to create, sponsor, coordinate, and provide speakers for workshops, conferences, and other forms of educational outreach including media presentations. Consumers are frequently the best spokespersons for their cause. Both professionals and the general public can learn substantially from the words of consumers.
Fourth principle:	*Nurture strengths-based alliances.*
Sample activities:	Social causes are often viewed in isolation. Yet, thoughtful analysis of how people can connect their strengths with the abilities of others is frequently a fruitful endeavor. Consumers and professionals need to consider who can contribute to a common cause. Collaboration with other consumer groups and allied professionals can yield additional resources as well as fresh ideas and approaches. Once again, consumers should take a primary role in identifying potential partners and in making contacts with any such groups of people.

Example: As researchers, social workers are familiar with the value of scientific information in creating social change. A prudent and logical step in most agency-based planning processes is to perform a community needs assessment. This often involves both the compilation of existing materials and the collection of new data. Consumers should consider how to coordinate and collaborate research endeavors with other consumer groups, agencies, and volunteer organizations. Beyond the procurement of useful information, careful consideration of the benefits of associations and alliances with other groups in conducting research is one way to extend the strengths orientation beyond the parochial boundaries of any single consumer group, agency, or social cause.

THE ROLE OF THE CONSUMER

A key to successful macro practice, as noted, is the social worker's ability to initiate and sustain meaningful consumer involvement. It is important that consumers be at the forefront of social change. Given the fact that consumers frequently come to the social worker in pain, demoralized, and at times involuntarily, encouraging groups of people, organizations, individuals, families, and communities to engage in an active consumer role can present a considerable challenge.

Yet, consumers of our services also possess a strong spirit and unmatched sense of resilience. When consumers are respected as human beings, feel dignified, and possess realistic hope, the possibilities for social change seem boundless. Unleashing and harnessing the passion and fire of consumers in constructive ways can be a powerful and rewarding experience, probably rooted as much in art as science.

Promoting the role of the **consumer** is a major task for social workers engaged in macro practice using a strengths orientation. Moore and Kelly (1996) provide insight concerning relevant activities for the role of consumer. Social workers should assist consumers in finding ways to do the following:

- Interface, on emotional, cognitive, and physical levels, with the service delivery system, providers, professionals, and leaders.
- Secure internal and external resources.
- Improve quality in human services.
- Advance the "consumer's viewpoint."
- Affect agency mission, structure, division of labor, and management practices.
- Shape organizational, community, and societal agendas.
- Create opportunities for teamwork, collaboration, and networking.
- Put forward a democratic, participatory orientation to decision making.

Although it may be difficult for some people to envision consumers as major stakeholders in human services, current research suggests this as a plausible and worthwhile pursuit. As an example, several progressive community-based long-term care programs have adopted a consumer direction (CD) perspective. Using this strategy, consumers "take more active roles in their care management, by hiring, training, supervising, and firing care providers. A limited number of existing studies show that CD consumers indeed feel they have more choice and control over their care compared to those under the traditional model" (Yamada, 2001, p. 83). Indeed, it only seems logical that consumers, the very people who stand to benefit most from programs and services, occupy a central and significant position in determining what is desired or needed in service delivery systems.

First and foremost, the role of consumer needs to be grounded in the quest for consumer participation, control, and rights in the context of human service relationships. Competing interests (e.g., from funding sources, politicians, administrators, and corporate partners) often act to prescribe the role of the consumer in very different, usually more passive or submissive, ways. Because social roles are defined and enacted through interaction with a myriad of others, it is important to realize that consumers and social work practitioners constitute only two of many sources of power influencing role expectations and behaviors.

Tower (1994) assures us that "social workers who adopt a consumer-centered orientation toward practice can play important facilitative roles. Consumers need good role models if they are to become more autonomous" (p. 195). Although people and organizations seldom yield control without resistance, the strength of consumers, professionals, and relevant others working collaboratively can be appreciable. Depending on the propensity of a social structure toward change, agencies can shift toward becoming more consumer-centered rather quickly. And, possibly most important, as "practitioners align themselves with the interests of consumers, including consumer input and control, the result will be greater self-determination among clients [consumers] and less ethical discord regarding paternalism with the helping professions" (p. 196).

THE SHIFTING OF POWER AND CONTROL

The acquisition of power and control by consumers can be expansive in nature, or it can result in a loss of control and power by others (e.g., providers of services, administrators, funding sources, and community leaders). The buy-in for any redistribution of power and control will certainly vary from person to person and among various special-interest groups and organizations. Some stakeholders will see the shift toward consumerism as meaningful and empowering. Others will vie to maintain control over service delivery systems and existing structures by minimizing or negating the possible contributions of consumers. Ultimately, the task is to avoid false or pseudo consumer participation and to "devise and implement additional procedures for including [endorsing] citizens [consumers] in public decision making" (Olsen, 1978, p. 400).

Interestingly, the repositioning of one's professional self from the role of helper or therapist toward that of a facilitator poses a challenge for many social workers. Seeking the talents and abilities of consumers, be they smaller systems, organizations, communities, or society, is an appreciable change from helping clients to resolve intrapsychic difficulties, interpersonal relations, life transitions, and structural conflicts—that is, from problem solving. Many social workers will grapple with a desire to "do more." In some respects, such a feeling is testimony to the importance of a strengths perspective. As consumers strive to use their talents and capabilities to "do more" in creating change, social workers and others stand to lose power and control. This does not mean that social workers will become passive but, instead, that they will use their expertise in relationship building, communication, and interpersonal skills in different, more empowering ways.

The commitment to advance the viewpoints and perspectives of consumers can leave social workers with a sense of loss. Allowing consumers to come to the forefront takes social workers and other helping professionals away from center stage. However, as consumers acquire power, use their abilities, and become formidable shareholders in planning and decision making, a feeling of worth and participatory governance soon takes hold. This can be exciting, enlightening, and refreshing for consumers, social workers, community leaders, administrators, and politicians alike.

Green and Lee (2002) suggest that social workers should strive to espouse professional "curiosity" and to assume "not-knowing or non-expert" positions in the effort to view each consumer's reality. After all, the consumer's "view of reality is socially constructed and is as valid as anyone else's. . . . To try to understand clients' [consumers'] realities we have to listen very closely to their problems and their stories" (p. 184). Here, consumers are viewed as "experts on themselves," and the role of social workers is to use their skills to actively ask questions and to direct their energies toward allowing consumers to teach us, use their competencies, and acquire needed resources (p. 185).

STEPS FOR USING THE STRENGTHS PERSPECTIVE IN MACRO PRACTICE

One of the most comprehensive models for conceptualizing phases or steps for using the strengths orientation in generalist practice is provided by Miley, O'Melia, and DuBois (2001). Their framework is particularly well suited to macro practice, as it can be applied to larger systems (organizations, communities, and society) as both consumers and target systems in promoting social change.

In recent years, traditional problem-solving models (involving assessment, problem identification, goal setting, planning, program, evaluation, and termination) have been modified for use with larger systems. For example, Kirst-Ashman and Hull (1997, p. 203) propose their IMAGINE model (*i*dea, *m*uster support, identify *a*ssets, specify *g*oals, *i*mplement plan, *n*eutralize opposition, and *e*valuate progress). Models such as this are certainly useful and reflect

Table 3.2 An Empowering Approach to Generalist Practice

Phase	Process	Activities
Dialogue	Forming partnerships	Build empowering social worker–client relationships that acknowledge clients' privileges and respect their uniqueness.
	Articulating situations	Assess challenging situations by responding in ways that validate clients' experiences, add transactional dimensions, and look toward goals.
	Defining directions	Determine a preliminary purpose for the relationship to activate client motivation and guide the exploration for relevant resources.
Discovery	Identifying strengths	Search for client strengths in general functioning, coping with challenging situations, developing cultural identities, and overcoming adversity.
	Assessing resource capabilities	Explore resources in clients' transactions with the environment, including connections to family, social groups, organizations, and community institutions.
	Framing solutions	Construct an achievable plan of action that utilizes client and environmental resources and leads toward desired goals.
Development	Activating resources	Implement the action plan by mobilizing available resources through consultancy, resource management, and education.
	Creating alliances	Forge empowering alliances among clients, within clients' natural support networks, and within the service delivery system.
	Expanding opportunities	Develop new opportunities and resources through program development, community organizing, and social action.
	Recognizing success	Evaluate the success of the change efforts to recognize achievements and inform continuing actions.
	Integrating gains	Wrap up the change process in ways that resolve the relationship, celebrate success, and stabilize positive changes.

SOURCE: From Karla Krogsrud Miley, Michael O'Melia, and Brenda DuBois, *Generalist Social Work Practice: An Empowering Approach*, 3/e, © 2001, p. 99. Published by Allyn & Bacon, Boston, MA. Copyright © 2001 by Pearson Education. Adapted by permission of the publisher.

elements of a strengths orientation and the growing movement toward strengths-based practice.

Miley, O'Melia, and DuBois (2001) have made a concerted effort to create dynamic yet flexible phases for conceptualizing macro practice, derived from an empowering and strengths-based approach. In their model, the emphasis in creating planned change becomes "cultivating client strengths and resources throughout all phases of the practice process" (p. 97). This thought-provoking and innovative approach encourages the social worker and consumer to thoroughly move away from a "what is wrong" logic to a more aggressive and opportunistic "what is available" mentality (p. 97).

The three basic phases in Miley, O'Melia, and DuBois (2001) model involve dialogue, discovery, and development. Keep in mind that the foundation of successful social work practice, micro or macro, is always predicated on consumer self-determination, respect for differences, relationship building, creating and maintaining healthy avenues of communication, and thoughtful reflection. Table 3.2 provides a thorough overview and description of Miley, O'Melia, and DuBois's (2001) dialogue, discovery, and development approach.

For social workers engaged in macro practice, this model offers a concrete framework for contemplation in relation to every consumer, meeting, and pursuit. It is not a lockstep approach but, rather, a general framework for identifying collaborative, consumer-based processes and activities for creating social change. With respect to macro practice, specific attention has been given to utilizing the strengths of consumers to expand and create new opportunities through program development, community organizing, and social action. This embraces several traditional forms of macro social work practice under the rubric of empowerment.

Use of the phases, processes, and activities identified by Miley, O'Melia, and DuBois (1997) appears appropriate regardless of the macro-practice role. Social workers assuming the roles of community organizer, researcher, planner, facilitator, and administrator, among others, can constructively adopt this framework as a guide for reflecting on various forms of role enactment.

USING DIVERSITY AND
CULTURAL VALUES AS STRENGTHS

The United States is a country rich with human diversity. It would be remiss not to examine diversity and cultural values as strengths when working with larger social systems. **Diversity** includes such factors as age, gender, race, religion, ethnicity, sexual orientation, social-economic class, and regional distinctions. Organizations, communities, and society differ appreciably in their composition in terms of these dimensions. This can be viewed both as problematic and as a source of power and strength. The challenge for consumers and social workers is to find ways to take advantage of the unique qualities and attributes of larger social systems as a regular function of macro social work practice.

As one example, Fong (2002) suggests "The strengths perspective applied to empowering people of color, especially immigrants and refugees, means to identify the critical traditional values and to assess how they might manifest themselves as strengths in the client's [consumer's] life" (p. 207). For the practitioner, this means an acute awareness of and sensitivity to **cultural values** and beliefs associated with relevant racial and ethnic groups for use in macro-level change. The possibilities here are endless, as different racial and ethnic groups can offer a variety of resources based on a specific cultural heritage—political ties, business connections, church affiliations, educational links, and family support.

Delgado (2000) suggests that "[t]he presence or absence of murals, playgrounds, gardens, and sculptures are indicators of a community's strengths. These types of projects also increase community exchanges and help strengthen a community's identity" (p. 59). Community-based projects and physical artifacts often reflect the presence of cultural heritage and are used as a means of promoting and fostering a sense of pride and empowerment with respect to cultural traditions. These endeavors need not be merely symbolic. For example, in addition to enjoyment, parks and playgrounds can be used as meeting places and venues for maintaining customs and togetherness. When strategically positioned, murals and sculptures serve as focal points as well as gathering spots.

It is safe to say that "most ethnic groups use cultural values as strengths" (Fong, 2002, p. 207). For social workers, the key is to help consumers identify ways to build on their cultural traditions and to use these assets as tools for acquiring power and access to opportunities and needed resources. Toward this end, social workers will need to develop the ability to understand specific dimensions of culture, as revealed by consumers and other sources, and to apply these factors to the consumers themselves and consumer efforts to affect their environment—**cultural competence** (Lum, 1999). This includes "learning and exposing ourselves to different cultures, languages, groups—[m]ulticultural learning is formal and informal, immediate and ongoing" (Marsh, 2004, p. 5). Specifically, cultural competence challenges social workers to assess cultural norms and behaviors as strengths in advocacy, planning, and organizational and community development (see the *NASW Standards for Cultural Competence in Social Work Practice,* 2001).

Hurdle (2002) describes culture-centered macro practice in terms of "recognition of the strengths of communities of color" (p. 189) and suggests, at times, "a need for interpreters or cultural mediators to ensure that communication is fully understandable" (p. 190). In the case of a Native Hawaiian community development project, special measures were provided to assure that "the project was based on the values and worldview of the Native Hawaiian communities it served, and [that] it built upon community strengths by integrating cultural practices into program delivery, such as the use of Native Hawaiian healers and dietary instruction" (p. 190). This was accomplished, in part, by a carefully constructed planning conference and the formation of task groups where consumers and other community representatives developed, implemented, and evaluated the "master plan" for the project.

SUMMARY

You have continued on an important professional journey. As a student of social work, you have been challenged to shift your professional outlook even further toward a strengths orientation. This involves promoting an appropriate organizational culture and climate for advancing the rights and strengths of consumers. Special emphasis has been given to consumers as major stakeholders in the service delivery system. Diversity and cultural values were examined as forms of consumer strength.

Also, an array of macro-practice roles were provided for your consideration. Each role definition contained an explicit slant toward the strengths orientation and emphasized consumer participation, power, and control.

Finally, you were asked to examine Miley, O'Melia, and DuBois's (2001) dialogue, discovery, and development model as one approach to implementing a strengths orientation in everyday practice. Their framework will be particularly valuable in relation to capacity building, enrichment, and the creation of opportunities, topics examined in subsequent chapters of this book.

A FEW KEY TERMS

organizational culture	organizational climate	diversity
decentralized decision making	macro-practice roles	cultural values
	consumer	cultural competence

USING INFOTRAC®
COLLEGE EDITION AND INFOWRITE

InfoTrac College Edition

Finding ways to enable consumers to participate in the decision-making process is a worthy goal in macro social work practice. Participation in decentralized decision making can take numerous forms. Often it is not necessary to reinvent existing practices.
    Complete the following exercise:

1. Go to InfoTrac College Edition.

2. Search under the Keyword Search using "consumer decision making."

3. Find two articles illustrating how consumers engage in decision-making processes. Be forewarned: Many of the articles will examine consumerism in the business world or in health care. These articles are appropriate to use.

4. Could the techniques or mechanisms described in your articles be applied to social service organizations? Why or why not?

5. If applied, would the procedures result in empowerment for consumers? If so, to what degree?

InfoWrite

This chapter emphasizes using cultural values and diversity as strengths in macro social work practice. For example, how might murals and playgrounds reflect cultural traditions and serve as a source of empowerment? Unfortunately, when people begin to think about the strengths of cultural traditions, they may also engage in stereotypical thinking. In order to refine your critical-thinking skills:

1. Go to InfoWrite.

2. Scroll to Critical Thinking.

3. Read the section focusing on "Recognizing Ethnocentrism and Stereotypes."

4. With classmates, identify a stereotype associated with Latino Americans.

5. If you are working with consumers of services to establish a monument, mural, or other form of public artwork to promote a specific cultural heritage, consider how consumers and professionals can guard against ideas and products that might advance harmful stereotypical thinking and ethnocentric beliefs. Create two brief vignettes depicting an appropriate and an inappropriate use of cultural values in promoting diversity via community–based projects or physical artifacts.

CASE EXAMPLE: The Virtues of a Bottom-Up Approach

The Central Shelter is a community-based drop-in center providing temporary overnight shelter and daily meals (lunch and dinner) to more than three hundred homeless people. Most of the consumers are unemployed, live on the streets, and are experiencing mental health and/or substance difficulties. Consumers are generally transient; they come to the Central Shelter for a warm meal and a place to sleep. The people served at the Central Shelter are predominantly African American.

The only stipulations for acquiring emergency shelter and food services are that people sign in and be non-disruptive. Food is served cafeteria style. Accommodations consist of two large auditoriums, separated by gender, with bunk beds. Consumers are required to leave the shelter each day by 9:00 A.M. There are no restrictions on how many times a consumer can return for food or shelter.

There is a small residential program connected to the Central Shelter for consumers wanting to move toward independent living. Requirements for the residential program are more stringent; they include sobriety, participation in an intervention program, and work duties in the kitchen or on the serving line. Upon graduation from the residential program, consumers move to a nearby affiliated housing program and seek employment in the community.

The Central Shelter employs a small staff, which includes social workers, administrative support, and cooks. The shelter relies heavily on the use of volunteers and on contributions from churches and families. The focus of leadership at the Central Shelter is a grassroots orientation. This means that the consumer council, consisting of women and men from both the emergency and the residential program, is the dominant force in policy and program development and in decision making, including decisions affecting delivery of services. The macro roles for the social workers are mainly those of facilitator, administrator, fund raiser, advocate, community organizer, educator, and group leader—all roles described earlier in this section.

Social workers and staff members at the Central Shelter have worked diligently to identify the strengths of consumers in developing the consumer council. This is a particularly delicate matter, as consumers at the Central Shelter come from varied backgrounds and are generally transient. Because of the prevalence of mental health and substance issues, consumers are also prone to relapses.

Consumer council meetings are held weekly and are open to all consumers and employees. The agenda is set by consumers and can include any relevant topics, excluding personnel matters. Decisions are made by vote after full discussion. Historically, the consumer council has been leery of entering into new relationships with funding sources out of fear of losing independence and the consumer-driven nature of the shelter. At times, this has meant losing funding in favor of maintaining autonomy.

Located in an impoverished section of the city near a symphony hall, the Central Shelter has recently come under attack by local leaders from the fine arts. The conductor of the city symphony has led an effort to encourage city officials to utilize the right of eminent domain to acquire buildings in this portion of town and construct a new fine arts center. This would not only involve displacement of the poor but also legally mandate the relocation of the Central Shelter and its affiliate programs.

Sadly, this venture pitted advocates for the fine arts, a well-funded and politically connected (predominantly white) group, against consumers at the Central Shelter and other coali-

tions for the homeless. Two sets of community-minded organizations were at battle for resources and rights in one of the poorest parts of town. Clearly, consumers at the Central Shelter viewed this as an affront to their presence, as well as a social class and racial issue. Consumers felt that the more affluent symphony-goers and supporters of the fine arts simply did not want to see or be near consumers frequenting the Central Shelter.

The consumer council at the Central Shelter stood firm in its resolve to keep the shelter at its current location. Given this direction, social workers encouraged the consumer council to frame a plan for strengthening the shelter's position in the community. After assessing the presenting situation and resource capabilities, consumers sought to keep the Central Shelter in its current location, enhance community understanding and knowledge of the importance of its services and functions, and build alliances with kindred organizations and associations.

In many respects, what first seemed to be a problem—the threat of displacement of the Central Shelter—quickly became an opportunity. The threat of relocation provided an impetus for consumers at the shelter to raise community awareness concerning their programs and services. Many people in the community had little experience or knowledge of the Central Shelter or had become complacent about this population. In cooperation with other human service organizations and advocacy groups for the homeless, consumers successfully informed council members of their situation, contacted local media sources, attended public meetings on the topic, and built upon existing resources for the shelter to further services and rights for the homeless.

(continued)

CASE EXAMPLE   (*continued*)

The virtues of a strengths-based, consumer oriented approach to macro-level change are many. This case example highlights the importance of establishing a strong, structural (e.g., organizational) means for consumers to exert power and control. At the Central Shelter, this structural means was the use of a consumer council. An active and vital consumer council allowed the expectations and desires of consumers to come to the fore. It served as a potent mechanism for subscribing to what Poole and Colby (2002) call a bottom-up philosophy.

It is also important to note that social workers worked with consumers to identify consumer strengths, opportunities, capabilities, and solutions. Social workers then used their expertise to help consumers form alliances and activate existing resources. Ultimately, social workers helped consumers find valuable ways to meet with council members, media representatives, and community leaders to secure resources and expand opportunities for the homeless. Consumers effectively used a democratic form of decision making to advance the "consumers' viewpoint," shape the community agenda, and collaborate with other human service organizations and associations (Moore & Kelly, 1996).

In this case example, race and social class were both salient factors.

As a consequence, it was especially crucial that citizens and various interest groups heard about needs, positions, perspectives, and stories directly from the mouths of consumers at the Central Shelter. There is no real substitute for hearing the gut-level trials and tribulations of consumers.

As a final observation, the Central Shelter is frequently described by citizens and helping professionals as being "run by the clients." Many people describe an organizational culture of "nonprofessionalism." Frequently, it is difficult to differentiate between consumers and employees at the Central Shelter. Depending on one's point of view, this could be seen as either a negative comment or a compliment.

Indeed, from a time and resource management perspective, delivery of services and decision making at the Central Shelter could arguably be more efficient at times. Yet, when consumers are put into action to use their capabilities and skills in interfacing with the service delivery system, human dignity and respect are maximized. From a strengths perspective, improving the quality of services and creating opportunities for advancement are inseparable from the centrality of the consumer role, even if some organizational inefficiencies may result.

THINKING CRITICALLY
ABOUT THE CASE EXAMPLE

1. Clearly, the Central Shelter embraces a bottom-up philosophy of leadership. Although this can be very empowering, what are some possible drawbacks of such an orientation? It may not be surprising that some people label the organizational culture as nonprofessional. Given these circumstances, envision concrete ways to promote and enrich relationships between consumers and professionals.

2. The Central Shelter supports temporary housing. As a result, people come and go on a regular basis. Does this constitute an asset or a problem with respect to membership on the consumer council? Assess the importance of continuity for both membership and leadership. What about the role of secondary consumers of services (e.g., family members or former consumers)? How do the perspectives of secondary consumers differ from those of primary consumers?

3. Are consumers of services always "experts on themselves"? As noted, many of the residents at the Central Shelter experience mental health and/or substance difficulties. How does this both enhance and limit their ability to participate in shared governance and build alliances with other organizations (e.g., the local symphony orchestra)?

REFLECTION EXERCISES

1. Many social work degree programs require agency visits, either course-embedded or otherwise. On your next visit to a social service organization, find out how consumers participate and exert control in decision-making or planning activities. Does the organization have a consumer council or some other form of group leadership with consumer membership? How are consumers seen as stakeholders in the agency? Do not be surprised if the agency personnel seem unaccustomed to or uncomfortable with the term *consumer*. Try to assess the organizational culture surrounding the use of a strengths orientation and decentralized decision making.

2. Ask a social worker to describe one of his or her macro practice roles. If you receive a puzzled look, ask the social worker how he or she works to create change with organizations or in her or his community or society. Be attentive to how professional involvement is described. What is the role of the consumer? For example, if the social worker is serving on a planning group for an upcoming workshop or conference, ask about consumer participation and ownership in the endeavor. Are any consumer groups involved as sponsors? If so, what is the level of consumer involvement?

3. Consider joining a consumer-based advocacy group or voluntary association. The particular organization you decide to join will depend on your interests and needs as well as community and societal conditions. Approach your membership in two ways: as a source of personal enlightenment and as an opportunity to contribute to a worthwhile cause. Make a special effort to be sensitive to notions of diversity and cultural competence. Strive to acquire "grounded knowledge" by becoming attuned to the history, culture, traditions, customs, language, and art forms associated with your newfound consumer group (Hurdle, 2002, p. 186). Identify other, kindred special-interest groups aligned and collaborating with your newfound consumer group. How did these associations occur and why?

SUGGESTED READINGS

Miley, K. K., O'Melia, M., & DuBois, B. (2001). *Generalist social work practice: An empowering approach.* Boston: Allyn & Bacon.

Moore, S. T. (1996). Quality now: Moving human service organizations toward a consumer orientation to service quality. *Social Work, 41*(1), 33–40.

O'Melia, M., & Miley, K. K. (2002). *Readings in contextual social work practice.* Boston: Allyn & Bacon.

Poole, D. L., & Colby, I. C. (2002). Do public neighborhood centers have the capacity to be instruments of change in human services? *Social Work, 47,* 142–152.

REFERENCES

Akerlund, M., & Cheung, M. (2000). Teaching beyond the deficit model: Gay and lesbian issues among African Americans, Latinos, and Asian Americans. *Journal of Social Work Education, 36,* 279–292.

Brody, R., & Nair, M. D. (1997). *Macro practice: A generalist approach.* Wheaton, IL: Gregory.

Delgado, M. (2000). *Community social work practice in an urban context.* New York: Oxford University Press.

Fong, R. (2002). Empowering multicultural clients by using cultural value and biculturalization of interviews. In M. O'Melia & K. Miley (Eds.), *Pathways to power: Readings in contextual social work practice.* Boston: Allyn & Bacon.

Green, G. J., & Lee, M. (2002). The social construction of empowerment. In M. O'Melia & K. Miley (Eds.), *Pathways to power: Readings in contextual social work practice.* Boston: Allyn & Bacon.

Hurdle, D. E. (2002). Native Hawaiian traditional healing: Culturally based interventions for social work practice. *Social Work, 47,* 183–192.

Kirst-Ashman, K. K., & Hull, G. H. (1997). *Generalist practice with organizations and communities.* Chicago: Nelson-Hall.

Landon, P. S. (1995). Generalist and advanced generalist practice. In R. L. Edwards (Editor-in-chief), *Encyclopedia of social work* (19th ed.)

(Vol. 2, pp. 1101–1108). Washington, DC: NASW Press.

Lum, D. (1999). *Culturally competent practice: A framework for growth and action.* Pacific Grove, CA: Brooks/Cole.

Marsh, J. C. (2004). Social work in a multicultural society. *Social Work, 49,* 5–6.

Mead, G. H. (1934). *Mind, self, and society.* Chicago: University of Chicago Press.

Meenaghan, T. M., Washington, R. O., & Ryan, R. M. (1982). *Macro practice in human services.* New York: Free Press.

Miley, K. K., O'Melia, M., & DuBois, B. (2001). *Generalist social work practice: An empowering approach.* Boston: Allyn & Bacon.

Moore, S. T., & Kelly, M. J. (1996). Quality now: Moving human services organizations toward a consumer orientation to service quality. *Social Work, 41,* 33–40.

National Association of Social Workers. (2001). *NASW standards for cultural competence in social work practice* [brochure]. Washington, DC: Author.

Netting, F. E., Kettner, P. M., & McMurtry, S. L. (1993). *Social work macro practice.* New York: Longman.

Olsen, M. E. (1978). *The process of social organization: Power in social systems.* New York: Holt, Rinehart & Winston.

Perlman, H. H. (1957). *Social casework: A problem-solving process.* Chicago: University of Chicago Press.

Pincus, A., & Minahan, A. (1983). *Social work practice: Model and method.* Itasca, IL: F. E. Peacock.

Poole, D. L., & Colby, I. C. (2002). Do public neighborhood centers have the capacity to be instruments of change in human services? *Social Work, 47,* 142–152.

Saleebey, D. (1992). *The strengths perspective in social work practice.* New York: Longman.

———. (2002). *The strengths perspective in social work practice.* New York: Longman.

Tower, K. D. (1994). Consumer-centered social work practice, restoring client self-determination. *Social Work, 39,* 191–196.

Walker, J. (2002). Building on strengths in community settings. *Focal Point, 16,* 3–4.

Weiman, K., Dosland-Hasenmiller, C., & O'Melia, J. (2002). Shutting off that damn bell: Raising the voices within. In M. O'Melia & K. Miley (Eds.), *Pathways to power: Readings in contextual social work practice.* Boston: Allyn & Bacon.

Yamada, Y. (2001). Consumer direction in community-based long term-care: Implications for different stakeholders. *Journal of Gerontological Social Work, 35,* 83–97.

4

Calling on Consumer
and Citizen Strengths

Chapter Content Areas

The Link Between Individual
Help and Social Environment

Policy Perspectives That Build on
Strengths

Inclusion as a Policy Theme

Developmental/Prevention
versus Remediation Approaches

Two Major Social Work
Movements: Settlement Houses
and the Charity Organization
Society

Individual Approaches:
Psychotherapy and
Psychopathology

The Power of Individual,
Residual Approaches

Emphasizing the Positive: The
Other Side of Social Work

Working from a Strengths
Perspective

Utilizing the Empowerment
Approach

The Social Development
Perspective

The Membership Perspective

Prevention and Resiliency

The Group-Centered Perspective

Implementing the Strengths
Perspective

Thinking from a Strengths
Perspective

Finding Opportunities for
Consumer Action

Structuring Services in Forms
That Build on Strengths

Nurturing the Organizational
Culture to Build on Client
Strengths

Developing Mechanisms for
Promoting Consumer and
Citizen Involvement

Promoting Participatory Action
Research

CONSUMER STRENGTHS
AND SOCIAL CHANGE

Chapters 1 through 3 introduced the concepts of macro social work practice, the strengths orientation as it applies to macro practice, and some considerations for practitioners who are using a strengths orientation in macro practice. Now our attention moves to empowerment, particularly unleashing and harnessing the strengths of consumers to create social action and produce social change.

Calling on the strengths of consumers to enact social reform is righteous and generally a good thing, but it is not easily accomplished in the context of everyday practice. Instead, social workers are confronted with competing demands and expectations for defining their practice. As examples, in the previous chapter, time considerations and organizational pressures to concentrate on micro- over macro-level activities in practice were explored. Similarly, Chapter 2 examined the influence of problem-centered approaches on macro-level intervention. In the beginning of this book, we elaborated on the influence of environmental forces in shaping macro practice.

Before turning our focus to specific hands-on techniques for eliciting the strengths of consumers, it is necessary to reconcile the calls for professional involvement in both smaller- and larger-scale change in practice. Social workers, regardless of their professional inclinations and level of specialization, will need to direct their energies simultaneously toward assisting consumers and their families and toward creating social change. The degree to which this goal can be attained constitutes a defining moment in the career of most social work practitioners.

THE LINK BETWEEN INDIVIDUAL
HELP AND SOCIAL EMPOWERMENT

Traditionally, social work has been conceptualized in ways that hide the connections between working with individuals and helping groups of people to reach out and resolve social issues. As explained in Chapter 1, a conventional view of social work has defined it in terms of different methods: casework, group work, community organization, and administration. An underlying assumption is that these are distinctive methods, applied at different times, in different situations, and by different social workers. Indeed, many social workers, especially at the graduate level, receive advanced training in a single method. Similar problems exist with distinguishing social work as micro or macro, direct or indirect, casework or environmental. Each of these dichotomies tends to deemphasize the unitary nature of social work.

Porter Lee, an innovator in social work in the late 1920s, described the dual mission of social work as "cause and function." *Cause* references the organizing, policy, advocacy, and social reform functions of social work intended to deal with social conditions. *Function* relates to work with individual consumers and their problems (Chambers, 1980, p. 20). Subsequent analysis of this thinking has suggested that social work must deal with the "cause *in* function," suggesting that these approaches should be seen as a connected whole. Social work, uniquely among the helping professions, pursues both macro and micro concerns simultaneously.

Rather than viewing social work as a collection of different methods, then, it is probably more useful and practical to embrace this **unified approach.** From this perspective, calling on the strengths of consumers is seen as both an individual and a collective endeavor. This is true regardless of whether a social worker feels more comfortable working at one level or another. It is important to note that for the practitioner "to adequately pursue social justice and deal with issues of power and oppression in a clinical context, this bifurcated structure of social work must somehow be unified" (Vodde & Gallant, 2002, p. 439).

Because of the individualistic nature of U.S. society and the predominance of the individual approach in social work, social work students are probably most familiar with case approaches through texts, field placements, and the general acceptance of counseling and therapy in our society. Students may have less exposure to macro approaches, which are typically more abstract. As a result, students may feel less comfort with and support for macro approaches.

Given this unified direction, it is imperative that social work be conceptualized as something more than therapy. On the other hand, social work practice should not be dedicated solely to large-scale, macro change. Social work practice should be seen as both of these—and much more. A unified approach means that macro social work need not be conceptualized as specialized or "advanced" social work practice. Macro practice is not a method to be instituted instead of, or in place of, work with individuals and families. Social workers can be "Jills and Jacks of many trades" and can call on the strengths of consumers in many different ways, simultaneously.

In Chapter 3, various macro-practice roles (advocate, educator, community organizer, political activist, etc.) were identified and described using a strengths orientation. With a unified approach, one way of depicting a sense of professional self as a social worker is to think of oneself as moving into and out of an array of social work roles (both micro and macro) in any given day. As the social worker consciously enacts various roles, she or he works to understand the presenting situation and social circumstances from the standpoint of the consumer and seeks ways for consumers to promote their strengths and interests—the essence of empowerment.

HOW POLICY PERSPECTIVES
SHAPE CONSUMER ACTION

Social welfare policy is frequently seen as lying along a continuum, from institutional (universal) to residual (selective) approaches (Popple & Leighninger, 1990, pp. 41–42). Universal approaches are predicated on the notion that programs are offered to consumers on the basis of needs and that eligibility requirements will not be unduly restrictive. Conversely, residual/selective approaches seek to serve fewer people, mainly those who are experiencing problems despite general support from family and the economy (market).

Similarly, Tice and Perkins (2002) discuss the problem-centered perspective and the strengths approach to policy development (pp. 10–15), which parallel the residual and universal approaches. Communities and societies espousing universal approaches to social policy and service delivery can be seen as more progressive and have to some extent already embraced consumerism and a strengths approach. Universal approaches more readily allow the strengths of consumers to come to the fore in the helping process, particularly in terms of program and policy formation and development. When social programs and policies are viewed as responsive to human needs, consumers become legitimized in their ability to exercise influence and control over their lives.

Conversely, residual and problem-solving approaches, characterized by formal eligibility requirements and means tests, are more likely to emphasize the partitioning of problems and social control. There is also a tendency to compartmentalize issues confronting consumers, which frequently leads to fragmentation of the service delivery system. Under these circumstances, social workers must make special efforts to underscore and reinforce the strengths of consumers and to explore appropriate means of promoting consumer empowerment.

Inclusion as a Policy Theme

It is important to examine social policies in terms of the extent to which they enhance the inclusion and well-being of all segments of a population. A major thrust of current European social policy is to recognize and promote the inclusion of marginalized groups. *Marginalized groups* are those that aspire to be accepted by others and to acquire a valued status in the social structure, but remain outside or peripheral to those in power. Structurally, social workers need to identify and analyze how specific groups of people become marginalized or excluded from the decision-making process and access to resources in a society.

A thorough consideration of ways to reduce or eliminate social barriers for marginalized groups is particularly germane to the implementation of the strengths perspective. For example, segregation, stereotyping, and discriminatory laws and policies often act as social barriers and constraints for marginalized groups of people. Ideally, the discovery of strengths, whether for individuals or for groups of people, is maximized when social policy initiatives exhibit an explicit commitment to equitable and just policies for all groups of people.

Although inclusion may be a less dominant theme in U.S. social policy discussions, our historical analysis of social change in the first chapter of this book serves as a small testament to the importance of inclusion as a policy theme. For example, embracing a War on Poverty in the 1960s was a bold societal and policy initiative to empower traditionally marginalized groups on the basis of race and class. Take a moment to consider the effects of President Lyndon Johnson's policies in relation to marginalized groups of people in the United States as compared to President Ronald Reagan's individualistic approach to social policy.

Four Social Service Arenas

Lofquist (1992) has suggested that social service activities can be conceptualized in terms of two dimensions: *purpose* (from prevention to remediation) and *focus* (from individuals to conditions). Using this logic, Lofquist proposes four basic human service arenas: (1) community development, (2) personal growth and development, (3) community problem solving, and (4) personal problem solving. Although social work operates in all four arenas, the bulk of social work activity currently tends to be the fourth arena, personal problem solving. A balanced approach to social work would place greater emphasis on arenas 1 through 3. Personal problem solving is most associated with remedial, problem-centered policy approaches, whereas community development and personal growth are more compatible with universal, strengths-based policy approaches.

Settlement Houses and the Charity Organization Society as Reflections of Different Policy Approaches Two noteworthy movements in social work, the settlement house and the Charity Organization Society (COS), developed in the late 1800s. Both were initiatives intended to deal with problems associated with rapid urbanization and industrialization in the United States. Yet, it is important to differentiate these approaches as two distinguishable responses to human need. A basic difference involved the role of the consumer in relation to the social environment. The settlement house movement reflected a more progressive approach, emphasizing consumer-driven opportunities and activities intended to enhance the normal development of individuals and groups, a combination of activities and actions captured in Lofquist's arenas 1 through 3. Conversely, the COS movement reflected a more remedial approach, focusing on causes of individual and family problems. Social workers helped those in need to overcome problems—Lofquist's arena 4, personal problem solving.

The Prominence of Individual Approaches, Psychotherapy and Psychopathology There are many reasons why individual remediation has prevailed over community development, social change, and preventive approaches in the United States. Dealing with individual problems rather than social issues more clearly embraces the prevalence of individualism in U.S. culture and society. Also, social work services intended to soothe individual problems rarely call for political upheaval or radical social changes. Instead, individual and family-based therapy tends to support the status quo—the existing social structure—and can be viewed as a type of manageable demand, amenable to cost-containment strategies (e.g., managed care).

When the focus is on individual-level help, there is an inherent tendency to "blame the victim" (Ryan, 1976). Such an outlook essentially absolves society, each of us, from any obligation to resolve larger social issues. Not only is this convenient, but it sends a message to the public that people in power should maintain their status as decision makers. Those with personal problems are frequently viewed as broken, weak, troubled, and incapable of effectively exerting power and influence. Such a negative outlook gives rise to efforts to find ways of helping people to better cope with the social environment, not to change it.

If you have entered the profession of social work with the primary goal of conducting therapy, do not be dismayed. Societal and social work values certainly support initiatives aimed at personal problem solving. In addition, as a social worker you will find yourself uniquely prepared to challenge "the assumptions constituting the problem narratives of individual clients and families in clinical practice" (Vodde & Gallant, 2002, p. 440). Such an outlook provides social workers with a broad vision for helping others that includes attention both to personal problems and to the power relations and social forces undergirding the difficulties confronting consumers of our services.

Early in the development of social work as a profession, Abraham Flexner, a major figure associated with the reform of medical schools, was asked to speak to a conference of social workers. In his address, he accused social work of not being a legitimate profession because it lacked an established, defined theoretical base (see Popple & Leighninger, 1990, p. 70). Freudian psychodynamic theory dealt with the cause of individual problems while suggesting interventions that might be helpful in dealing with problems at a personal level.

As a result, in the early years of our profession, social workers probably adopted Freudian theory too uncritically. Well into the 1960s, social workers were busy trying to modify Freud's thinking to include environmental change and adaptations. Meanwhile, clearly defined theoretical frameworks for macro social work were not forthcoming and remained far less developed than individual approaches. Many factors contributed to this phenomenon. But it is important to recognize that macro approaches were typically founded on sociological theory and were never intended for application to helping others. Additionally, as suggested earlier, individual-level orientations were more compatible with the political needs and desires of people in power and providers of funding.

The Power of Individual, Residual Approaches A closer examination of the reasons for the dominance of both individual and residual approaches in American social work can be quite revealing. Those involved in human services should realize that individual and remedial approaches serve many purposes:

- They minimize pressures to change society and its various institutions.
- They reinforce and justify current institutional arrangements and configurations.
- They maintain the existing class structure and hierarchy.
- They elevate the perceived power of the profession and professionals by emphasizing professional expertise over the power of consumers.
- They define the role of professionals as control agents or "fixers."
- They establish boundaries between professionals and consumers, where professionals are designated as powerful and consumers as subordinate.

THE POSITIVE SIDE OF SOCIAL WORK:
PERSPECTIVES AND CONCEPTS

There have been many critiques of what is seen as an overemphasis on psychological approaches and pathology in American social work. As one notable example, Specht and Courtney (1994) in *Unfaithful Angels,* emphasize the importance of public social services and programs that more fully acknowledge the strengthening of communities and larger systems—in the settlement house tradition.

Encouragingly, the past several decades in the United States have seen a rekindled interest in a variety of approaches (holistic, positive, and social models) that lend themselves to a more comprehensive view of social work practice and consumer well-being. These orientations often act to enrich and stimulate thought, dialogue, and action concerning the significance of social factors in practice.

The social worker who approaches social work practice using a unified approach attempts to integrate "traditional" and "community-oriented" approaches (Hadley, Cooper, Dale, & Graham, 1987). Traditional approaches are reactive, provide services at arm's length, are based on professional responsibility, and are focused on the individual client. In contrast, community-oriented approaches are preventive; they are proactive; they provide services in relation to the community; they are based on shared responsibility; and they stimulate the building of social networks (pp. 8, 9). Given a community orientation, consider the possible contributions of the following perspectives.

The Strengths Perspective

As stated earlier, Saleebey (2002) has written extensively about the "strengths perspective" in social work. We have already identified this as a broad, positive approach that can inform social work practice at many levels and in multiple domains. Saleebey suggests a number of key concepts in using the strengths approach: empowerment, membership, resilience, healing and wholeness, dialogue, and collaboration (pp. 9–12), as well as the following general principles: "every individual group, family and community has strengths"; adversity may be harmful but "also may be a source of challenge and opportunity"; aspirations of individuals, groups, families, and communities must be taken seriously; "we best serve clients by collaborating with them"; and "every environment is full of resources" (pp. 13–17).

These concepts and principles can be applied to multiple facets of social work, but they seem particularly appropriate for macro social work and readily usable for community-oriented practice. Analyzing and using strengths with a particular sensitivity to community assets has identifiable merits. It provides a definable context for practice—one's community—and draws on the spirit of the settlement house movement, mainly social activism and reform. "The messages inherent in the settlement house work were 'do with' their neighbors to effect changes in environmental conditions and broaden opportunities for individuals" (DuBois & Miley, 2002, p. 35).

In many respects, the unification of the strengths perspective with a community orientation seems natural. It successfully identifies the community as a social entity full of natural helpers and resources—be they family members, neighbors, friends, businesses, churches, clubs, or other groups of people. In addition, a strengths–community orientation draws attention to the importance of people coming together to effect change, one of the defining tenets of macro social work practice.

The Empowerment Approach

Judith Lee (1994) discusses the usefulness of an empowerment approach in social work. Whereas empowerment certainly involves individual consumers, it also calls upon social workers to engage groups of people in assessing collective strengths and seeking opportunities for change. Indeed, one could argue that a major role of social workers, from this perspective, is to facilitate the formation of groups, commonly community-based groups. Consumer groups are intended not only to provide support for members but also to identify resources and seek ways to advocate for policies and practices aimed at improving their collective situation.

Social workers need to be careful not to restrict empowerment in everyday practice to an individual-level construct. If this were the case, empowerment would become little more than a new wrinkle on traditional, pathology-based helping. Instead, one responsibility of a social worker can be seen as providing "safe havens" for consumer interaction, much like the settlement houses of yesteryear. These havens can be physical dwellings or other media (including electronic) that encourage open and productive communication among consumers.

A good example of the empowerment approach as applied to community work is the Family Unity Camp for HIV/AIDS-affected youth. A TEAM ("Together Everyone Achieves More") approach was implemented:

> Rochester-area AIDS counselors and volunteers have found that
> traditional approaches do not work for HIV/AIDS affected youth.
> The last thing young people want to do is talk about the pain they
> have experienced. What they want is to connect with others, have fun
> and serve their community. The youth leader program was designed to
> move youngsters from "helpee" to "helper." (Taylor-Brown, Garcia, &
> Itin, 2002, p. 11)

The Family Unity Camp gives youth and their families a place to congregate and examine issues of common importance. The program has been a success because it is guided by an empowerment–strengths orientation and allows youth and families to meet and work "in a less clinical context, which lessens resistance" (p. 11). Taylor-Brown, Garcia, and Itin (2002) offer this argument for the virtues of an empowerment approach: "The deficit orientation is reinforced by

© Thomson Higher Education/Heinle Image Bank.

delivery of services framed in a reactive mode, responding in times of family crisis rather than offering preventive or developmental services that respond to a child's experience of death in a normative way" (p. 11).

The Social Development Perspective

Social development is a term that has been used extensively, particularly at the international level. James Midgley (1995), a South African–born leader in U.S. social work education, has written extensively about social development as an orientation in social work practice. As used by Midgley, "social development" combines community development and economic development approaches. For example, this perspective has increasingly informed post-apartheid social policy and social work practice in South Africa (Gray, 1998).

In this book, the relationship between macro social work practice and efforts relevant to social development have not been a central focus. The International Federation of Social Workers (IFSW) is an organization dedicated to promoting international cooperation and action to foster social development and welfare across the globe. Indeed, the general principles and tenets of empowerment and the strengths orientation can be applied to and are suitable for international social work and social development.

The Membership Perspective

Falck (1988) presents a "membership perspective" for human services. This orientation involves the ability to act as a conduit between the individual and society as each reaches out to the other to seek fulfillment (p. 11). Falck's writings concentrate on the connectedness of all people. Rather than perceiving users of social services as passive recipients of help, an orientation toward membership assumes that every person has the ability to make contributions to her or his immediate situation, social circumstances, and society as a whole: "Identity of each member is bound up with that of others through social involvement. A member is a person whose differences from others create tensions that lead to growth, group cohesion, and group conflict. Human freedom is defined by simultaneous concern for oneself and others" (p. 30).

Important themes in the membership perspective include affiliation, connectedness, mutual contribution, and mutual support. Consumers are viewed as potentially active and productive members of groups, their community, and society. Using this outlook, social workers seek ways to help consumers affirm and legitimize their membership status in the social world.

Prevention and Resiliency

Special note should be made of the concepts of prevention and resiliency, which are closely associated with the strengths perspective. Ideally, consumers would be spared exposure to negative situations and circumstances. **Prevention** involves the extent to which the environment can be modified to prohibit social ills from occurring. It is a hands-on stance with respect to social-economic development that advocates for consumer-based policies and programs intended to thwart difficulties before they emerge. "Proactive involvement is directed toward developing equitable social and economic policy . . . to prevent problems for individuals and society before they occur" (DuBois & Miley, 2002, p. 55).

Resiliency can be viewed as a protective factor, which helps individuals, groups, and communities to overcome adversity. Resiliency is promoted by the successful development of supportive structures and the ability of consumers to contend successfully with problems (Benard, 1992). In relation to communities, resiliency involves the ability to persevere, bend, and adapt to changing conditions. As people evaluate the assets, resources, and capacities of various social systems, resiliency is often overlooked.

The Group-Centered Perspective

The group-centered approach is an attempt to capture the theoretical underpinnings of the settlement house and group work movements (Alcorn, Epstein, & Rasheed, 2001). It highlights the importance of group affiliation and the role of social workers in encouraging consumers to participate actively in various group memberships.

This line of thinking goes beyond the use of group work as a therapeutic method in micro practice. Consumer linkage with and participation in groups is a means of empowerment—an avenue for social advocacy and for producing social change. Social workers work with consumers to establish, maintain, and enrich groups. These groups use their capabilities to position themselves and lobby for rights and opportunities in organizations, the community, and society.

Affiliation

In one way or another, each of the aforementioned models relates to the social aspect of human existence—the value of **affiliation.** As social beings, all humans need socialization, affiliation, and a feeling of belonging. Human beings benefit both individually and collectively from social interaction and affiliations of all sorts.

Social work is not alone in recognizing the value of formal and informal affiliations with others. In *Bowling Alone,* political scientist Robert Putnam (2000) attributes the recent decline of civic engagement in the United States to the demise of group affiliations. A basic cornerstone of a civilized democratic society is the ability of citizens to express their concerns and interests effectively via group affiliations. Without this ability, the overall social structure can be ignorant of and unresponsive to the ever-changing needs of its people. Consequently, Putnam calls for a concerted effort to rebuild the prominence and power of social grouping as a means of enriching civic discourse and engagement.

IMPLEMENTING EMPOWERMENT
AND THE STRENGTHS PERSPECTIVE

Empowerment and the strengths perspective require social workers to function in ways that may be new and unfamiliar. Here are some practical suggestions for calling on the strengths of consumers in everyday practice. Some ideas are action oriented; others are more abstract. Several of these offerings have been touched upon in previous chapters; others will be elaborated on in later chapters.

First and foremost, strive to identify yourself as a social worker dedicated to implementing empowerment and a strengths orientation whenever necessary or appropriate. No single theory or orientation can ever account for all of human existence or be used in every instance for helping others. Life is far too complex. But, as much as possible, do your best to adopt these notions as guiding constructs in framing your practice.

1. *Use the language of strengths and empowerment in place of pathology-oriented terminology.* Ideally, at some point, the concepts and terms associated with the strengths perspective will become the pervasive and accepted language of practice. Many Americans, including social workers and consumers, view helping in terms that do not maximize the potential of individuals and groups to affect and change their situations and environment. You have been introduced to many new and important strengths-based and empowerment-oriented concepts. Include words like *consumer, strengths, resiliency, empowerment, affiliation,* and *group-centered* in your everyday practice vocabulary.

2. *Respect consumers.* A crucial value for social workers is respect for consumers. When people respect consumers, they become better listeners. Respect is a prerequisite for understanding situations and developments

from the point of view of consumers. Social workers need to show confidence in the belief that consumers have abilities and rights. This needs to be a given. How can helping professionals pursue means to empower the consumers of services if we ourselves do not believe in their potential for effecting change? Think of consumers as being experts in their areas of concern. Address and interact with consumers in a manner that dignifies their experiences and knowledge, much as you would with a well-informed colleague. Indeed, consumers have insight and information from which we all can benefit. Believe in the power of consumers to affect their life circumstances.

3. *Avoid "taking over" for consumers or trying to "save" victims through professional expertise, insight, and wisdom.* Human service professionals have historically been socialized to "help" clients, and the traditional mode for many professionals has been to provide direction and expertise to assist in resolving consumer problems. Social workers are different from other professionals in that they are not only knowledgeable about problem-solving but also adept at building partnerships with consumers to maximize their strengths in producing change. A general principle in macro social work practice is to avoid the temptation to "do things" for people. Often, consumers are best suited to accomplish tasks and attain goals for themselves. Control is the major issue here. When you mobilize consumers' involvement and activate their ingenuity, dependency is minimized and self-sufficiency is maximized.

4. *Develop active listening skills.* Perhaps one of the most important skills for the social worker is the ability to be an active listener. Consumers possess an incomparable knowledge of their life circumstances and a commanding view of their situations. Social workers have to learn how to elicit and listen carefully to consumer insight. This involves careful attention to consumers' stories. Through the use of interviews, group work, and well-organized meetings, the voice of the consumer can be heard, documented, and channeled for use in creating social change.

5. *Strive for a positive, optimistic attitude, and search for strengths in larger social systems.* How often have you heard people say that social workers and consumers of services have little or no power? It is easy to focus on helplessness and the negative aspects of a situation—the problem or problems. But focusing on the negative is often overwhelming, counterproductive, and fatalistic. Negativism is an inherent component of problem-centered approaches, as "the problem" takes center stage. Resist this temptation. Strive to discover the positive elements of any given state of affairs. Believe that consumers can make a difference and that change is inevitable. Optimism is contagious. Once you begin, it will become easier and easier to identify strengths, capabilities, and positive attributes in consumer groups, organizations, communities, and a society.

6. *Acknowledge the power of "grounded knowledge."* **Grounded knowledge** is information derived from experience and everyday observations.

Consumers are frequently rich in experience derived from their trials and tribulations. Although consumers may look to social workers for theoretical, book, and research knowledge, give due recognition to the value of life experiences and examine ways that this type of information can be structured, disseminated, and used to create social change.

Promoting Opportunities for Individual and Collective Action

Consumers often require encouragement to become involved, as they feel powerless and helpless. An important function for social workers is to stimulate and initiate consumer involvement. Think of yourself as a spark, a motivator, and an organizer. Your job is to identify and promote ways of allowing people to seek opportunities—for themselves. Here are a few techniques to kindle collective action.

1. *Promote connections and affiliations for people with similar circumstances.* Social workers can nurture opportunities for people facing similar circumstances to organize themselves. This can be as simple as referring consumers to existing advocacy groups and organizations. It can also involve organizing meetings, identifying means of transportation, scheduling, and other activities aimed at effectively bring people together. When people assemble to champion a cause and share experiences, the benefits are often plentiful. The power of collective thought often far outweighs that of individual contemplation. A primary goal for any social worker involves the facilitation and enrichment of empowerment-based consumer groups.

2. *Affirm the power of the collectivity.* There really is strength in numbers. It often takes a number of people and/or a few influential individuals to facilitate social change. Particularly in U.S. society, people must be convinced of the virtues and power of working together. Often, people confront difficulties on an individual basis. Our society tends to reward those who set out to brave the world alone. As a social worker, acknowledge and reward collective action. Assert with consumers, administrators, and people in positions of power that the ideas and perspectives of the people drawn together can be enlightening, empowering, and revealing. All citizens are potential recipients of insight gained from consumer input and strategizing. Certainly, business and industry have profited from such wisdom through the use of focus groups and other group methodologies.

3. *Identify natural leaders.* Social workers need not assume the role of group leader. Once a group is organized and processes are underway, the group is free to identify a leader from its ranks. It is often difficult for social workers and other helping professionals to yield and relinquish power. But consumers have an uncanny way of focusing attention on issues that might not be thought of or raised by others. Consumers bring to the table a host of personal attributes and assets. Your role as a social worker is to help to identify consumer leaders and then to nurture their abilities.

4. *Look for opportunities to equalize power.* The negative circumstances that often surround consumers of services can result in a perception of power-lessness. One function of the social worker is to help consumers and consumer groups to find ways to exert influence. When consumers gain a fuller, more comprehensive understanding of their situation (socially, politically, economically, and otherwise), they can more effectively seek ways of maximizing their clout. Help consumers see the "big picture" in terms of opportunities for equalizing power.

5. *Endorse groups for empowerment.* Efficacy in macro social work is often linked to the actions of groups of concerned people, not just to individual efforts. Whenever practical, reinforce and promote the use of groups as a form of participatory governance. Attempt to build an expectation or a tradition in your geographical area and community that recognizes the value of citizen groups in decision-making processes.

Structuring Services to Build on Strengths and Promote Empowerment

Social services designed in ways that promote a strengths perspective are probably more the exception than the rule. There are a number of techniques for structuring services to accentuate and build upon consumer and community strengths and to encourage social empowerment. Here are a few useful ideas:

1. *Provide services as physically close to people as possible.* It is easy for administrators and helping professionals to feel comfortable in their own space. For many, there is a sense of security and a feeling of power associated with "going to the office" in a central location inhabited by other professionals. Yet, decentralized offices in neighborhoods (e.g., in community-based buildings, churches, and schools) are much closer to where consumers live and more practical for bringing people together. Think of your office area as a venue for facilitating consumer gatherings, in the settlement house tradition, not simply as a space for conducting therapy.

2. *Promote community-based outreach.* Take active steps to contact prospective consumers where they live. Do not wait for them to come to you. Be proactive in identifying and contacting consumers who share common interests and in creating opportunities for consumers to assemble. Help organize block parties, town meetings, and chat rooms to facilitate grassroots consumer involvement.

3. *Combine macro and micro social work.* Even social workers whose principal role is working with individuals and families can and should function as macro social workers and promote empowerment. Such involvement needs to be supported and rewarded organizationally by the sponsoring institution. For example, the Alliance for Children and Families, which has been historically identified with social casework, has increasingly recognized that its affiliated agencies are engaged in a wide variety of

community-based projects. Indeed, the Alliance has worked to advance a unified approach so that social workers are educated and trained in a manner that embraces micro and macro social work simultaneously (Ryan, DeMasi, Heinz, Jacobson, & Ohmer, 2000).

Developing Mechanisms for Ensuring Consumer and Citizen Involvement

The focus of the social worker needs to be centered squarely on the voices and views of consumers. Functionally, this involves building organizational cultures where consumer strengths and perspectives take center stage. Whenever and wherever possible, consumers and other citizens should be included in a meaningful fashion in program planning and organizational decision-making processes. This can be facilitated in several ways:

1. *Include consumer views in the planning process.* Often agencies plan programs without taking the ideas and perspectives of consumers into account. This results in programs that are unresponsive to consumer needs and are underutilized. Strategically mandate consumer membership and participation on planning committees.

2. *Organize consumer meetings.* Social workers often are called upon to call, organize, and facilitate consumer meetings. These gatherings allow consumers to express views and interests and to evaluate the prospect of collective action. Establish mechanisms to document the sentiments of consumers for use in planning processes and organizational decision making.

3. *Create advisory boards.* Advisory boards can be useful means of incorporating the thoughts of consumers in agency deliberations. Although such input is rarely binding, advisory groups and boards can give leaders a sense of consumer sentiment and opinion. When advisory board advice is appreciated and used in earnest, it constitutes an invaluable source of knowledge for service agencies and makes service delivery more relevant and effective.

4. *Form consumer groups.* Allow creativity to reign. You can probably identify natural occurrences that bring consumers together, perhaps in relation to orientation programs, voluntary associations, celebrations, or local cultural events. Consider every occasion as an opportunity, formally or informal, for feedback on how consumer groups perceive and experience your agency and its services.

5. *Encourage meaningful participation of consumers on boards of directors.* Many agencies and planning organizations appoint consumers and other types of community representatives as directors on governance boards. This can be a powerful step. However, measures need to be taken to ensure that consumer members of the board are not marginalized in terms of their participation. As an example, newer members of boards often feel

intimidated in the face of existing relationships among more seasoned board members and their own general lack of information concerning board functions and responsibilities. If consumers serve only a short term or some other form of rotating term, meaningful board membership can be compromised. Additionally, some boards do an appreciable portion of their business in subcommittee sessions, so that meetings of the full board become almost perfunctory. When consumers are given unimportant subcommittee assignments, they are for all practical purposes diverted from the decision-making process.

6. *Provide structured opportunities for consumers to give back to the organization.* Many social service organizations have embraced peer counseling and mentorship programs in a systematic fashion. In the case of organizations using self-help and mutual aid groups, consumer involvement is a basic underlying principle of service delivery.

7. *Survey consumer views.* Periodic surveys of consumers and potential consumers will yield important information and allow agencies to effectively target population groups at risk, evaluate program delivery systems, and prioritize resource allocation.

8. *Promote participatory action research.* Far too often, social scientists and professionals approach research questions using perspectives or applying values that fall short of a full appreciation of the real-life experiences of consumers. Consumers can be insightful partners in the research process, particularly practice-focused research. This topic will be explored in much greater depth in a subsequent chapter; suffice it to say here that it is often wise to include the perspectives and orientations of those affected by an issue in theory formation and development in research (Feagin & Vera, 2001, p. 165).

Seeking Allies

Consumers, social workers, and social service agencies do not function or perform optimally when working in isolation. Although the down side of forming **alliances** is a propensity to diffuse one's purposes and goals, nurturing and developing partnerships and alliances between and among groups and organizations is crucial for acquiring information and building a consumer-oriented power base. The following are a few suggestions for finding **allies:**

1. *Encourage interagency networks and partnerships.* There are many different ways for social service agencies to work together. The possibilities here seem almost endless (e.g., cluster groups, pooling of resources). Consumers interface with a wide variety of service organizations and volunteer associations. Once again, call upon and rely on the knowledge of consumers as a potent perspective for conceptualizing interagency networks and partnerships.

2. *Get involved in professional and consumer associations.* Groups like the National Association of Social Workers (local, state, and national chapters) provide

opportunities for workers to share information and to advocate on behalf of clients. Depending on your area of practice, a number of other professional associations will most likely warrant your consideration. Make a special attempt to align yourself with consumer associations. For example, in the area of mental health, the National Alliance for the Mentally Ill (NAMI) is an influential consumer-based association in many communities.

3. *Embrace allies in your agency.* It is important, particularly when seeking consumer-driven modifications of policies and programs, to identify colleagues with a similar commitment to progressive change. Team building within an organization, both formal and informal, is an important consideration. Form alliances with other professionals committed to developing a consumer orientation to program delivery in your agency.

SUMMARY

This chapter offered a more detailed analysis of issues related to the implementation of empowerment theory and a strengths perspective in macro practice. Social work has often emphasized individual and remedial approaches over macro and prevention approaches. This is in part a reflection of the importance of individualism in our culture. In reality, social work practice includes a variety of approaches involving multiple system sizes (e.g., individual, family, group, organization, community, and society). Similarly, a number of theories and perspectives, many highlighted in this chapter, can be used to inform and assist social work practitioners who wish to embrace empowerment and the strengths perspective.

In considering the various practical suggestions offered in this chapter, remember that some of the most important virtues of a social worker are flexibility, adaptability, and the ability to think and act in a professional manner. The philosophical underpinning and tenets of empowerment and the strengths perspective are best incorporated into practice in a manner that corresponds to the specific will and desires of consumers. Whatever your social work role or position, establishing and building systemic means of enhancing consumer participation and decision making in service delivery will most likely be one of your more important and rewarding tasks.

A FEW KEY TERMS

unified approach	resiliency	alliances
social development	affiliation	allies
prevention	grounded knowledge	

USING INFOTRAC®

COLLEGE EDITION AND INFOWRITE

InfoTrac College Edition

Consumers can resolve issues and create change through unified efforts. The idea of citizen participation is essential to social work's principles of self-determination and empowerment. The relationship between citizen participation and the strengths perspective discussed in this chapter is emphasized in the following exercise.

1. Go to InfoTrac College Edition.

2. Search under the Keyword Search using "citizen participation."

3. Review the articles that describe citizen participation.

4. Read at least five citations on citizen participation.

5. Compile a list of the methods used to achieve citizen participation.

6. Describe how the methods correspond to prompting opportunities for individual and collective action as defined in this chapter.

InfoWrite

In this chapter, grounded theory is described as information derived from everyday observations. Apply the concept of grounded theory to your respect for others.

1. Go to InfoWrite.

2. Scroll to Modes of Exposition.

3. Click on "Process."

4. Read the section on "Explaining How Something Works."

5. Reflect on your personal inter-action style. Consider decisions you have made about the use of language, tone, relationships, or time. Provide at least two examples of how your obser-vations over a period of time influenced your respect for other people.

CASE EXAMPLE: Embracing Consumers in Social Action

Sarah Baxter has been employed as a social worker at the Pineville Coun-seling Center for about three years. She has spent the vast majority of her time working with individual clients one-on-one. Indeed, her official classi-fication as a social worker is Therapist I.

In recent months, Sarah has noticed that her caseload is increas-ing. It has reached a level where it is difficult to keep current on the status of her cases. Lately, only consumers facing the grimmest of circumstances command her attention.

Sarah has also noticed that a number of consumers are recipients of TANF (Temporary Assistance to Needy Families). Many of these people are very anxious because eligibility determiners in the local TANF pro-gram have been threatening to cut recipients from financial assistance. Employment in the region is difficult to obtain, as the local economy has been in a steady slump for over a year. The word among consumers is that

(continued)

CASE EXAMPLE   *(continued)*

---

decisions regarding termination from TANF seem arbitrary and show little sensitivity to the individual needs of families.

Using empowerment theory, the strengths perspective, and suggestions expressed in this chapter, identify and debate with your classmates some practical considerations for embracing the current sentiments of consumers. At present, Pineville Counseling Center sees group work in purely therapeutic terms—as billable hours of treatment. How could group work be envisioned differently—in a less remedial, more progressive manner?

Brainstorm ways that macro social work practice, particularly social empowerment and a strengths perspective, could establish itself in this type of working environment. Remember that although Sarah's consumers are struggling economically, they are experts concerning their unique life circumstances and social situation. Imagine, if consumers were to establish an active voice at Pineville Counseling Center and in the community, what kinds of social change might be considered.

THINKING CRITICALLY
ABOUT THE CASE EXAMPLE

1. Many negative stereotypes are associated with consumers of public assistance. Identify information and data sources describing the experiences of recipients of TANF. Do research findings dispel or support stereotypic thinking?

2. In this case example, information about local economic conditions appears sparse. How might you collect and evaluate information from consumers of TANF concerning employment, availability of housing, and day care services?

3. Pineville Counseling Center emphasizes billable hours of treatment as a measure of organizational success. Analyze the value of "billable hours" from the perspective of consumers and with respect to macro-level change.

REFLECTION EXERCISES

1. Social work degree programs in universities are known for requiring agency visits, volunteer experiences, and/or field education. As a result, you are probably familiar with some type of social service agency. Using an agency familiar to you, make a list of the ways this agency embraces empowerment, a strengths perspective, consumerism, and/or macro social work practice. Next, list the ways this agency reinforces a traditional (problem-solving), micro, and authoritative model of practice. Compare the two lists with respect to size and organizational commitment. Does the agency support a unified approach? How? How could processes be improved?

2. There is no substitute for experience and participation when attempting to learn more about the power of consumers and consumer groups. Attend a town or community meeting that has been organized in relation to a social cause. Pay attention to the roles played by consumers of services and other vested citizen groups in the meeting. How do the passion and focus of consumers differ from those of other interested parties, including professionals?

3. Pick up a copy of your campus newspaper and circle an article describing a concern for students on your campus. As one example, it is not uncommon for students on many campuses to express concern over a living wage for university custodial and food service workers. Is this merely a gripe column, or are students legitimately interested in confronting an issue? If it appears to be a legitimate concern, identify potential allies in relation to this cause. Candidates might include student clubs, faculty groups, sympathetic administrators, alumni, community entities, and national organizations.

SUGGESTED READINGS

Bens, C. K. (1994). Effective citizen involvement. *National Civic Review, 7*, 32–39.

Hyde, C. A. (2004). Multicultural development in human services agencies: Challenges and solutions. *Social Work, 49*(1), 7–16.

O'Looney, J. (1994). Model collaboration and social services integration. *Administration in Social Work, 18*(1), 61–87.

Poole, D. L., & Colby, I. C. (2002). Do public neighborhood centers have the capacity to be instruments of change in human services? *Social Work, 47*(2), 142–153.

REFERENCES

Alcorn, S., Epstein, M., & Rasheed, M. (2001). *The group centered perspective.* Unpublished paper. Aurora, IL: Aurora University School of Social Work.

Benard, B. (1992). Fostering resiliency in kids: Protective factors in the family, school and community. In *Prevention Forum, 12*(3), 1–16.

Chambers, C. A. (1980). Social service and social reform: A historical essay. In F. R. Breu & S. J. Diner (Eds.), *Compassion and responsibility: Readings in the history of social welfare policy in the United States.* Chicago: University of Chicago Press.

DuBois, B., & Miley, K. K. (2002). *Social work: An empowering profession.* Boston: Allyn & Bacon.

Falck, H. S. (1988). *Social work: The membership perspective.* New York: Springer Publishing.

Feagin, J. R., & Vera, H. (2001). *Liberation sociology.* Boulder, CO: Westview Press.

Gray, M. (Ed.). (1998). *Developmental social work in South Africa: Theory and practice.* Cape Town: David Philip Publishers.

Hadley, R., Cooper, M., Dale, P., & Graham, S. (1987). *A community social worker's handbook.* London: Tavistock Publications.

Lee, J. A. B. (1994). *The empowerment approach in social work practice.* New York: Columbia University Press.

Levine, M., & Perkins, D. V. (1997). *Principles of community psychology: Perspectives and applications* (2nd ed.). New York: Oxford University Press.

Lofquist, W. A. (1992). Mental models and fundamental change: A path to human service transformation. *New Designs for Youth Development, 10*(2), 28–34.

Midgley, J. (1995). *Social development: The developmental perspective in social welfare.* London: Sage Publications.

Popple, P. R., & Leighninger, L. (1990). *Social work, social welfare and American society.* Boston: Allyn & Bacon.

Putnam, R. (2000). *Bowling alone: The collapse and rise of American community.* New York: Simon and Schuster.

Ryan, W. (1976). *Blaming the victim.* New York: Vintage Books.

Ryan, W. P., DeMasi, K., Heinz, P. A., Jacobson, W., & Ohmer, M. (2000). *Aligning education and practice: Challenges and opportunities in social work education for community practice.* Milwaukee, WI: Alliance for Children and Families.

Saleebey, D. (2002). *The strengths perspective in social work practice* (3rd ed.). Boston: Allyn & Bacon.

Specht, H., & Courtney, M. (1994). *Unfaithful angels: How social work has abandoned its mission.* New York: Free Press.

Taylor-Brown, S., Garcia, A., & Itin, D. M. (2002). Family unity camp. *Social Work Today, 2*(20), 10–11.

Tice, C. J., & Perkins, K. (2002). *The faces of social policy: A strengths perspective.* Pacific Grove, CA: Brooks/Cole.

Vodde, R., & Gallant, J. P. (2002). Bridging the gap between micro and macro practice: Large scale change and a unified model of narrative-deconstructive practice. *Journal of Social Work Education, 38,* 439–458.

5

Enriching
Organizational Life

Chapter Content Areas

Organizations

Bureaucracy

Organizational Goals

Systems Model

Subsystems

Open System

Organizational Culture

Elements of Culture

Organization Development

Internal Organization
Developers

External Organization
Developer

Organizational Politics

PREPARE: An Assessment of
Organizational Change Potential

Empowerment

Organizations, such as private and public social service agencies, must be
well informed and flexible if they are to maintain and thrive in an ever-
changing environment. Organizations must be adaptable in order to
assess current and future needs, envision possible service strategies, and engage in
often far-reaching change. Such change might involve introducing training programs for staff, designing new programs or services, developing new community-
based collaborations, serving new consumers, and securing new funding streams.
Perhaps most challenging, organizations are often required to establish their own
policies and procedures based on guidelines that specify where, how, when, and
to whom services are to be provided.

It is essential that social workers examine and engage in organizational life
because of the environment within which contemporary social problems exist.
For example, consider the complexities of poverty, substance abuse, violence,
and health care. In all these situations, a maze of organizations and subsequent
services has been designed and operates to address the needs of people in their

communities. Indeed, organizations have far-reaching influences on people's lives. Think about the impact organizations have had in your own life. More than likely you were born in a hospital, were educated through a system of schools, belonged to various clubs or associations, attended a religious gathering, and were employed in various settings. Organizations are at the core of all of these services, memberships, and activities, so it should come as no surprise to you that macro social work practice involves studying these important social systems. This point is expressed by Etzioni (1964) in his classic book on organizations:

> We are born in organizations, educated by organizations, and most of us spend much of our lives working for organizations. We spend much of our leisure time paying, playing, and praying in organizations. Most of us will die in an organization, and when the time comes for burial, the largest organization of all—the state—must grant official permission. (p.1)

This chapter will acquaint you with the basic concepts of organizations, including the idea of organizations as open systems. Sections on organization development and the role of organization developers present a number of techniques by which macro practitioners can help organizational systems improve their functioning. Empowerment, leading to consumer participation and a healthy organizational culture, is a central theme throughout the chapter.

THE CONCEPT OF ORGANIZATION

Probably most social workers define *organization* on the basis of their agency experiences. As with other complex terms, everyone's definition is right and simultaneously wrong. Basically, an organization is a group of people intentionally organized to accomplish a common goal or set of goals. Organizations have also been defined as "institutionalized strategies geared to the achievement of more of less specific objectives through an orderly arrangement of many individuals" (Hollander & Hunt, 1976, p. 466).

Organizations are important because of their pervasiveness and power. Historically, the influence of organizations can be traced to the Great Depression, when large-scale public organizations were first introduced for the provision of human services. The programs of the New Deal created an infrastructure of organizations at the federal level that became both the foundation of the welfare state and the first large government human service **bureaucracies** (Netting, Kettner, & McMurtry, 1998). Large public bureaucracies and nationwide networks of affiliated agencies in the private sector greatly changed the size and complexity of human service organizations. As stated by Perrow (1979):

> Because of the superiority as a social tool over other forms of organization, bureaucracy generates an enormous degree of unregulated and often unperceived social power; and this power is placed in the hands of very few leaders. (p. 7)

As the size and sophistication of organizations changed, so did the role of macro practitioners within these organizations. Trends such as the size of human service organizations, their complexity, the diversity of services, and changes in standard budgetary policies all forced administrators to seek new skills. Implicit in these changes was a shift in the orientation of macro practice from external considerations to internal considerations, including operational efficiency and program effectiveness. At this juncture, the practice of social work supported a high degree of specialization based on professional training. Individuals were given specific job assignments and organized in levels based on both education and expertise. Finally, social workers became accountable for achieving certain goals related to consumers and the organization as a whole.

The goals of an organization include some that are explicit (deliberate and recognized) and others that are implicit (operating unrecognized). Organizational goals include (1) *vision,* an image of how the organization should be working; (2) *mission,* an overall purpose; (3) *values,* priorities in the organization's activities; and (4) *strategies,* several overall general approaches to reaching goals.

The importance of goals in human service organizations relates to the need for a standard by which to measure the success of social workers and of the organization. That is, effective performance, on whatever level one operates, must be related to some standard of evaluation. This goal model of evaluating an organization's effectiveness is built on Weber's (1947) studies of bureaucracy and assumes that organizations are designed to achieve specific ends, and that decision makers purposively act in accordance with goals (Maynard-Moody, 1987, p. 172). Goals are the organizing principles around which procedures, staff responsibilities, and structures are built.

Take a moment to consider the goals of your field agency and your role in achieving those goals. Then answer the following questions:

- How are agency goals made public?
- What values are integral to the organization's goals?
- How does your work address the organizational goals?
- What is the association between consumers and organizational goals?

Sometimes social workers have difficulty understanding the concept of organizational goals because they work primarily on a one-to-one basis and do not visualize the organization as a unit. Although professionals can readily understand that individuals have purposes and objectives, they have difficulty comprehending that organizations can also have specific objectives (Neugeboren, 1991). Their orientation to direct service gives them a perspective that inhibits thinking on a "systems" level.

Organization as a System

Social work practice with individuals is based on systems theory to support the holistic assessment of people in their communities. It also helps to think of organizations as systems (Katz & Kahn, 1978). Simply put, a system is an organized collection of parts that are highly integrated in order to accomplish

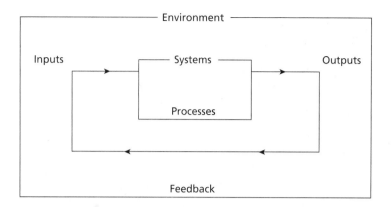

FIGURE 5.1 The Open System Model

SOURCE: From F. Ellen Netting, Peter M. Kettner, and Steven L. McMurtry, *Social Work Macro Practice*, 2/e. Published by Allyn & Bacon, Boston, MA. Copyright © 1998 by Pearson Education. Reprinted by permission of the publisher.

an overall goal. As illustrated in Figure 5.1, systems have inputs, processes, outputs, and **feedback.** *Inputs* to the system include resources such as money and people. These inputs come through *processes* in a coordinated fashion to achieve the goals established for the organization. *Outputs* are tangible results produced by the processes in the system such as services for consumers. Finally, *feedback* is a special form of input whereby a system receives information about its performance. Feedback can be either positive or negative. Positive feedback is input about a system's positive functioning, whereas negative feedback suggests an organization's malfunctioning (Kirst-Ashman & Hull, 2001). It is important to note that if one part of the system is changed, the nature of the entire system changes. Thus, there is a circular relationship between the overall system and its parts.

This approach is based on the work of biologist Ludwig von Bertalanffy (1950), who believed that lessons from fields such as ecology, which concerns organisms' interdependence with their surroundings, provide a basis for conceptualizing other phenomena as systems engaged in environmental interactions (Netting, Kettner, & McMurtry, 1998). In this model, "consumers" or organizations are viewed not as isolated entities driven primarily by internal psychological needs. Instead, they are seen as social beings whose personalities and behaviors can be analyzed in terms of their constant interaction with the world around them. As *open systems*, organizations both give to and draw from elements external to themselves. The key to understanding organizations lies in this ongoing process of exchange with critical elements (e.g. , culture, community, family) that constitute their personal environments.

Several features distinguish human service organizations from others. Most important, they work directly with people whose characteristics or concerns they address. The "raw material" for these organizations is the people themselves. The

© Thomson Higher Education/Heinle Image Bank.

interactions between service providers and consumers of services are the core production process. The output and justification of existence of such organizations is the protection, promotion, and enhancement of the well-being of the people they serve.

The effect of systems theory is that macro social workers can examine organizations from a broader perspective. Specifically, systems theory has brought with it an interpretation of patterns and events in organizations. Social workers are noticing the interrelations of the organizational parts, the need for coordination, and the benefits of collaboration. More attention is given to feedback, assessment, and evaluation in order to focus on structures and strategies that promote behaviors that determine events rather than simply reacting to events.

A major strength of the systems model is the encouragement it gives to social workers to think of themselves as part of a network that, as a totality, can serve consumers in a coordinated fashion. Ideally, by using the systems model, social workers will develop structures that nurture relationships between the agency and other systems. Methods of coordination with community groups, funding sources, government agencies, other helping agencies, educational institutions, professional organizations, and a variety of other systems would need to be identified (Lewis, Lewis, Packard, & Souflee, 2001).

Complete the following exercise as a means of integrating the information on organizations with systems theory. During the exercise, consider your professional responsibility as a social worker to continuously assess the effectiveness of organizations as a means of improving services (Kirst-Ashman & Hull, 2001).

Select at least two dissimilar agencies and contact social workers and administrators. For each agency, gather the following information: (1) the organizational goals; (2) methods to achieve the goals, (3) forms of inputs; (4) various processes such as services and treatment modalities, outputs, or ways that effectiveness is determined; and (5) ways that feedback is solicited and used.

With the agency information in hand, how do you explain the differences in the agencies' goals? Consider the similarities and difference between the agencies' input, process of service provision, and effectiveness measures.

Organizational Culture

The totality of the subsystems that make up an organization develops shared experiences—what Schein (1985) refers to as **organizational culture.** In this sense *culture* involves a sense of group identity that permeates decision making and communication within the organization. More specifically, organizational culture is

a pattern of basic assumptions—invented, discovered, or developed by a given group as it learns to cope with its problems of external adaptation and internal integration—that has worked well enough to be considered valid and, therefore, to be taught to new members as the correct way to perceive, think, and feel in relation to those problems. (Schein, 1985, p. 9)

Why should macro social workers be concerned with organizational culture? As with viewing organizations using a systems model, culture provides insight into an organization's successes and values. It has a strong influence on the behavior of an organization over time. Further, the influence of culture is predictable. The information gathered from culture is crucial for social workers because it spells out the informal rules of behavior and expectations while providing a value system within which to operate.

Values are the foundation of culture. Organizations that stand for something, such as social justice or self-determination, have an explicit philosophy that drives the service delivery system. Macro social workers who pay attention to values ensure that the organization is consumer-centered and based on the principles of the social work profession. Finally, the organizational values are known and shared by all workers and consumers of organization services.

How does organizational culture develop and how does it continue even as individual organization members come and go? According to Ott (1989, p. 75), organizational culture has three sources or determinants:

1. The broader societal culture in which the organization resides
2. The nature of the organization's business
3. The beliefs, values, and basic assumptions held by the organization's leaders

The three sources are not necessarily independent of one another. Rather, an organization's culture is the sum of the composite of the three general sources. Consequently, each organizational culture is unique.

How does a social worker begin to read or diagnose a culture in order to understand the unique features of an organization? Somewhat as a clinical social worker does with a client, a macro social worker conducts a holistic assessment of an organization through a process. Other than values, of particular interest are the role models for employees and consumers to follow. Such models might be leaders within the organization. However, any person can demonstrate what it takes to be a successful participant in the organization. The organization's rituals, as displayed in celebrations and honors, also show how employees and consumers are expected to behave. Finally, the cultural network or the manner of communication within the organization provides insight into the ways values are transmitted and the expected patterns of interaction.

Figure 5.2 provides a list of cultural elements to review in conjunction with the organization assessment. A beginning point for the assessment process is studying the physical setting. Are the organization's buildings well maintained, accessible, and appropriate for the services offered? What are the decorations like? For example, what hangs on the walls? Who are the organization's neighbors? Are they a possible source for collaborative relationships? Is the organization located in close proximity to its consumers?

The organization's statements about itself and its services reveal much about its values and resultant culture. Spend time reading annual reports, press releases, policy and procedures manuals, educational material designed for consumers, and brochures. Is the message the same in all print and nonprint material? Follow up the review of information with an examination of how consumers are treated when they enter the organization. Is there a comfortable reception area? Does the organization appear informal or formal, and why? Are people called by their first names or their titles? How are consumers referred to and how are they addressed?

The diagnostic profile of an organization should include interviews with staff. It is important to ask people questions about their history in the organization and their perception of the organization's history. What are described as the organization's successes and failures? How does the organization celebrate events or accomplishments? On the basis of the interview process, begin to consider the type of people who work at the organization and why. Consider lengths of employment with the agency, recruitment procedures, and reward systems.

Finally, observe how people spend their time. How much time is spent on paper or computer work? What are interpersonal interactions like in terms of frequency and spontaneity? Is the organization's language formal or casual? Does humor seems to be appreciated and, if so, in what way? Pay particular attention to anecdotes and stories that seem to pass through the organization.

The cultural diagnosis requires the use of multiple methodologies, especially qualitative and ethnographic strategies. It gives social workers a fix on the organization's culture, particularly whether it is weak or strong, focused or

anecdotes, organizational

art

assumptions, patterns of basic

assumptions, shared

assumptions that people live by

attitudes

behavioral regularities

being

beliefs

beliefs, patterns of shared

celebration

ceremonies

climate, organizational

cognitive processes, patterns of

commitment to excellence

communication patterns

consensus, level of
(about myriad organizational variables)

core

customs

doing things, way of

enactment (per Weick, 1977)

ethic, organizational

ethos

expectations, shared

feelings

glue that holds an organization together

habits

heroes

historical vestiges

identity

ideologies

interaction, patterns of

jargon

justification for behavioral patterns

knowledge

language

links between language, metaphor
and ritual

management practices

manner

material objects

meaning, patterns of

meanings

meanings, intersubjective

mind-set

myths

norms

philosophy

physical arrangements

practical syllogisms

purpose

rites

ritualized practices

rituals

roots

rules, informal system of

scripts, organizational

sentiments

source of norms, rules, attitudes, customs,
and roles

specialness, quality of perceived
organizational

spirit

stories, organizational

style

symbols

thinking, way of

traditions

translation of myths into action and
relationship

understandings, tacit

values

values, basic or core

values, patterns of shared

vision

way

world views

FIGURE 5.2 Alphabetical Listing of Elements of Organizational Culture

SOURCE: Adapted with permission from *The Organizational Culture Perspective*, by J. S. Ott (Pacific Grove, CA: Brooks/Cole, 1989), p. 53.

fragmented (Deal & Kennedy, 1982). Organizational culture serves as a source of energy and focus, providing meaning and direction for organization members. Organizational culture not only gives an organization its unique identity—it *is* the unique character or personality of an organization. People in organizations need culture for identity, purpose, feelings of belongingness, communication, stability, and cognitive efficiency.

Many of the elements of organizational culture are present in the following case example. Read the case and analyze the cultural elements of the agency.

CASE EXAMPLE

Located by a church and across from the street from a family-owned restaurant, the counseling center is a primary service agency for the rural county area. With a staff of fifteen, the agency has been in operation for over twenty years. It serves as a placement site for undergraduate and graduate social work students in the state's university.

The building is old but well maintained. As Amy Wieland, a consumer, enters the agency, she is greeted by name by a receptionist. Amy replies in kind. Her appointment is scheduled in ten minutes; while waiting, she has a cup of coffee provided in a reception area. The reception area is comfortably furnished. There are recent magazines and the local paper to read. On the walls are photos of local scenes and a plaque honoring the outstanding employers of the year, recognized for their community service contributions.

The social worker greets Amy by name and with a handshake at the designated appointment time. They walk back to the worker's office together. In the hallway, they pass the agency's director, who speaks to Amy about a career fair that the agency will host in the next month.

What do the cultural elements tell you about the values and philosophy of the agency? How would you describe the relationships illustrated in the case? Is this an agency where you think you would like to work or receive services? Why or why not?

ORGANIZATIONAL DEVELOPERS

As you begin to examine the structure, functioning, and culture of organizations, try to consider the organization as a client. Macro social workers who work with dysfunctional organizational systems are called *organization developers.* According to Rieman (1992), organization developers enhance knowledge, improve skills, modify attitudes, and change behaviors in order to provide better services to consumers. They use organization development to initiate organizational change, improving the effectiveness of the organization and its members (Brueg-gemann, 1996).

Organizational Development

Organizational development (OD), historically one of the most commonly used consultative methods in business and industry, is increasingly being used in human service organizations. In OD, the consultant or organization developer and the client organization jointly assess an organization's change needs and develop an action plan for addressing them. To change the way an organization solves its problems, the organization developer may use any one of a vast numbers of possible interventions, including these common ones:

- Group process interventions such as team building
- Intergroup process interventions, including conflict resolution strategies, intergroup confrontation meetings, and joint problem-solving sessions
- Training programs designed to enhance organizational skills and using innovative educational strategies such as simulation and gaming
- Survey feedback or the gathering and sharing of diagnostic data about the organization and its current norms and processes
- Action research, which involves broad participation in the development of change strategies based on structural research and behavioral science technologies
- Change in organizational structure based on group agreement about suggested alterations (Lewis et al., 2001, p. 285).

The basic assumptions on which organizational development is premised are as follows:

1. The answers to many of these questions will vary depending on the perspective of different constituent groups.
2. Clear and widespread consensus on these issues is rare within organizations.
3. The broader information sources (horizontal and vertical), the nearer the conclusions will be to reality.
4. The data-gathering process itself offers a unique opportunity to build trust and clarity (Feinstein, 1987).

On the basis of these premises, the role of the organization developer is to establish a wide communication loop, receiving information from key constituent groups as the process goes on.

The Role of an Organization Developer

Of primary importance are two objectives: the organization developer encourages the organization to regard the conclusions and recommendations as its own, and the developer facilitates the broadest possible participation in the change effort. In this way, the organization developer is preparing subsystems of the organization to accept and understand recommendations for change. Thus, the key to defining an intervention through OD is not the specific strategy used but the democratic involvement of organization members (especially consumers) who might be affected by the change. All organizational development is done under the assumption that the organization must be able to deal effectively with future needs. This assumes that the organization and its members must gain purposeful control over the change process.

According to Brueggemann (2002), there are two types of organization developers. The first is a developer internal to the organization. This is an individual or an employee of the organization (e.g., a mental health center) who works exclusively for and with consumers, employees, and administrators of the agency. Internal organization developers must be cautious and thoughtful in their recommendations because they will have to live with the changes they recommend (Robbins, 1992). Furthermore, they come under constant scrutiny of consumers and their colleagues.

In contrast, external organization developers work either as private consultants or as members of an organizational development firm; they provide management consultations, training, and problem solving to many different organizations and agencies. Although external consultants can offer objective perspectives because they are from outside the organization, they often do not have an intimate understanding of the organization's history, goals, and procedures. As a result, external consultants may have a tendency to institute drastic changes because they do not have to live with the results.

Whether working as an internal or external organization developer, the process is a collaborative venture involving various stakeholders, especially consumers. Harrison (1987) describes the steps in organization development as follows:

- *Scouting:* The organization developer seeks to determine how ready and able the members of the organization are to follow through on a project and to change their behavior and their organization.
- *Entry:* The organization developer and stakeholders of the organization negotiate about their expectations for the project and formalize them in a contract specifying the timing and nature of the developer's activities.
- *Diagnosis:* The organization developer gathers information about the nature and sources of the organization's problems and its unique strengths, then analyzes this information, examines possible solutions, considers ways to improve effectiveness, and provides feedback to the organization through presentations, reports, and interviews.
- *Planning:* Organization developers and stakeholders of the organization jointly establish objectives for the project's action phase and plan any steps (interventions) to be taken to solve problems and improve effectiveness.
- *Action:* The organization implements these plans with the help of the developer.

- *Evaluation:* The organization and stakeholders assess the impacts of the action phase and consider further actions. Under ideal conditions, an independent researcher evaluates project outcomes.

- *Termination:* If no further action is planned, the project terminates. The project may break off earlier if clients or developers become dissatisfied with it (Brueggemann, 2002).

Organizational Politics and Change

A distinguishing feature of both internal and external organization developers is **organizational politics.** According to Gummer and Edwards (1985, p. 14), the concept of an organization as a political system offers a particularly useful scheme for understanding organizations and for developing ideas that lead to effective practice with them. A central feature of political decision making is its explicit recognition of conflict as a normal part of organizational life, and the provisions it makes for transforming potentially disruptive conflicts into negotiated settlements.

How does this relate to the role of organization developers? An essential skill for the organization developer is the ability to identify sources of organizational power that can be used to produce support for desired policies and programs. In other words, power is viewed as the ability to make things happen or get things done in an effective manner. Consequently, the ability to assess the structure and operation of power is a central attribute of the organization developer.

Building on the idea of organizational power and the personal power of social workers, Kirst-Ashman & Hull (2001) introduced a way of assessing **organizational change potential,** which they call "PREPARE: An Assessment of Organizational Change Potential." It is designed for organization developers and other macro practitioners to use in considering organizational problems and possible change in a general way (pp. 108–109). The elements of PREPARE are summarized in Figure 5.3. The steps associated with the process follow:

> STEP 1. PREPARE: *Identify Problems to be Addressed.* Most organizations have problems that have a negative impact on the work environment. The first step for the organization developer is to identify and prioritize problems in the context of the organization's culture. Consider if and how the problems have an impact on consumers. Are the problems significant enough to warrant a change effort? Will the staff and consumers support the proposed change?

> STEP 2. PREPARE: *Review your Macro and Personal Reality.* Evaluate the chances of introducing a successful macro change. To do this, consider the organization's environment, including its subsystems, resources, funding sources, culture, and staff composition. What are the constraints to change,

Step

1. P   Identify **PROBLEMS** to address.
2. R   Review your macro and personal **REALITY**.
3. E   **ESTABLISH** your macro reality.
4. P   Identify relevant **PEOPLE** of influence.
5. A   **ASSESS** potential financial costs and potential benefits to consumers and the organization.
6. R   Review professional and personal **RISKS**.
7. E   **EVALUATE** the potential success of the macro change process.

FIGURE 5.3 PREPARE: An Assessment of Organizational Change Potential

SOURCE: From *Macro Skills Workbook: A Generalist Approach,* 2nd edition, by Kirst-Ashman/Hull Jr., © 2001. Reprinted with permission of Wadsworth, a division of Thomson Learning: www.thomsonrights.com. Fax: 800-730-2215.

such as the political climate, regulations, or cultural components? Consider your own skills, qualities, and relationships. How will your assets affect the change effort?

STEP 3. PREPARE: *Establish Primary Goals.* What goals do you think you can accomplish? Establish a sense of direction for your proposed interventions that supports the strengths of the organization's culture. A concrete course of action defines a system of accountability.

STEP 4. PREPARE: *Identify Relevant People of Influence.* Who will help in the change effort? Consider both consumers and employees of the organization in terms of their commitment to and energy for change. Identify possible opponents to change. How will you address their resistance?

STEP 5. PREPARE: *Assess Potential Financial Costs and Potential Benefits to Consumers and the Organization.* Think about the costs associated with the macro change. Is the cost reasonable given the financial situation of the organization and the anticipated benefit of making the change?

STEP 6. PREPARE: *Review Professional and Personal Risks.* Does the proposed change effort place you in jeopardy of losing your job or contract? How will it affect your chances for career mobility? How will you be perceived by consumers? Will any of your relationships become strained as a result of the macro change?

STEP 7. PREPARE: *Evaluate the Potential Success of the Macro Change Process.* After reviewing the PREPARE process, decide whether the change effort deserves your commitment and the organization's time and resources. Should the effort be initiated, delayed, or canceled?

CASE EXAMPLE

You have been employed by an urban mental health facility for approximately three years. During that time, you established yourself as a productive organization developer by assessing the need for staff training, formalizing the Program Advisory Committee, introducing consumer focus groups to evaluate services for adolescents, and initiating a community service recognition program.

The administrator is concerned about a decrease in consumer contact hours and asks you to review the admissions packet to ensure that the material is relevant. Your review indicates that the forms are at least twenty pages long and take well over an hour to complete. The font used on many of the forms is small, the text is complicated, and personal questions related to marital status, finances, and resources are asked without a clear reason for doing so. Further, the admissions packet is available only in English and is written at a tenth-grade level of reading difficulty. The admissions packets are printed, processed,

and filed by three workers who have been employed by the agency for a number of years.

The center's catchment area has a high portion of people over the age of sixty-five. An increasing number of residents are Hispanic, with strong Roman Catholic affiliations.

1. What are some possible problems with the admissions packet? What are some of its strengths?

2. What are some constraints on any proposed change effort? Are resources available to assist with the change?

3. What are some possible goals related to the admissions packet?

4. Who are the people relevant to the change effort? What is the possible relationship between the admissions packet and the decrease in consumer contact? How will you test this relationship?

5. Are any professional or personal risks associated with the proposed change?

SOURCE: Adapted from Kirst-Ashman & Hull (2001), p. 124.

EMPOWERMENT

The concept of *empowerment*, when applied to an organizational setting, brings together the material presented in previous chapters with the information on organizations and the role of the organization developer. Saul Alinsky, the social activist who wrote *Reveille for Radicals* (1969), laid the foundation for the empowerment process by stating that an organization functions to achieve power to realize the people's program—a set of principles, purposes, and practices commonly agreed upon by the people. Building on the work of Alinsky, Solomon (1976), concluded that the term *empowerment* described the process of assisting "clients who manifest powerlessness to develop their latent powers and to exert these powers to obtain needed resources" (Hepworth & Larsen, 1993, p. 495). Her more comprehensive definition of empowerment is as follows:

> a process whereby the social worker engages in a set of activities with the client . . . that aim to reduce the powerlessness that has been created by

negative valuations based on membership in a stigmatized group. It involves identification of the power blocks that contribute to the problem as well as the development and implementing of specific strategies aimed at either the reduction of the effects from indirect power blocks or the reduction of the operations of direct power blocks. (Solomon, 1976, p. 19)

When applied to an organization, the empowerment process pulls together diverse elements or subsystems and builds on their strengths to improve the social and economic conditions of consumers. This is accomplished through the three interlocking dimensions of empowerment (Lee, 1994, p. 13). The first is the development of a more positive and potent sense of self. In the context of an organization, this dimension refers to a coherent philosophy supported by goals that build on the strengths of the organization. The positive image of the organization is conveyed to consumers through such avenues as print and nonprint material, interpersonal communication, and formal as well as informal celebrations. The second interlocking dimension is the fund of knowledge an organization accumulates in order to understand the realities of its environment. Consumers are a major source of such knowledge, as are employees, other agencies, and funding sources. Finally, Lee (1994) concludes that organizations must cultivate resources and strategies for the attainment of personal and collective goals. This dimension clearly speaks to the relationship between empowerment, collaboration, and the formation of a community with a broad-based constituency.

Organizational development themes included in the empowerment process involve democratic procedures, voluntary cooperation, self-help, development of indigenous leadership, and educational objectives to foster empowerment (Rothman & Tropman, 1987). Organization developers, then, emphasize organizational building based on the assumption that there is common good that people working together can realize (Brager & Specht, 1973).

When empowerment is an organizational aim, social workers will find themselves questioning both public-policy issues and their role in relation to dependent people. Specifically, social workers committed to the empowerment of their organizations will challenge policies or programs designed *to use on* consumers rather than actively designed *in conjunction with* consumers. Further, social workers will confront the "paradox that even people most incompetent, in need, and apparently unable to function require more than less control over their own lives; and that fostering more control does not necessarily mean ignoring them" (Rappaport, 1985, p. 18). In this way, empowerment presses a different set of metaphors upon the social work profession than the traditional helping model.

The empowerment ideology contains at least two requirements (Lee, 1994). It demands that macro social work practitioners examine many diverse settings in which people are already handling their own problems, in order to learn more about how they do it. Simultaneously, it demands that social workers find ways to apply what they learn from people handling life problems to organizational settings through policies and programs. In light of both of these

Organization: _____ Social worker: _____ Date: _____

Concerns/Problem Situation

Briefly summarize the problem areas or concerns.

Briefly describe the perceived strengths of your organization.

List concerns/problems in order of priority from highest to lowest.

Subsystem	Obstacles	Strengths	Effect on Problem Situation
Internal policies and procedures			
External policies and procedures			
Professional staff pattern			
Support staff pattern			
Workload			
Organizational support			
Professional autonomy			
Degree of trust among administrators, professional staff, and support staff			

FIGURE 5.4 The Organizational Empowerment Assessment

SOURCE: From Collaborative Social Work: Strengths-Based Generalist Practice, 1st edition, by Poulin. © 2000. Reprinted with permission of Wadsworth, a division of Thomson Learning: www.thomsonrights.com. Fax: 800-730-2215.

requirements, the organization is viewed as a resource to help people gain control over their lives.

Including empowerment in organizations requires many intervention tools such as those included in this chapter: examining subsystems, diagnosing culture, and assessing the potential for organizational change. These tools enhance organizational functioning and, in turn, consumer empowerment, through social investigation, humane policies, and program development (Simon, 1994). As described in Figure 5.4, another intervention tool is an organizational strengths-based assessment. Designed to assess the strengths and obstacles within an organization, the strengths-based assessment helps macro social workers and consumers to focus on present organizational conditions in order to direct future change efforts.

As with building on the strengths of people, developing organizational strengths shifts from the search for a monolithic way of doing things and providing services. By contrast, the strengths assessment offers a bottom-up process that starts with people telling administrators what social policies and programs are necessary. This means that the outcome of empowerment will not only look different depending on the life problems being confronted, but may even look different within each setting in which it operates. The strengths assessment suggests that diversity rather than homogeneity in organizations should dominate if the operating process is one of empowerment.

In conclusion, there are two vital components of success with organizational empowerment. The first involves absolute commitment to an empowerment ideology as displayed in language and action. The other is an ongoing collaboration with the professional community and service consumers, who are viewed as invaluable resources. This interactive venture is empowering in itself. The end result is a new and vibrant organizational culture, based not on dependence, professional expertise, and passive acceptance but, rather, on the power and dignity of people.

ORGANIZATIONAL CHANGE
FROM WITHIN THE ORGANIZATION

Organizational change *is* possible, particularly when leadership and professionals are committed to consumers. Changing an organization from within is a double endeavor.

As a means to prompt organizational change "from within," consider the merits of creating an *improvement team* (Brueggemann, 2002, p. 338). Forming a group or committee of consumers and workers to discuss improvement ideas at a social service agency can be a valuable mechanism for discussing a number of topics (e.g., quality assurance, policy development, innovative programming, procedures, and climate issues).

The establishment of an improvement team recognizes that organizational change is inevitable, is necessary, and can be positive. The primary goal of the improvement team is to discuss important issues and timely topics—"to ask people to talk about what matters to them, not to ask people to support what matters to you or the leaders. . . . Dialogue is key" (Brueggemann, 2002, p. 338).

SUMMARY

Many of you entered your educational and field experiences thinking that your primary function in social work would be that of a clinician working with individuals and families. Perhaps you did not give much attention to the larger systems that influence your life and the lives of consumers.

This chapter calls attention to organizations and asks you to make the transition from thinking about interventions on the micro level to conceptualizing methods of enriching the life of organizations through macro interventions. The bridge between these practice areas is empowerment. In the larger context, the empowerment process ensures that program design, policies, and organizational development promote consumer self-determination, power, and dignity.

A FEW KEY TERMS

bureaucracies	organizational culture	organizational politics
feedback	organizational development	organizational change potential

USING INFOTRAC®
COLLEGE EDITION AND INFOWRITE

InfoTrac College Edition

After reading this chapter, you should have an idea of the complexities and significance of organizations. To apply some of your newly acquired knowledge, do the following:

1. Go to InfoTrac College Edition.

2. Under the Subject Guide, search for "organization."

3. Review the long list of articles that describe an array of national and international organizations.

4. Select an article under one of the organization categories that is of interest to you.

5. On the basis of the article, assess the organization in the context of community change as defined in "PREPARE: An Assessment of Organizational Change Potential."

6. Prepare your findings in the PREPARE format to present to the class.

InfoWrite

Critical thinking is a critical component of social work practice. It involves evaluating what other people say or write to determine whether to believe their statements. The following exercise encourages you to use your critical thinking skills to assess a newspaper article that describes a particular community organization.

1. Go to InfoTrac College Edition.

2. Under Subject Guide, search on "community organization."

3. Select an article of interest on a community organization.

4. Read the article.

5. Go to InfoWrite.

6. Scroll to Critical Thinking.

7. Read the information presented on critical thinking.

After reading the article on community organization and the section on critical thinking, answer the following questions:

1. Does the article reflect a political or cultural bias? Explain why or why not.

2. Does the information included in the article reflect the time period and current social conditions? Support your response with examples.

3. Why is the article useful to you as a future social worker?

4. What are some of the insightful comments contained in the article?

CASE EXAMPLE: The Virtues of Karen's Korner

Karen's Korner is a cluster of four two-bedroom apartments owned by The First Church of the Resurrection. The buildings were donated to the church by the heir of Karen Conners, a local philanthropist. Upon receiving the gift, the social outreach division of the church earmarked the dwellings for transitional living for single mothers through a cooperative agreement with Target Services, a local agency serving homeless mothers with small children.

Target Services provides case management services for residents at Karen's Korner. Congregation members at The First Church of the Resurrection have formed a Karen's Korner group to maintain the apartments and to function as a landlord. Residents pay a modest rent, $200 a month, and are provided with utilities.

Residents of Karen's Korner do not view themselves as consumers of services at their temporary residence. Special effort has been taken to avoid stigmatization by church members and professionals at Target Services. Apartments have a "home feel," and residents are empowered with a sense of ownership over their lives. They can paint and decorate

(continued)

CASE EXAMPLE *(continued)*

---

apartments to their tastes. Residents are expected to follow a few basic rules and maintain a professional working relationship with social workers from Target Services.

In this case example, Target Services and The First Church of the Resurrection have formed a cooperative arrangement. They share important elements in their organizational cultures that have facilitated a successful partnership.

Both organizations demonstrate commitment to empowerment and destigmatization. Their organizational culture and goals emphasize short-term (transitional) services, inter-agency collaboration, flexibility, minimal exertion of authority and control over the lives of consumers, and responsiveness to feedback from consumers and partner organizations.

This brief example constitutes a clear illustration of the virtues of an open–system approach to organizational development. The ability of leaders, professionals, consumers, and citizens to be open and proactive in forming interorganizational alliances is a noteworthy attribute. It suggests a level of maturity, as organizations are ready and willing to change, adapt, and enter relationships when called upon.

THINKING CRITICALLY
ABOUT THE CASE EXAMPLE

1. Religious sponsorship of human services and social programs is common in the United States. In the case of Karen's Korner, it appears that The First Church of the Resurrection has been a source of empowerment. Imagine yourself as a resident at Karen's Korner: How might Target Services and the host church better utilize the talents of the residents?

2. Do faith-based organizations typically afford flexibility in social programming and service delivery? How might this differ depending on denominational auspices and church leadership?

3. The case example asserts that Target Services and The First Church of the Resurrection represent "a level of maturity" (e.g., readiness to change, adapt, and enter into relationships with other organizations). What constitutes organizational maturity? List and describe other criteria for a mature organization. Is organizational maturity similar to personal maturity? If so, how?

REFLECTION EXERCISES

1. An essential element of an organization involves feedback. Examine a social service organization and identify modes of consumer feedback. Examine feedback in terms of both form and content. How do consumers provide feedback, and what kinds of feedback (information) are elicited? How does consumer feedback align with measures of organizational performance? How could consumer feedback be enhanced?

2. Construct a job description for an organization developer (OD) at a social service agency. This can be a part-time, full-time, or contract position. Tailor the expectations and responsibilities of the OD to the unique organizational culture of the agency. How would the strengths of consumers be utilized by the OD through organizational development? What is the relationship between the OD and administrators, as well as other salient stakeholders?

3. Locate the entryway or lobby of the social work program at your university. Take a moment to examine the decorations (e.g., pictures, plaques, and postings), furniture, and layout of the program. What does the physical setting tell you about your educational program? What is being emphasized? What is missing? As social work students, do you have any ownership in the setting? If you desired to do so, could students affect the physical nature of the program? Why or why not?

SUGGESTED READINGS

Claiborne, N. (2004). Presence of social workers in nongovernmental organizations. *Social Work, 49*(2), 207–217.

Etzioni, A. (1964). *Modern organizations.* Englewood Cliffs, NJ: Prentice Hall.

Kusmer, K. L. (1972). The functions of organized charity in the Progressive Era: Chicago as a case study. New York: *Journal of American History, 60*(3), 657–678.

REFERENCES

Alinsky, S. (1969). *Reveille for radicals.* New York: Vintage.

Brager, G., & Specht, H. (1973). *Community organizing.* New York: Columbia University Press.

Brueggemann, W. G. (2002). *The practice of macro social work.* Chicago: Nelson-Hall.

Deal, T. E., & Kennedy, A. A. (1982). *Corporate cultures: The rites and rituals of corporate life.* Reading, MA: Addison-Wesley.

Etzioni, A. (1964). *Modern organizations.* Englewood Cliffs, NJ: Prentice Hall.

Feinstein, K. W. (1987). Innovative management in turbulent times:

Large-scale agency change. In F. M. Cox et al. (Eds.), *Macro practice: Strategies of community organization.* Itasca, IL: F. E. Peacock.

Gummer, B., & Edwards, R. L. (1985). A social worker's guide to organizational politics. *Administration in Social Work, 9*(1), 13–21.

Harrison, M. (1987). *Diagnosing organizations: Methods, models, and processes.* Newbury, CA: Sage.

Hepworth, D. H., & Larsen, J. A. (1993). *Direct social work practice.* Pacific Grove, CA: Brooks/Cole.

Hollander, E., & Hunt, R. (Eds.). (1976). *Current perspectives in social psychology* (4th ed.). New York: Oxford University Press.

Katz, D., & Kahn, R. L. (1978). *The social psychology of organizations.* New York: Wiley.

Kettner, P. M., Daley, J. M., & Nichols, A. W. (1985). *Initiating change in organizations and communities: A macro practice model.* Monterey, CA: Brooks/Cole.

Kirst-Ashman, K. K., & Hull, G. H. Jr. (2001). *Macro skills workbook: A generalist approach.* Pacific Grove, CA: Brooks/Cole.

Lee, J. A. B. (1994). *The empowerment approach in social work practice.* New York: Columbia University Press.

Lewis, J. A., Lewis, M. D., Packard, T., & Souflee, F. (2001). *Management of human service programs.* Pacific Grove, CA: Brooks/Cole.

Maynard-Moody, S. (1987). Program evaluation and administrative control. In F. M. Cox et al. (Eds.), *Macro practice: Strategies of community organization.* Itasca, IL: F. E. Peacock.

Netting, J. E., Kettner, P. M., & McMurtry, S. L. (1998). *Social work macro practice.* New York: Longman.

Neugeboren, B. (1991). *Organization, policy, and practice in the human services.* New York: Haworth Press.

Ott, S. J. (1989). *The organizational culture perspective.* Pacific Grove, CA: Brooks/Cole.

Perrow, C. (1979). *Complex organizations: A critical essay* (2nd ed.). Glenview, IL: Scott, Foresman.

Poulin, J. (2000). *Collaborative social work: Strengths-based generalist practice.* Itasca, IL: F. E. Peacock.

Rappaport, J. (1985). The power of empowerment language. *Social Policy, 16*(2), 15–21.

Rieman, D. S. (1992). *Strategies in social work consultation: From theory to practice in the mental health field.* New York: Longman.

Robbins, S. (1992). *Essentials of organizational behavior* (3rd ed.). Englewood Cliffs, NJ: Prentice Hall.

Rothman, J., & Tropman, J. E. (1987). Models of community organization and macro practice: Their mixing and phasing. In F. M. Cox, J. L. Erlich, J. Rothman, & J. E. Tropman (Eds.), *Strategies of community intervention: Macro practice* (4th ed.). Itasca, IL; F. E. Peacock.

Salami, G. R., & Pfeffer, J. Who gets power—and how they hold on to it: A strategic contingency model of power. *Organizational Dynamics, 5,* 3–21.

Schein, E. (1985). *Organizational culture and leadership.* San Francisco: Jossey-Bass.

Simon, B. L. (1994). *The empowerment tradition in American social work: A history.* New York: Columbia University Press.

Solomon, B. (1976). *Black empowerment: Social work in oppressed communities.* New York: Columbia University Press.

von Bertalanffy, L. (1950). An outline of general systems theory. *British Journal for the Philosophy of Science, 1*(2), 493–512.

Weber, M. (1947). *The theory of social and economic organizations.* (A. M. Henderson & T. Parsons, trans.). New York: Macmillan. (First published in 1924.)

6

Developing Community Resources and Capacities

Chapter Content Areas

Community

Trends in Community Practice

Overview and History of Community Organizing and Community Work

Community Practice Theory

Useful Theoretical Perspectives in Community Practice

Practice Roles

Strengths-Oriented Community Practice Principles

Community Development

Community Liaison, Interagency Partnerships/Networks, and Collaboration

WHAT IS COMMUNITY PRACTICE?

Although **community** is a word that is frequently used in everyday conversation, it is a slippery concept to define. The term *community* often elicits a particular image or images—a small town with its main street, the neighborhood in which you grew up, or the apartment complex where you reside. Obviously, "community" is a commonly used expression in our vocabulary, but it is also a term that can have multiple meanings.

Even people working professionally with communities experience difficulty in settling on a definition. Generally speaking, community can be conceptualized in two different, but related ways: (1) that which is shared and (2) an area with a common geography. In all likelihood, the richest connotation for social work practice involves the connotation of sharing.

Community as Sharing or Collective Affiliation

Increasingly, you hear discussions of the importance of nongeographic communities—"communities of interest." These include professional communities (e.g., the social work community), ethnic communities (e.g., the African American community), and religious communities (e.g., the St. Rita Parish community). In using the term *community* in relation to nongeographic entities, an assumption is made that people in a community possess common, shared experiences and identity. In these instances, the extent to which a community exists can be described by the amount of sharing that transpires in any given situation. It also is understood that community involves close communication, common bonds, and face-to-face relationships or "Gemeinschaft" (Lyon, 1987, pp. 7–8). In this sense, members of a community are viewed holistically (together) as a single entity.

A community is distinguishable from a society in several important ways. A society is not typically characterized by face-to-face relationships. Societal membership is at a distance and impersonal. Furthermore, societies (countries) operate by means of rules, intended to treat members alike—in similar or prescribed ways. This is functional but not personal. Communities, both localities or communities of interest, usually engage people in more personal ways and can thus serve as *mediating structures* between individuals or families and the more impersonal society.

Self-Help/Mutual-Aid Groups as Community

Most of us are familiar with self-help groups, also called mutual-aid groups. In our society, these groups seemingly exist for every conceivable human issue. Examples include alcoholism (Alcoholics Anonymous) and mental illness (Recovery, Inc.).

Self-help groups typically function as nongeographic communities, in that their members share a particular condition and life experiences associated with it. In a sense, self-help groups and other nongeographic communities take on some of the more important activities and responsibilities that traditionally were assumed by geographic communities and neighborhoods. Mutual-aid groups can be very important to consumers, as these groups often recast problems either as normal or as opportunities, facilitate the mobilization of collective resources, and empower individuals to help themselves through helping others.

Geographic Communities

The most traditional way of conceptualizing a community involves geographic location. Each of us lives in some kind of a community. Your community could be a densely populated urban neighborhood, a sprawling suburb, or a small town in rural America. People in large metropolitan areas often identify a small section of the city as their community. For college students, their university campus often represents a physical community.

In geographic communities, people have neighbors. As a consequence of the availability of transportation and various means of communication (e.g., telephones and computers), many people in industrialized communities enjoy the ability to control and place limits on face-to-face interaction with their geographic neighbors. In the past, direct contact with neighbors, local businesspeople, and residents of the neighborhood was difficult to avoid. Indeed, the ability to regulate one's engagement and social interaction with neighbors suggests the existence of "communities of limited liability" (Hassinger & Pinkerton, 1986).

However, it is important to note that Americans do not enjoy equal access to technological advancements in our society. Indeed, the local geographic community (neighborhood) is often considerably more important to certain demographic and social-economic groups than to others. For people with limited access to transportation (e.g., the poor, older adults, children, and persons with disabilities), neighbors living within walking distance constitute a very real and viable resource. In impoverished communities, neighbors learn to rely on one another for many things, including child care, food, supplies, tools, knowledge, skill, and ingenuity.

In social work practice, a crucial consideration with regard to any geographic community involves its potential for human sharing and exchange. Unfortunately, limited resources and a collective sense of pessimism characterize many impoverished geographic communities. Under these circumstances, community members become immobilized and fail to recognize the many assets and strengths that surround them. In many instances, this is not intentional. Instead, the physical design and construction of space in neighborhoods (e.g., the positioning of dwellings, public buildings, businesses, and recreation areas) has a limiting effect on social interaction. The appropriate design and use of physical space in a geographic community is a key factor in promoting human exchange and sharing, as noted in Newman's (1972) *Defensible Space.*

Functions of Communities

The significance of community in U.S. society is complicated, multifaceted, and changing. For some people, one's community represents a bastion of goods, services, amenities, and opportunities for relationship building. For others, a community can serve as a source of personal identity. How many times have you heard, "I came from such-and-such side of town"?

Warren and Warren (1997) identify a number of specific functions of geographic communities. These include the following:

- *Sociability arena:* A neighborhood can be a place to establish and sustain friendships.
- *Interpersonal influence center:* Thinking and perception are influenced by those around us, including neighbors.
- *Mutual aid:* This can be as basic as "borrowing a cup of sugar" or as complicated as providing day care for a neighbor's child.

- *Status arena:* Neighborhoods often reflect the social status of their residents. Certain neighborhoods, such as the Upper East Side of Manhattan, can easily be recognized as a community inhabited by people of high social-economic means.

- *Identity and meaning:* When neighbors share values and common perspectives, a community can be a powerful referent for personal identity and meaning.

- *Site for human services:* Communities support and provide a working context for a variety of social services. From the earliest developments in social work (the Charity Organization Societies and settlement houses), social service delivery has been shaped by and grounded in neighborhood settings.

The British context, in particular, offers insight into providing services on a "patch" basis, whereby a team of workers, perhaps representing different agencies, provide services to a defined neighborhood or "patch" (Adams & Krauth, 1995). Many agencies continue to do outreach—perhaps better referred to as "inreach"—to local communities.

Trends in Community Practice

Community practice has traditionally been acknowledged as a specific mode of practice in social work. However, it is also a type of practice that has continued to evolve and now carries a variety of connotations.

Community Practice Rather than Community Organization *Community organization* is a phrase that has traditionally been used to describe social work intervention at the community level. Increasingly, *community practice, community-based practice, community-based service delivery,* and *community building* are all terms used to describe social work at the community level.

In recent years, *community practice* has evolved as a more inclusive expression than *community organization.* In many instances, *community organization* has been narrowly used in social work circles to specify one of a number of community intervention options. Meanwhile, *community practice* has taken on a much broader meaning.

Two terms capture the range of activities within community practice: community building and community-based service delivery. *Community building* suggests that the community's own abilities to confront and take care of issues are being mobilized and used. In this vein, terms such as *community empowerment* and *competent communities* are also relevant. Community building assumes that community members are engaged in strategies and techniques that can be used to intentionally enhance a community. This entails creating opportunities for people in the community to become more involved in making decisions concerning important issues and the general quality of life in the community.

Community building can take many forms and use many methods. Examples include the development of issue-specific focus groups, a neighborhood crime-watch group, a block club that sponsors block parties to enhance social interaction among residents, a cultural group that brings amateur musicians together, and a child care cooperative.

Collectively, neighbors can positively affect the social image of a given area, both internally and externally. Neighborhood groups often publish local newspapers, host house tours, sponsor cultural events (e.g., parades, flower shows, and concerts), and create symbolic items (e.g., tote bags, T-shirts, hats, and signs) in an effort to promote their neighborhood. For current residents, these activities tend to accentuate the benefits of community life. Meanwhile, prospective residents are introduced to the virtues of becoming a member of a community.

Nongeographic communities can use similar techniques to increase member involvement and to facilitate positive changes in the perception of a particular condition. In doing so, they too are building community. In particular, Naparstek (1999) suggests that community building is comprehensive and integrative, facilitates new forms of collaboration and partnerships, strengthens existing social networks, utilizes and builds on a variety of neighborhood assets, and makes a concerted effort to target specific neighbourhoods and groups of people to enhance participation.

The term *community-based service delivery* acknowledges that agencies often provide valuable and much-needed services in a neighborhood or community setting. Geographic communities vary considerably with regard to the availability of community-based services within their bounds. Similarly, communities of sharing rely on and vie for convenient service delivery based on their interests.

Community building and community-based service delivery are not mutually exclusive. Community practice involves both notions. Effective social work practice with communities promotes effective service delivery systems in and for communities and also involves working with community members to build collective capacities.

In contemporary community practice, interorganizational collaboration in promoting social change is both expected and encouraged—particularly by funding sources. When community-based organizations communicate and collaborate with one another, assets and resources can be more effectively used (e.g., through the elimination of duplicative services and programs). In addition, collaborative efforts between organizations can serve to bring together, organize, and structure the interests of consumers to garner political influence and establish prominence in decision-making processes. When members of social service agencies, voluntary associations, and planning groups act collaboratively, a unique synergy can be formed.

Overview and History of Community Organizing/Community Work

The Charity Organization Societies The Charity Organization Societies (COS), described in Chapter 1, were an attempt to develop a mechanism to coordinate the work of the many small charities that had emerged in many cities in the United States. A national office, for many years under the leadership of

Mary Richmond, served as a way of providing the local COS with helpful information and support. Several features characterized the work of the local COS. Foremost, the COS offered a systematic means of coordinating social service delivery and operations, focusing both on individual capabilities and on the impact of social conditions. Indeed, the aforementioned *Social Diagnosis* (1917) was written by Mary Richmond to assist in the training of charity workers.

To minimize duplication of cash assistance from more than one charity, recipients of assistance from any charity would be registered with the central COS office in a city. A worker from the COS, sometimes called a "friendly visitor," was assigned to provide service to families in a specific geographic district of the municipality. The workers, predominantly women, then set out to determine the need for assistance and underlying causes precipitating the request for help. The work of the COS became more refined over the years, and increasingly workers relied on the use of modern counseling techniques rather than moralistic approaches.

Much of the macro work of the COS focused on organizing the efforts of separate charities and developing a rational system for service delivery. The COS described its method as "scientific charity." By contemporary standards, however, it was probably more of a systematic approach than a truly scientific endeavor.

During the 1930s, the COS was unable to meet the extraordinary need for cash assistance created by the Great Depression. As a consequence, the government assumed the burden of providing financial assistance, with the bulk of the funding provided by the federal government. The administration of financial programs was turned over to local and state governments.

With less responsibility for monetary relief, the mission of the COS evolved toward an increasing emphasis on family counseling. Local affiliates soon changed their names to incorporate the term "family service," and a national association formed, called Family Service America (FSA). In recent years, partially as a result of merger, FSA has become known as the Alliance for Children and Families. Family service agencies are among the oldest and best established agencies in communities throughout the United States.

As a result of this history, family service agencies have continued to emphasize community-based approaches in providing services and advocating for policy formation and development. In addition, many social workers would argue that the community orientation and approach offered by the COS constituted the very origin of social planning in the United States.

The Progressive Era and the Settlement House Movement   The settlement house movement was an early attempt to ameliorate problems associated with rapid urbanization and massive immigration. Settlement houses were neighborhood centers that provided a variety of programs. Staff, often young (traditional college-age) women, moved into a neighborhood and lived in settlement houses. Volunteers with middle- and upper-class backgrounds hoped to experience firsthand conditions in poorer communities and thus to become better informed.

© Thomson Higher Education/Heinle Image Bank.

The specific services provided in a neighborhood were determined by each settlement house, but typically included preschool education as well as programs for school-age children, adolescents, and adults. These services were commonly offered using some form of group format. Clubs, classes, and mass activities (e.g., open gym sessions) were the staple of most settlements. Emphasis was placed on promoting healthy development, prevention, and group intervention. Classes included music, arts, crafts, cooking, and activities accentuating ethnic heritage, as well as literacy programs. As suggested in earlier chapters, the group orientation and outlook associated with the settlement house movement served as an important backdrop for the development of group work as a distinct method in social work practice. Similarly, the recreation and adult education movements often trace their historical roots to this same settlement house movement.

It is important to note that while the vast majority of settlement houses were concerned about local neighborhood conditions, settlement houses also were free to approach issues in more individualized ways. As an example, many settlement houses established a system of neighborhood associations as a mechanism to encourage local residents to organize into smaller social units. Each neighborhood association would prioritize concerns and then identify its unique strengths and abilities for addressing and resolving issues. Settlement houses were also involved in broader social issues. For example, staff at Chicago's Hull House, headed by Jane Addams, were associated with major reforms such as the development of juvenile courts and provided national leadership in government and for major nonprofit associations. As you will recall, the settlement house movement was strongly associated with the "progressive movement," which championed reforms in labor, health, housing, and food production.

Settlement houses continue to do important work, although they are now more likely to be known as community or neighborhood centers. A national organization, the United Neighborhood Centers of America, Inc. (www.unca. org) continues to serve as the coordinating body for such agencies. The settlement houses clearly fit into both the community development and the social advocacy models.

Community Chest, the United Way, and Councils of Social Agencies
Larger communities in the United States typically establish a United Way. Originally known as "community chests," these organizations provide an organized system of community-based fund raising for nonprofit agencies. United Ways solicit contributions from local residents and employees to develop a funding pool ("chest") to help underwrite nonprofit, voluntary agencies. On an annual basis, employers often ask for contributions from their workers, usually through payroll deduction plans.

United Ways are also highly involved in making determinations concerning local community needs and decisions about how funds should be allocated to various agencies. Traditionally, United Ways have worked via a committee structure (e.g., committees dedicated to allocations and appropriations and to evaluation and planning) composed of volunteers from the community. Top donors, both companies and individuals, frequently vie to make sure that their representatives secure positions of authority on the more powerful committees of the United Way.

This is an interesting—and potentially self-serving—practice for making committee appointments. Using an empowerment orientation, it would seem imperative that consumers have adequate representation with regard to decisions involving the prioritizing and funding of local services. From a strengths perspective, the recruitment of able and well-suited stakeholders (consumers and others) for committee membership also seems prudent and wise when developing community capacities.

International Community Development Following the end of World War II, there was a surge of interest in the notion of community development. Some of this interest came from the British Colonial Office, which was interested in improving local conditions in British colonies. This was particularly true in east Africa, an area soon to become independent (Midgely, 1995). Writers such as Biddle (1965) and Batten (1957) contributed to the development of this approach.

A central theme of community development in this context was that local (village) residents could be mobilized to identify problems and to develop imaginative, tailor-made solutions. A major emphasis of community development involved building on the strengths of community members and teaching the skills needed for successful engagement in the community development process. Priority was given to "low" or "appropriate" technologies requiring little expertise that could be more easily implemented at the grassroots level. The community development approach was broadly accepted by many developing countries and continues to enjoy widespread support among major foundations and organizations in the Americas (e.g., the U.S. Agency for International Development). This approach has also been used as a mechanism for community engagement within poorer, disenfranchised areas in the United States.

The Civil Rights Movement and the War on Poverty As you will recall from Chapter 1, two movements in the 1960s helped to shape macro practice and are particularly relevant when considering community practice. The civil rights movement attempted to address historic patterns of exclusion, segregation, and discrimination. It was instituted by minorities and their allies and involved the use of a variety of innovative strategies for change (e.g., lawsuits, legislative initiatives, sit-ins, passive noncompliance, and demonstrations). Social workers and consumers united with community leaders across the United States to employ new techniques—often times labeled "radical"—to advance the cause of racial minorities. A newfound sense of strength, opportunity, and unbridled passion emerged, as minorities united and rallied behind more progressive forms of community leadership.

The so-called War on Poverty was an attempt by government to deal with both civil rights issues and the rediscovery of poverty (Harrington, 1974). The most visible federal agency was the Office of Economic Opportunity (OEO), which sponsored a number of community-oriented programs, including the Head Start preschool program, Job Corps (a training program for unemployed young adults), and the Community Action Program (CAP).

In some respects, the CAP was a forerunner of empowerment theory, as it was based on the principle of "maximum feasible participation" of the poor. CAP established local organizations with a mandate that a majority of the board of directors would be people experiencing poverty or their representatives. The CAP program encouraged local residents to plan programs in relation to their needs and provided funding for locally initiated projects. In many cases, residents were able to secure employment in these programs.

Ultimately, a wide range of programs were funded through CAP, many of which included a strong emphasis on social advocacy and on organizing poor residents. Some of these programs were controversial, and clashes with established institutions and political structures were not uncommon. The CAP and similar programs encouraged people to become engaged in the social-political life of their communities. This meant that people had to overcome the apathy and sense of hopelessness that often accompany poverty.

As an encouraging by-product of this process, many local leaders emerged during the 1960s and 1970s, some of whom sought and won political office. Equally important, many traditional social agencies and organizations achieved a beginning-level awareness of the importance of involving users of services in identifying needs and designing programs.

Saul Alinsky Though not part of the antipoverty program, a key figure during the War on Poverty years was Saul Alinsky, who worked with several Chicago neighborhoods, particularly Woodlawn and Back of the Yards. His approach to community organizing was to identify issues involving marginal-ized people and to confront established institutions and leadership concerning their role in perpetuating these problems.

Alinsky typically used dramatic, confrontational approaches designed to draw attention to causes. His tactics had the potential to embarrass powerful people; they were designed to persuade the local power structure to negotiate in good faith with representatives of consumer groups.

For a brief description of Alinsky's overall approach, see the work of Lyon (1987, pp. 121–125). The Industrial Areas Foundation in Chicago, founded by Alinsky, continues to serve as a national training center for community organiz-ers. Alinsky's approach is an aggressive and confrontational form of social advocacy. It is empowering in that it uses the strengths of consumers and their allies to challenge local power brokers over decision-making processes.

Refinement of Community Practice Theory

The Contribution of Jack Rothman and Others The 1960s and 1970s saw a rapid increase in the amount of theoretical material related to community orga-nization. In Chapter 1, the work of Jack Rothman (1979) was introduced. You will recall that Rothman classified community approaches into three major modes: (1) locality (community) development, (2) social planning, and (3) social action. This line of reasoning was indeed helpful to many social workers. Roth-man's predecessors had attempted to develop single, unified approaches to com-munity work, while often failing to recognize a range of approaches, each containing different assumptions and goals. Through the advancement of a vari-ety of community strategies and models, community practitioners could now consider and debate which approaches best fit consumer strengths, identified needs, organizational cultures, and community conditions. Although Rothman (1979) recognized that his three modes of intervention were not pure and that "mixing and phasing" of the strategies would be needed, his classification scheme successfully allowed community practitioners and consumers to consider differential assessment and intervention at the macro level.

Other writers focused on delineating other aspects of community practice. Perlman and Gurin (1972) brought attention to the process (e.g., steps or phases) involved in community practice. Meanwhile, Warren and Warren (1977) identified a typology of neighborhoods that helped social workers and consumers understand the qualitative aspects and importance of the kinds of neighborhoods under consideration. These and other theoretical materials are examined in greater detail toward the end of this chapter.

Current Approaches: Freire; Kretzmann and McKnight The ideas of several contemporary writers have contributed substantially to the literature examining community practice. Paulo Freire, a Brazilian educator, is known for his critique of traditional approaches to teaching. Freire believed that con-ventional approaches in education employ a "banking" approach, where the teacher is revered as the expert and is expected to transmit (deposit) knowledge to students. Freire suggests that what is really needed, particularly in relation to the interests and needs of the poor, is a collective or "popular education." Using his shared approach, oppressed groups of people are encouraged to identify local issues of concern and critically analyze the roles of various social institutions (e.g., social welfare, education, family, polity, and religion) in improving conditions.

Using Freire's logic, a process of reflective consciousness raising, labeled **conscientization,** is seen as a vital step in enabling marginalized groups of people to understand that difficult social circumstances are neither inevitable nor self-inflicted (Feagin & Vera, 2001). Through active dialogue and reflection, community members learn about the relevance of external factors to their lives. As this awareness develops, an emphasis is placed on political action and the importance of policy formation and development.

The professional's role is to stimulate consciousness and to work with people in a cooperative fashion, as coinvestigators, to use and develop their abilities and strengths to produce change. Prominence is given to a process or "praxis" centered on critical reflection. Ultimately, people contemplate and make decisions concerning any actions to be taken and the consequences of strategies and tactics to be used (Hope & Timmel, 1995; Schneck, 2002).

John McKnight and his colleague Jamie Kretzmann (Kretzmann & McKnight, 1993) have promoted the philosophy of "asset-based" community work. This approach explicitly promotes a strengths-based approach over the traditional problem orientation to community work. A major emphasis of their work is on identifying the strengths (assets) of a local community through a process of "assets mapping." The term *community assets* is often defined in a very broad, encompassing fashion. In addition to physical resources (buildings, parks, etc.), community assets can include citizen participation, associations, leadership, formal and informal resources, interorganizational networks, shared values, a sense of community, the ability to wield power, and engagement in critical reflection (Delgado, 2000).

In discussing Kretzmann and McKnight's asset-based approach, Delgado (2000) makes an interesting distinction through his preference for the term **capacity enhancement** over *capacity development*. Delgado suggests that "enhancement" recognizes the existence of inherent capacities to build upon, whereas "development" implies that assets may not yet exist in a community. Indeed, a strengths-based perspective for community engagement assumes the presence of many different kinds of assets that can be used and built upon in macro-level intervention.

Useful Theoretical Perspectives
in Community Practice Strategies

Rothman's Models: Locality (Community) Development, Social Planning, and Social Action For decades, Rothman's (1979) three modes or strategies of community practice (locality development, social planning, and social action) have served as a basis for examining community-level change. (As a point of clarification, the term *community development* may be preferable to *locality development,* as it includes the possibility of using such approaches with nongeographic as well as geographic communities.) In addition, Rothman's three strategies are similar to those identified by James Christenson (cited in Lyon, 1987, pp. 115, 126): (1) self-help (community development), (2) technical assistance (social planning), and (3) conflict (social action).

Since his original publication, Rothman has continued to develop his thoughts concerning community organizing. In particular, he has suggested the need for a more elaborate range of strategies than his original three modes. As a result, several writers have worked to identify and describe additional types of community work.

For example, Taylor and Roberts (1985) put forward five models of community work. These include Rothman's original models with the addition of community liaison and program development. Taylor and Roberts also suggest that models of community practice should be analyzed and evaluated in relation to the amount of energy and action that is agency-driven versus consumer-determined.

Marie Weil (1996) has identified eight models of community practice. To Rothman's original modes she has added organizing functional communities, community social and economic development, program development and community liaison, coalitions, and social movements. In each mode, the theme of building on the strengths of consumers through collective reflection and critical analysis (among consumers and with professionals) is an important element. Though not always the case, the decision as to which strategies to utilize in community practice should be a primary function of the will of consumers.

To assist the reader, Rothman's paradigm, along with Taylor and Roberts's two additional modes of community intervention, is summarized in Table 6.1. Chapter 7 examines program development and social planning in greater depth, while, Chapter 9 is concerned with social action and political empowerment. Later in this chapter, community development and community liaison are examined in closer detail.

A Complementary View of Strategies: Collaboration, Campaign, Contest Three useful strategies have been identified for bringing about change at the community level and within organizations. These are collaboration, campaign, and contest (Netting, Kettner, & McMurtry, 2001).

The least confrontational and least conflict-oriented technique involves **collaboration,** where the intent is to minimize power differentials between actors and to seek agreement among the various players. Collaborative efforts are particularly appropriate and effective when relevant parties exhibit relatively few differences, are open to change, and espouse compatible goals. Collaboration closely aligns with Rothman's "locality development," as both emphasize the "pulling together" of sentiment and the establishment of workable alliances between groups of people (i.e., capacity building). Collaborative efforts often assist and empower people in acquiring or gaining political influence.

Table 6.1 Strategies/Models of Community Practice

Model	Auspice	Change Accomplished by:	Typical Worker Roles
Program development	Fully sponsor-determined	Campaign	Administrator, implementer
Social planning[a]	7/8 sponsor-determined	Campaign	Analyst, planner
Community liaison/networks	1/2 sponsor-, 1/2 client-determined	Collaboration[b]	Broker, mediator
Community development	7/8 client-determined	Collaboration	Teacher, coach
Social action/political empowerment	Fully client-determined	Contest[b]	Advocate, agitator, negotiator

[a]Bold type indicates Rothman's original strategies.

[b]Collaboration and contest are approaches aimed at attitudinal change. A "contest strategy" involves power and confrontation.

SOURCES: Derived from the work of Rothman (1979), Taylor and Roberts (1985), and Netting, Kettner, McMurtry (2001).

A **campaign** strategy is more confrontational, as it involves convincing individuals or groups of the rightness of a particular plan, proposal, or direction. This is often an important tactic in Rothman's "social planning," as it assumes that one actor, often a paid professional, has expertise and special knowledge concerning the issues at hand, as well as viable resolutions. Examples of campaign tactics would include educational efforts (e.g., community forums, distribution of information, media presentations) aimed at convincing organizations and public officials of the merits of a plan or policy.

Unfortunately, campaign approaches can be structured in ways that minimize the ability and knowledge of consumers and ordinary citizens to determine appropriate courses of action, in favor of professional expertise and consultation. Special attention must be given to the strengths of consumers (e.g., experiences, public speaking, media presentations) when attempting to sway public sentiment.

Collaboration and campaign both involve "attitude change," as each seeks to alter or sway people's attitudes. In both approaches, pressure is brought to bear to convince others of the merits of a particular goal or plan. However, neither strategy endorses coercion or strong-arm, confrontational tactics as means of gaining acceptance.

A **contest** strategy, by contrast, condones and is dedicated to a much more open use of conflict and confrontation as a means of promoting change. Tactics used include legal challenges, protest, bargaining and negotiation, civil disobedience, and demonstration. The contest approach fits nicely with Rothman's social action model, as contest tactics aim to promote and advance the equalizing of power between unequal actors through collective (planned) action.

Although they are presented separately here, it is not uncommon for consumers and community practitioners to implement these approaches in concerted, often stepwise, ways. For example, larger community-based public agencies often can wield greater power over decision makers than voluntary associations of consumers. A group of consumers advocating for needed change in organizational policy might first approach the agency with their request using collaboration and then resort to a campaign strategy. If both strategies were to fail, then the consumer group would likely entertain a contest strategy as a means of achieving their goals.

Conversely, consumers might conclude that the best first step is to mount a pointed, high-profile protest concerning the unreasonableness and insensitivity of the agency's policy. Functionally, the use of contest strategies in community-based change often serves to grab the attention of authorities, so that good-faith discussions using collaboration or campaign can then take place.

Of course, these are calculated decisions, not to be taken lightly. The ramifications of employing any of these strategies, but especially a contest tactic, need to be fully explored. Most important, determinations of this kind need to be made and fully endorsed by consumers. The role of the social worker is to encourage and assist consumers in defining their strengths and in making informed decisions. Some consumer groups are well organized and equipped to confront power differences and public opposition. Other consumer groups need assistance in nurturing and developing their capabilities. Regardless, an overall self-assessment of the strengths of consumers is a necessary step before implementing any community change tactic.

Community Practice and Process

Reflective examination of helping processes has been an ongoing theme throughout the history of social work. As you will recall from earlier chapters, the term *problem-solving model* refers to a system of logical, sequential steps that is used as a framework for engaging consumers in planned change.

In this book, social work intervention has been viewed through two lenses: that of the strengths perspective and that of empowerment. This is an important departure from traditional forms of problem solving. Yet, problem-solving models contain some important redeeming features. For example, social workers have traditionally focused on distinct beginning, middle, and ending phases when conceptualizing community-level change. It is helpful to understand that community change, like other forms of social work practice, can be conceptualized and structured in terms of phases or steps. Phases of intervention keep consumers and professionals focused on the issues at hand and present considerations for each step in the process.

Perlman and Gurin (1972) are recognized in the social work literature for their early contribution in devising a detailed process for conceptualizing intervention at the community level. Though problem oriented, Perlman and Gurin (1972) pose two noteworthy, parallel themes for consideration—analytical and interactional. *Analytical* references the importance of theoretical knowledge in practice. Of course, this would include the work of Rothman and many others, but it also serves as a reference to more recent works, including the strengths perspective and empowerment theory. The term *interactional* gives credence to interpersonal, relational, and group-building skills in community practice.

Indeed, many social workers would argue that the strength of our profession lies in these two areas. First, social workers are particularly adept in facilitating analytical assessment (with consumers) and examining a community, or any other social system, from a multitude of perspectives, including the strengths orientation. Second, by virtue of their education and professional development, social workers have excellent interpersonal and organizational skills. This is particularly true when working with individuals, families, and consumer groups in communities.

Many social workers would agree that interpersonal skills and the ability to view phenomena from multiple viewpoints are two crucial elements when considering social advocacy. Professionals and consumers must work together in communities to assess both strengths and barriers, so that they can successfully identify relevant issues and actors and calculate meaningful change. Knowledge, information, theoretical wisdom, analytical abilities, relational skills, and practical experiences are some of the cornerstones of successful community intervention.

Neighborhood Typologies

Warren and Warren (1977) have identified a classification system for neighborhoods on the basis of three key factors: (1) identity, (2) interaction within the community, and (3) links to external resources. Their scheme is particularly useful for helping workers and consumers to identify assets and attributes in communities. A total of nine community types are provided, using the aforementioned criteria. Insight into the neighborhood type can yield information concerning community assets, areas for capacity building, the focus of work, and the pace of change efforts. Although the Warren and Warren scheme was developed to describe geographical neighborhoods, many of their ideas (e.g., identity, modes of interaction, and external linking capabilities) seem applicable as well to communities of interest.

Worker Roles

When engaged in community practice, it is useful to consider some of the specific roles that are appropriate for social workers in macro social work practice. Many of these roles (e.g., social planner, administrator/organizational leader, evaluator, community organizer, advocate, educator, political activist, group leader, researcher, fund raiser, grant writer, policy analyst, committee/board member, and program developer) were examined in Chapter 3.

When considering the community, as either a consumer or a target system for change, several additional roles have particular relevance. For example, the role of *mediator* is important, particularly in collaborative strategies. Social workers often seek ways to reconcile differences between groups of people.

This involves accentuating group commonalities and shared strengths, while learning to minimize or accept differences.

Similarly, in collaborative strategies, social workers often serve as *brokers*. Expertise and knowledge concerning community-based agencies, services, associations, and organizations allow social workers to become active agents in negotiating agreements and associations between various actors and social entities. Once again, this "brokering" is performed in response and as a complement to consumer participation and determination.

With respect to contest tactics, social workers can be seen as active participants in rousing the interests and ire of consumers. Although the term *agitator* carries negative connotations, social workers often work with consumers to bring important issues to the forefront. Envision a social worker with a bullhorn in hand making announcements at a rally, or a social worker helping consumers to create and distribute pamphlets. To the extent that social workers enter the fray of raising public consciousness and awareness concerning community issues, they can be rightfully viewed as agitators.

Using Community Organization Theory to Improve Practice

Knowledge and theory in an applied field such as social work are intended to improve the effectiveness of practice. The following points, stimulated by the scholarly works and perspectives examined in this chapter, are offered as means of sharpening your community practice.

1. *Determine the focus of community organizing.* Clarify whether the target for change is the community, the consumer (client) system, or both. In other words, who are you working for, and with, as a social worker? As much as possible, have consumers define the issues at hand and the scope of your work within the community context. Is *community* defined geographically or as a community of sharing? With consumers, determine the assets of your employing agency as well as the usefulness of relevant individuals, organizations, resources, and other entities in the community.

2. *Decide which community practice strategies are most appropriate.* Rothman (1979), Taylor and Roberts (1985), and others provide social workers with conceptual models for engaging in community practice. Contemplate the overall direction being called for in your practice. Once again, this is a participatory process that beckons for direct involvement and ownership by consumers. Everyone benefits when a clear sense of direction is defined and determined in community practice.

3. *Agree on which roles you are assuming as a social worker.* Which role or roles do you plan to perform? What expectations and behaviors are associated with these roles? The will of consumers concerning role assumption and definition is crucial. It is important to remember that a primary obligation is for the social worker to act as a coinvestigator, working in tandem with

consumers. Whatever your role (e.g., advocate, mediator, organizer, policy analyst), consumer endorsement legitimizes, directs, and places limitations on your status and actions. As suggested earlier, it will be helpful to discuss role enactment in the context of the particular types of strategies being employed—collaboration, campaign, and/or contest.

4. *Identify the type of neighborhood/community involved.* Warren and Warren (1977) suggest that neighborhoods can be differentiated by type—classified according to identity, interaction patterns, and ability to access external resources. Given these dimensions, work with consumers to identify community strengths and assets.

5. *Outline with consumers a process or steps for proceeding with planned change, and estimate a reasonable timeline.* What do previous research, local experience, up-to-date information, and contemporary theory suggest with respect to consumer plans? Nurture and develop relationships, channels of communication, and dialogue with consumers and relevant actors to maximize the probability of success (Perlman & Gurin, 1972). Agree on a reasonable timeline for pursuing change. Consider embedding critical junctures or turning points as identifiable elements in the process.

6. *Establish mechanisms for ongoing evaluation.* Consumers and professionals should be engaged in ongoing review of efforts directed at community change, using both formal and informal means. Mechanisms could include the use of consumer meetings, organization and special-interest group feedback, group discussions, surveys, commissioned focus groups, and review by external professional research bodies. Information derived from multiple indicators using a variety of sources often yields some of the best, most thought-provoking feedback.

Specific Principles Using a Strengths Perspective

The following are a few helpful suggestions for everyday community-based practice using the strengths perspective:

Worker role:

- Be clear about your roles in community organizing. Are you an advocate, group leader, evaluator, facilitator, administrator, or what? Strive to ensure that your role definitions allow for the strengths of consumers to emerge, develop, and take primacy.

- Listen! Practice active listening skills. People need to tell their story, often in detail. The thoughts, perceptions, feelings, and decisions of consumers constitute the foundation, the bricks and mortar, of macro social work practice and community-level change.

- Avoid the temptation to tell the group what you believe are their problems and their strengths. This should be a process of discovery, aimed at consumer ownership and empowerment.

- One of your most important tasks involves process. Help the group to reach a sense of consensus on the topics to be addressed and on consumer strengths in pursuing community change. Often the social worker plays a useful role in clarifying issues and tactics and in keeping the consumer group on task. Helpful undertakings can include finding a meeting place and times, formalizing agendas, making clear what needs to be done before the next meeting, reiterating the agreed-on division of labor, assisting leadership efforts, summarizing agreements reached during meetings, and spelling out the next steps in the process.

- Allow people to do for themselves and to assume their own form of leadership in community change. The social worker should perform roles endorsed by consumers. The temptation for some people is to ask the social worker to resolve problems. The goal of social work is to empower people to address their own issues and to build capacities for use in the future. If the worker takes on an issue for a community group, people will miss opportunities, collectively and individually, to enhance their abilities.

- Be honest about your abilities, your professional limitations, and the resources available at your agency. For community change to be successful, there must be an appreciable investment (of time, energies, and funds) from many parties. Early in the process, consumers need to be aware of these types of obligations.

- Be clear with the group that you and your agency may not be able to support some goals or tactics.

Process considerations:

- Think about community-level change as beginning in smaller ways, through individual contacts and small-group meetings (e.g., in homes or at community centers). This will allow consumers to build momentum, assess their strengths, and develop a proper pace for subsequent actions. To begin community change efforts with a large forum is often premature, grandiose, and ineffective.

- Assist consumers in establishing a climate that promotes successful action. The group should be conceptualized as achievement-oriented, not simply a "talking group." Identify and clarify the purposes of the consumer group or association.

- Get people involved in the change process, and nurture respect for even the most basic form of participation.

- Don't forget that community-level change can be fulfilling. People get involved in community groups for a variety of reasons, including social ones, and these motives should be recognized. Some people are better than others at addressing the social-emotional needs of members. For example, basic efforts, like serving refreshments, may increase participation and make work more enjoyable.

- Strike a good balance between process (how goals are achieved) and product (actual goal achievement). Consumers need to experience some degree of success in order to sustain interest, but the process of achieving goals is also important in its own right. Be attentive to both process and product in relation to human capacity building. Becoming skillful and able actors in the community is valuable, regardless of goal attainment.

- Encourage group members to avoid the tendency to plan so many activities that people become overwhelmed and bow out of planned change. In community work, as with other forms of intervention, activities need to be prioritized on the basis of overall group goals and probability of success.

- Identify the major stakeholders with respect to your consumer group. These individuals will most likely constitute the leadership and will play a major role in decision making. Take measures to ensure that consumer leadership is receptive and responsive to the strengths and concerns of other consumers.

- Timely follow up and feedback are important ingredients in sustaining consumer interest in community change. Some form of regular contact with each member should take place between meetings. Phone calls, fliers, and e-mails help ensure a flow of information and can facilitate active engagement.

Organizational considerations:

- The organizational structure of a community group should reflect the functions and tasks that are needed. Organizational structure should provide support and consultation for decision making, but need not be any more complicated than is required to get the job done. Social workers working with community groups should advise them to avoid creating more offices or committees than needed.

- Similarly, procedures need not be more complicated than is needed to achieve group goals. At times, *Robert's Rules of Order* can be too complex. Encourage consumers to adopt inclusive processes, where people are encouraged to voice opinions, use their talents and abilities, and participate freely in decision making.

- Assume that consumer participation will vary over time. Some people will come and go, particularly in the early phases. Nurture and develop individuals for leadership roles, and consider multiperson (co-leadership) models. Organizations often exhibit greater endurance when they are less reliant on a single person for leadership.

- Allow for multiple levels and kinds of participation by consumers. Some people may desire only occasional or intermittent involvement.

People who choose not to talk may like to engage in tangible actions (e.g., creating a Web site or distributing fliers). Consumers with political connections may prefer contacting community leaders. As with the settlement house movement, consumers benefit when organizational climate is open, warm, inclusive, and receptive.

Tropman (1997) has written a useful book for social workers practicing with community groups. Specific attention is given to developing leadership and the effective use of group meetings.

Community Development

Of all the community practice models, **community development** perhaps best lends itself to the strengths perspective. Community development work "promotes education in civic pride and civic consciousness, and sees in community itself an arena where the public interest can become a living force" (Brueggemann, 2002, p. 169). Community development assumes that there are inherent strengths in communities that can be mobilized to resolve issues and vitalize the community as a whole.

Community development is a particularly helpful approach for marginalized groups seeking to gain control over their conditions, circumstances, and well-being. Social workers help consumers to organize themselves (e.g., to identify their desires, abilities, knowledge, and resources) and to structure a plan of action to raise community awareness and create change. Youth can provide leadership in their communities to address social and economic issues that affect both young people and the wider community (Checkoway, 1998). Minorities can develop social support systems to help mitigate problems resulting from long-standing institutional discrimination. Community development employs democratic processes and procedures to cooperatively address community concerns and needs.

Community development work can be particularly invigorating, as it emphasizes and promotes consumer consciousness, pride, and engagement in community progress (political, economic, and social). For more specific information about community development processes, Swaenpol and DeBeer (1996) offer interesting insight and suggestions.

Community Liaison, Interagency
Networks/Partnerships, and Collaboration

Social workers have always been concerned with service coordination, interagency networks, and partnerships. They realize that no single agency has the resources to address the many needs of consumers of services. A variety of mechanisms have potential for enhancing coordination, including collaboration, coalitions, partnerships, and community involvement teams. Morrison, Howard, Johnson, Navarro, Plachetka, and Bell (1998) provide several examples of different models of service coordination.

Community partnering can help agencies achieve more effective and efficient service for consumers and can be a vehicle for securing additional support or sharing resources for programming. When contemplating potential partners, consumer participation and involvement are vital. For example, consumers are keenly aware of the cluster of services they commonly use. For families with children, schools, preschool programs like Head Start, the local child and family services agency, the family guidance clinic, and after-school programs may be logical. For older adults, a partnership between senior centers, nutritional programs, and health agencies would make more sense. Another set of partnerships could be clustered with respect to physical disability. When examining the potential of partnerships, the hopes and desires of consumer groups are a primary consideration, as well as the assets that consumer associations and groups bring to partnership building.

Community schools are one mechanism for enhancing coordination of services at a neighborhood level (Morrison et al., 1998). Because public schools are conveniently located in neighborhoods, serve most children, and have good facilities, they are natural sites for coordinated services. Both counseling and recreation/development services can be offered in school settings during school hours and after school. In some communities, nonschool agencies can partner to provide noneducational services.

Although a strong value is placed on coordination and partnership efforts in social work, these ventures can be difficult. Factors that can enhance success include the presence of formal authority (e.g., county commissioners and city leaders) supporting the collaboration, the ability to build strong relationships and trust between partners, and a commitment to examining and changing organizational processes and practices. Other important considerations with respect to interagency coordination include clarification of agency interests, a realistic view of the size and scope of the coordination efforts, the ability to formalize arrangements, and continuity of agency leadership.

Exchange theory is a useful theoretical perspective when examining the notion of interagency coordination and partnerships (see Blau, 1964). A fundamental tenet of exchange theory is that social organizations engage in an ongoing process of social exchange—give and take of resources. Organizations seek interaction and partnerships with other social entities that can satisfy or address their needs. Hence, social service agencies will be more likely to engage in coordination efforts when they perceive that there is something of value to be gained (Schmidt & Kochan, 1997).

General Guidelines for Community Liaison Work

Consumers, social workers, and other stakeholders are encouraged to perform these **community liaison** functions collaboratively:

- Assess the costs and benefits of a potential liaison for all parties (e.g., consumers, agencies, and the overall community).

- Examine the fit between prospective agencies in a community. Which agencies are most critical to the success of liaison efforts?

- Identify the competence of each potential organizational partner as well as the goodness of fit (e.g., mission, goals, and auspice) and degree to which organizations can complement one another.

- Specify the nature of exchange relationships between organizations (e.g., staff, funding, consumer eligibility).

- Secure support and endorsement from the high officials in each organization.

- Agree on a lead facilitator responsible for convening meetings, summarizing ideas during the meetings, arranging for minutes, and maintaining communication with participants between meetings.

- Commit agreements and associations to writing.

- Promote honest, open communication and awareness between organizations.

SUMMARY

This chapter was dedicated to an examination of community practice and the importance of the community in supporting people and achieving mutually defined goals. *Community* was defined as either a geographic community or a community of sharing. Many considerations and practical suggestions were provided for social workers engaged in helping people to build community capacities. In addition, a variety of theoretical orientations were examined for use in community practice.

A recurring theme in this chapter involved using the strengths of consumers in community building. The role of the social worker in community practice was viewed as being defined by the hopes and desires of consumers. In the tradition of the COS and settlement house movements, a primary responsibility of the social worker is to seek ways to promote community consciousness and empower consumers of services.

Finally, community development and community liaison work were examined. These orientations are particularly aligned with the tenets of strengths-based practice and emphasize consumer participation and ownership in creating social change.

A FEW KEY TERMS

community	capacity enhancement	contest
community practice	collaboration	community development
conscientization	campaign	community liaison

USING INFOTRAC®
COLLEGE EDITION AND INFOWRITE

InfoTrac College Edition

Community development is examined throughout this chapter, especially since it lends itself to the strengths perspective. This exercise is designed to enhance your understanding and application of the strengths perspective to community development. Be prepared to share your comments with your classmates by using a flip chart or PowerPoint presentation to document your responses.

1. Go to InfoTrac College Edition.

2. Search under the Keyword Search using "community development."

3. Select an article that highlights community development in a rural area in the United States or in another nation.

4. Read the article and apply the specific principles of the strengths perspective discussed in this chapter to the following questions:

   a. In the context of the article, what would you see as your social work role or roles? Explain why.

   b. List what you think are the main issues affecting the community.

   c. What consumers would you solicit to tell their story? Why do you think their personal narratives would be important to the community development effort?

   d. What investment behaviors are necessary for community change to occur?

InfoWrite

Much of the material presented in this book could be used in preparation for researching and writing a thesis on macro social work practice. To demonstrate this point:

1. Go to InfoWrite.

2. Scroll to The Writing Process.

3. Read under the bullet, "Developing a Thesis."

4. Define at least three possible theses that could be written from this chapter in conjunction with the other chapters of the book you have read.

5. Read under the bullet, "Supporting a Thesis."

6. Referring to your possible theses, indicate the strengths and weaknesses of each type of support for the theses.

7. Order your three theses and their corresponding supports according to their research feasibility.

8. Explain your ordering process.

CASE EXAMPLE: Beginning the Process of Community Development

Dorothy Rutter is a social worker at a community center located in a lower-income inner-city neighborhood. In recent months, various consumer groups at the center have been pressuring administrators and professionals to increase the organization's prominence and involvement in the neighborhood. Dorothy's consumers have been very vocal about their hope and desire for the center to become a more active player in community affairs. Consumers from several programs at the center have expressed an interest in having Dorothy take on a professional leadership role in promoting community involvement.

Before making any kind of commitment, Dorothy asked for each program at the center to query membership with respect to interest in community asset and capacity building. Prior to organizing a community-wide meeting, Dorothy sought to identify and understand the factors prompting a call for community involvement and intervention. She asked a few of the consumers who had stepped forward if they would be willing to hold small information-finding meetings in their homes.

As these meetings progressed, Dorothy actively listened to consumers' concerns and to their motivations for engaging in community work. Relationship building and establishment of trust and respect were primary considerations. Dorothy was careful not to make assumptions about what was of interest to consumers. Dorothy acted primarily as a facilitator to clarify issues, prompt information gathering, and assist consumers in identifying their potential strengths with respect to community development.

Dorothy worked with consumers both to clarify issues and to help identify consumer strengths. Several themes quickly emerged that were shared by a number of people. Police services and activities for youth were noted as concerns at each of the meetings. As part of the agenda of each meeting, Dorothy ascertained the interest of consumers in taking further action to address the identified issues. Volunteers were sought to serve as a committee for subsequent meetings and to establish a grassroots organization.

Dorothy knows that her role needs further specification and that decision making is a consumer right and responsibility. She is supportive of consumer efforts to confront issues, but she also points out the merits of community building. As a community organizer, she helps people to think about prioritization, community capacities, and goal acquisition. To keep the group on task, Dorothy periodically summarizes consumer decisions and plans.

At this point, consumers have decided to plan a larger community meeting at the center and to establish a formal committee to further assess the situation concerning police policy relations and youth. Dorothy and the consumers alike see her role as that of a facilitator and educator. She will continue to work with consumers and community leaders to further specify community and consumer strengths, seek opportunities for improving police relations, explore possible alliances with other community organizations, and eventually seek an appropriate course of action.

Dorothy is excited about the prospect of working with consumers in the process of community development. She sees an emerging civic consciousness and awareness concerning police relations. One of Dorothy's top responsibilities as a social worker is to help consumers of services to position themselves in a manner that allows their talents, abilities, and resources to be used in the best possible fashion to enrich the community.

THINKING CRITICALLY
ABOUT THE CASE EXAMPLE

1. In this case example, Dorothy views herself as a facilitator—clarifying issues, assisting consumers, organizing meetings, and prompting information gathering. With respect to developing community resources, is Dorothy working with a geographic community, a community of sharing, or potentially both types of community organizations? Why is this clarification important?

2. It appears that a concern in the community involves police relations. What would constitute helpful sources of information concerning police–consumer relations? How might these sources of information differ depending on the approach used (e.g., collaboration, campaign, or contest).

3. Critique the manner in which Dorothy engaged consumers in this case illustration. For example, Dorothy "asked a few of the consumers who stepped forward . . . to hold small information-finding meetings." Is this a good practice? Why or why not?

REFLECTION EXERCISES

1. Go to the U.S. Census Web site (www.census.gov) and use the tools provided there to develop a profile for your community. Include both demographic and housing information. Determine the census tract for your area. Compare census tract and ZIP code information. How might this type of information be useful to consumer groups in the community? Can you envision consumer leadership using this type of data from the Internet?

2. Using the brief vignettes that follow, discuss and debate with classmates appropriate activities and directions for the social worker. Be sure to include thoughts about how consumers would participate in decisions concerning the participation of the social worker. These vignettes can also be used for group exercises or role plays in class. In each of the situations, ask yourself these questions:

   - As a social worker, what are some possible roles in community practice?

   - What are potential goals for consumers?

   - What preparations are needed?

   - Which model or models of community practice should be considered?

   - How might you anticipate the process evolving?

   - What contingency plans should be considered?

1. Students in your neighborhood score poorly on standardized testing (proficiency exams). You have been asked to meet with a group of parents from the local school district. Identify some options with respect to your initial steps. If parents have arranged a meeting with the school administrators, consider ways of preparing for such a meeting. How can you help ensure that consumers, not professionals, are directing the process?

2. You are employed at a community health center. In a cost-cutting move, city council members are questioning program utilization and effectiveness at your agency. Politicians are looking to reduce spending and eliminate programs. Consumers and agency professionals have already heard about the intentions of council members. Professional staff members at the health center are highly invested in several programs. The sentiment of consumers concerning program implementation and efficacy is far less clear. Several consumers have asked you to assist them in efforts to maintain current programming.

3. You have been working with a community group that has expressed a concern about trash pickup in the neighborhood. The group does not want to be confrontational but would like to seek ways to remedy the situation. What are some initial thoughts concerning data gathering, potential alliances, and the value of networking?

SUGGESTED READINGS

Alinsky, S. (1972). *Rules for radicals.* New York: Vintage.

Kahn, S. (1970). *How people get power.* New York: McGraw-Hill.

McKee, M. (2003). Excavating our frames of mind: The key to dialogue and collaboration. *Social Work, 48*(3), 401–408.

Williams, B. (1948). *Lillian Wald: Angel of Henry Street.* New York: Julian Messner.

REFERENCES

Adams, P., & Krauth, K. (Eds.). (1995). *Reinventing human services: Community and family-centered practice.* Hawthorne, NY: Aldine de Gruyter.

Batten, T. R. (1957). *Communities and their development.* London: Oxford University Press.

Biddle, W. W., with Biddle, L. J. (1965). *The community development process: The rediscovery of local initiative.* New York: Holt, Rinehart and Winston.

Blau, P. (1964). *Exchange and power in social life.* New York: Wiley.

Brueggemann, W. (2002). *The practice of macro social work.* Belmont, CA: Wadsworth/Thomson Learning.

Checkoway, B. (1998). Involving young people in neighborhood development. *Children and Youth Services Review 20,* 765–795.

Delgado, M. (2000). *Community social work in an urban context: The potential of a capacity-enhancement perspective.* New York: Oxford University Press.

Feagin, J. R., & Vera, H. (2001). *Liberation sociology.* Boulder, CO: Westview Press.

Harrington, M. (1974). *The other America: Poverty in the United States.* New York: Macmillan.

Hassinger, E. W., & Pinkerton, J. (1986). *The human community.* New York: Macmillan.

Hope, A., & Timmel, S. (1995). *Training for transformation: A handbook for community workers* (rev. ed.). Gwero, Zimbabwe: Mambo.

Kretzmann, J. P., & McKnight, J. (1993). *Building communities from the inside out: A path toward finding and mobilizing a community's assets.* Evanston, IL: Center for Urban Affairs and Policy Research, Northwestern University.

Lyon, L. (1987). *The community in urban society.* Chicago: Dorsey Press.

Midgley, J. (1995). *Social development: The developmental perspective in social welfare.* London: Sage Publications.

Morrison, J. D., Howard, J., Johnson, C., Navarro, F. J., Plachetka., B., & Bell, T. (1998). Strengthening neighborhoods by developing community networks. In P. L. Ewalt, E. M. Freeman, & D. Poole (Eds.), *Community building: Renewal, well-being, and shared responsibility.* Washington, DC: NASW Press.

Naparstek, A. J. (1999). Community building and social group work: A new practice paradigm for American cities. In H. Bertcher, L. F. Kurtz, & A. Lamont (Eds.), *Rebuilding communities: Challenges for group work.* New York: Haworth Press.

Netting, F. E., Kettner, P. M., & McMurtry, S. L. (2001). In J. E. Tropman, J. L. Erlich, & J. Rothman (Eds.), *Tactics and techniques of community intervention.* Itasca, IL: Peacock Publishers.

Newman, O. (1972). *Defensible space: Crime prevention through urban design.* New York: Macmillan.

Perlman, R., & Gurin, A. (1972). *Community organization and social planning.* New York: Wiley.

Richmond, M. E. (1955). *Social diagnosis.* New York: Russell Sage Foundation. (Originally published in 1917.)

Rothman, J. (1979). Three models of community organization practice, their mixing and phasing. In F. M. Cox, J. L. Erlich, J. Rothman, & J. C. Tropman (Eds.), *Strategies of community organization* (3rd ed.). Itasca, IL: Peacock Publishers.

Schmidt, S. M., & Kochan, T. A. (1997). Inter-organizational relationships: Patterns and motivations. *Administrative Science Quarterly, 22,* 220–234.

Schneck, R. (2002). Revisiting Paulo Freire as a theoretical base for participatory practices for social workers. *Social Work/Maatskaplike Werk, 38*(1), pp. 71–80.

Swaenpol, H., & DeBeer, F. (1996). *Community capacity building: A guide for fieldworkers and community leaders.* Cape Town, South Africa: Oxford University Press Southern Africa.

Taylor, S. H., & Roberts, R. W. (1985). *Theory and practice of community social work.* New York: Columbia University Press.

Tropman, J. E. (1997). *Successful community leadership: A skills guide for volunteers and professionals.* Washington, DC: NASW Press.

Warren, R. B., & Warren, D. I. (1977). *The neighborhood organizer's handbook.* Notre Dame, IN: University of Notre Dame Press.

Weil, M. O. (1996). Community building: Building community practice. *Social Work, 41*(5), 481–499.

7

Social Planning

Chapter Content Areas

Social Planning

Rational Model

Political Model

Empowerment Model

Strengths Model

Promoting a Strengths
Perspective

Strategic Planning

SWOT Analysis

Task Environment

Mission and Vision Statements

Marketing

Planning Phases

Consumer Participation

The NIMBY Phenomenon

Resource Considerations

Planning as a Cooperative,
Educational Process

Sustainable Development

WHAT IS SOCIAL PLANNING?

Social planning is an activity typically associated with community practice, community organizing, and leadership in human services. Indeed, it is an important function in any community or society. Social planning involves processes that allow people to collectively explore assets and areas for improvement, develop plans of action, and evaluate the effectiveness of policies and programs in creating large-scale social change.

Planning involves mapping out or making arrangements for doing something. As a student, you engage in personal planning when you develop a strategy to complete a class assignment or study for an examination. Although this type of planning is an individual endeavor, the benefits of collective thought and contemplation are many. The veteran learner knows that conversations with other students yield valuable information and insight for approaching projects, exams, and papers.

Social planning is a cooperative process, associated with the strengthening of organizations, communities, and societies through the development and successful implementation of social policies and programs. In its most general form, social planning is an ongoing course of action, both formal and informal, in which consumers, citizens, leaders, and professionals work together to brainstorm and develop strategies to improve human functioning and the social environment.

As one might imagine, social planning is related to and often performed in conjunction with a variety of other social work roles and functions. For example, it is imperative that social planners keep abreast of policy initiatives and developments as well as current research depicting "best practices" and effective interventions in promoting social change.

Similarly, social planning is closely related to community practice and administration. Community-based leaders and practitioners are almost always engaged in some type of social planning, whether it is building a new community center, forming a task force, promoting a fund drive, or lobbying for a legislative initiative to provide opportunities for consumers. Therefore, it is important to view social planning as being encompassing, contextual, and a primary function in the professional life of social workers.

As with most forms of social work practice, a multitude of approaches can be used to conceptualize and engage in social planning. Although this book is dedicated to an analysis of the strengths orientation, social planning has traditionally been approached from a problem-solving (deficit) orientation. For many people, social planning has been and continues to be a mechanism to address, correct, and resolve social problems and injustices.

Although the problem-solving orientation toward social planning is a social work mainstay, it is only one possible approach. As suggested in previous chapters, seasoned social workers know the virtues of using an **eclectic approach**—considering a multitude of theories, approaches, and models for use in psychosocial intervention. As a rule, it is helpful to analyze social processes and phenomena in a variety of ways, being careful to cue into the voices, passion, and will of consumers. Social planning, by definition, involves numerous actors and vested interest groups. As a result, it is important from the outset of the social-planning process to be attentive to the tone or approach being advocated by various stakeholders.

CONSUMER AND CITIZEN
PARTICIPATION IN SOCIAL PLANNING

Historically, the profession of social work has demonstrated a rich commitment to identifying and fostering modes of consumer and citizen participation in grassroots (community-based) social planning. Some of the most basic tenets of grassroots planning include "rituals of engagement; the sharing of power; a culture of participation characterized by safety, respect, and high expectations;

and skilful, yet humble, facilitation to create solidarity and equality within the group" (Zachary, 2000, p. 71).

Typically approaching social planning in a nonauthoritarian manner, the tradition of social work practice has often relied on the ability of professionals to mobilize consumers and citizens to rally behind causes, win battles, and build a sense of "we-ness" among people. Kahn (1991) and Staples (1984) highlight the benefits of broad-based participation over personal power in leadership and planning processes.

WAYS OF APPROACHING
SOCIAL PLANNING

When working with people, it becomes obvious fairly quickly that consumers, professionals, citizens, business leaders, politicians, government leaders, community organizers, social planners, and administrators conceptualize social planning from varied perspectives and often differ in the approaches they offer to create social change. For example, politicians typically view social planning as a question of political clout and alignment: What are the best ways for people to position themselves in a manner to effect change?

Meanwhile, business leaders tend to see social planning in terms of cost-effectiveness and judicious investment of resources: Can we afford to do this? Would such plans make economic sense? And, although no single approach can capture the magnitude and complexity of social planning, each of the following approaches has merit and constitutes a unique source of insight concerning planned change.

Rational Model

The first inclination of many people is to think of social planning as a rational process. When a community or societal issue arises, they think: Let's bring a group of people together (e.g., commission, committee, task force) and, in an analytical and objective manner, assess the situation, define the problems, establish short-term and long-term goals, plan a course of action to reach the specified goals, and evaluate the effectiveness of the plan. Does this sound familiar?

The basic premise surrounding a rational approach in social planning involves the ability of people to sort out, understand, weigh, and agree on social problems and ways to address and resolve identified problems. A rational approach requires a careful examination of the values of society and relevant social groupings and the impact of these value orientations in acquiring information, considering policy alternatives, and anticipating outcomes. DiNitto (2000) states, "Rationality requires the intelligence to calculate correctly the ratio of costs to benefits for each policy alternative. This means calculating all present and future benefits and costs to both the target groups [the segment of the population intended to be affected] and nontarget groups in society" (p. 5).

Ideally, the rational approach to social planning allows participants to identify and study the roles and relevance of various actors, groups, social forces, and value orientations (social, political, and economic) in developing policy and program options. Because social problems and issues are typically complex and value-laden, multiple views of causation, solution, and outcome can be anticipated. Although consumers and social workers can strive for rationality in social planning, it is reasonable to assert that social planning is never completely rational, often gives way to subjectivity, seldom results in complete agreement among actors concerning the causes of social problems and the desired outcomes, and is vulnerable to political views and ideological beliefs.

Political Model

Many people, professionals and nonprofessionals alike, would argue that social change and social planning are inherently political. In this view, individuals and special-interest groups participate in a process of vying and positioning themselves to secure a greater share of limited resources (e.g., employment, prestige, money, goods and services). This is based in the somewhat hedonistic view that political persuasion and influence are rooted in an ongoing quest to acquire or sustain assets and power.

Given this premise, social planning constitutes a process by which actors work to garner support to acquire what they want, whenever it is desired. For example, influential individuals and groups of people portray needs, issues, and assets in terms that support and reinforce their preferred status in the social-economic ladder. In contrast, consumer groups and professionals often define social issues and policies in ways that address their needs and hopes.

Political action committees, special-interest groups, unions, voluntary associations, agencies, and political parties are examples of organizations that compete with one another to shape public policy and social programming. Each group presents its case through impassioned oratory, debate, lobbying, promulgation of information, campaigning, contributions, and public declaration of ideals and values. The intent of each political faction is that leaders and social planners will examine and address social change from their own vested point of view. Ideally, in a democratic society, the role of government and leadership is to develop a system and sets of rules that allow for and encourage free expression and appreciation of different opinions. Open discourse allows for the balancing of interests in public-policy formation and development and in social programming (DiNitto, 2000).

BOX 7.1

Social workers have a political action committee. It is called PACE—Political Action for Candidate Election. This organization makes contributions to political candidates that further the views and perspectives of social workers and their consumers via legislative initiatives.

Unfortunately, it is frequently a challenge to promote the voices and perspectives of consumers in the process of social planning. Influential people and groups often have ready access to information supporting their positions, develop an inside track to decision makers and power brokers, and approach planning in a sophisticated and savvy manner. People in power are adept at using behind-the-scenes means of persuading others to adopt their point of view.

To complicate matters, time and again, it is the political dimension that presents consumers and social workers with barriers to active participation in social-planning processes. The social worker's employing agency may prohibit her or him from engaging in political activities during work hours. Subtle pressure can be exerted to avoid "rocking the boat" of power brokers. Contacting influential people may be frowned on or even prohibited by the agency in fear of losing financial support. It is easy to see how the careful analysis of various actors and groups and their political stances, ties, and clout is a prudent step in the social-planning process.

Empowerment Model

So far, social planning has been described as a social, participatory process. Typically, social planning is conceptualized in terms of planning groups and coalitions. Stakeholders and representatives in a society, community, or organization are brought together to engage in planning. For social workers, there is a special interest is the inclusion of consumers of services in each and every planning process.

How professionals and others think about consumers often shapes how people interact with consumers. When consumers are viewed as equals, full members, and coparticipants in planning processes, their role is validated and their perspective valued. Social workers bring to the planning group a degree of expertise and knowledge. Consumers possess talents and skills, and they are also experiential experts. Consumers have firsthand knowledge of conditions and factors that others cannot fully understand.

It is important to note that social planners can be influential in producing change in a community or at the national level. They have the capability of exerting influence by putting forward strategies, plans, and recommendations. "The promise—or the threat—of empowerment lies in its socio-political dimension, its potential to generate collective thought, action, and research" (Ramon, 1999, p. 43). Hence, empowerment in social planning can be judged by the extent to which consumers become active players in designing policies and programs affecting their lives. In empowerment theory, this is furthered by assisting consumers to advocate for themselves (directly) and helping consumers "to build alliances with others for affirmation, support, consciousness raising, and social activism" (O'Melia, 2002, p. 9).

To the extent that empowerment involves issues of power and the redistribution of power in the planning process, empowerment-based social planning certainly can be seen as political. Consumer participation in social planning

represents a sense of **inclusion**—the idea that consumers, like other people, belong at the decision-making table. This often requires a reorientation of leaders, professionals, and others to acknowledge consumers as worthy stakeholders and rightful members of the social-planning group.

In order for consumers to be major stakeholders in the planning process, a sense of trust needs to be nurtured and developed. Members of planning groups form working relationships based on mutual respect and trust. The successful establishment of working relationships is a key ingredient in the planning processes.

If you have the occasion to attend and observe a social-planning meeting, attempt to assess who is actually hearing comments offered by others. Try to distinguish between passive listening and actually hearing (processing) the points being raised. Many times, hearing (cognitively processing) information at a planning meeting is based on relationship, current or past. If social planners know and respect someone, they are more likely to ponder the information or positions he or she is presenting.

Whitmore and Wilson (1997) offer distinct principles that, when applied to planning groups, encourage consumer participation in empowerment-based social planning. These include creating the possibility of nonintrusive collaboration, establishing mutual trust and respect, encouraging common analysis of problems and strengths, promoting a commitment to solidarity, emphasizing equality in relationships, focusing explicitly on process (participatory and inclusive), and recognizing the importance of language in promoting collegiality and permitting the strengths of members to emerge.

Strengths Model

As previously noted, the ability to shift from identifying problems in organizations, communities, and society to examining and building strengths, assets, opportunities, and capabilities of people and larger social systems can be a formidable task. In social planning, embracing a strengths perspective involves adopting a mind-set of looking at the physical and social environment as "rich with resources: people, institutions, associations, families who are willing to and can provide instruction, succor, relief, resources, time, and mirroring" (Saleebey, 2002, p. 91).

Strengths-based social planning seeks ways to utilize existing strengths in organizations, communities, and society to enrich the environment and create opportunities for people. Unfortunately, consumers, professionals, and community leaders frequently lose sight of the resources and competencies that surround them. This is often accompanied by a sense of entrapment, where people lack confidence, feel inadequate, experience stifled ambition, and possess a limited view of the potential for change in the environment (Rapp, 1998, p. 102). Of particular concern is the ability to reach out to consumers and tap their strengths in the planning process. This is especially true when consumers have a history of alienation from planning processes and feel disenfranchised and unmotivated to share their thoughts concerning planned change.

Nonetheless, the strengths of consumers are real and vital elements for consideration and inclusion in the planning process. The key in macro-level social work practice is identifying ways to allow for the strengths of consumers and environmental assets to emerge and be used. The following suggestions are offered for consideration in macro social work practice:

1. Seek ways to reach into the environment in social planning. **Inreach** refers to a conscious, concerted, and active process of reaching or tapping into consumer groups, organizations, and associations for participation in social planning.

2. Build structures that include consumers and recognize strengths in the environment at each step of the planning process. Communities and organizations that are serious about social planning from a strengths orientation create a visible and identifiable assets-based arm, unit, committee, or institute as an integral component of their organization or community. This produces a clear pathway and linkage to consumers and partners for collaboration. It also provides a forum where consumers can be viewed as partners in social planning. Does your school or university sponsor a community-building collaborative?

3. Recognize social advocacy as an explicit function in social planning. People advocate for positions, perspectives, policies, programs, and practices in self-serving ways as a part of the planning process. This is not necessarily bad, if it is recognized and if consumers have an adequate voice. Encourage people and groups to be up front about advocating for their interests and to take responsibility for their vested interest in social planning and efforts directed at planned change.

4. Bring social planning to the public. Meetings should be open and accessible to the general public, with solicitation of input. Social planning best uses the strengths of the environment when it functions in highly visible and inviting ways. Avoid private, backroom (e.g., lunch) meetings where people gather and secretly devise schemes to affect social planning.

5. Think of social planning as a collaborative process: Who should be, could be, and/or needs to be included in planning? It is very important to contemplate *who is and is not represented at the planning table*—people, groups, organizations, and constituencies.

6. Educate the general public about the perspective of the consumer. People need to be informed about social issues and causes through the voices and eyes of consumers. Use appropriate means of advancing this perspective (e.g., print and broadcast media, publications, and public testimonials).

7. Make building coalitions a strategic priority. Reach out to groups and organizations that share a common interest in attaining consumer goals. This can enhance the consumer power base and maximize the potential for success.

8. Endorse programs and interventions emphasizing prevention and the building of the strengths of people, organizations, communities, and society. Delgado (2000) advocates for a capacity enhancement orientation whereby communities develop plans and projects to accentuate common, core features and values. This includes the formation and strengthening of social programs and services and can extend to the strategic use of physical space (e.g., through murals, gardens, playgrounds, and sculptures).

9. Present human services and social programs as investments rather than costs. Typically, the long-term benefits of social programs and services are not emphasized. The general public and special-interest groups need to be able to appreciate the investment value of these programs and to see the concrete dividends they provide for the greater whole, whether on the community or the societal level.

STRATEGIC PLANNING FROM AN ORGANIZATIONAL STANDPOINT

Social workers typically participate in social planning as part of their organization, agency, or program. **Strategic planning** occurs when organizations take a concerted look at themselves in the context of their environment and in relation to other social structures. Periodically, sometimes as a part of a five- or ten-year plan, agencies examine how they operate and look at the long-term viability of the agency and its programs.

It is often useful to think of social service agencies as adaptive organisms or entities that seek sustenance (e.g., resources and consumers) and nurturance (e.g., acceptance and support) from their surroundings. Of course, a comprehensive analysis of the practicality of any organization involves sound input from multiple sources and a variety of vantage points. The goal of strategic planning is to obtain an objective and critical view of the organization that describes both its strengths and areas that need strengthening. On the basis of this information, a vision can be formed that looks forward and guides the agency in a fruitful, productive, and rewarding direction.

The SWOT Analysis

A variety of approaches have been used throughout the years to structure strategic planning. One approach is a systematic analysis of the strengths, weaknesses, opportunities, and threats of an organization, often known as the SWOT analysis. Strengths and weaknesses are internal attributes of an organization, whereas opportunities and threats come from the external environment.

Although the precise methodology varies, organizations typically empower or commission a strategic planning group (e.g., a steering committee) to conduct a SWOT analysis. Employees from the various programs and divisions of the organization complete a SWOT assessment tool, and their comments are summarized. Similarly, external stakeholders are asked for their views.

In strengths-based SWOT analyses, the goal is to effectively tap into the abilities of consumers to identify various organizational strengths, weaknesses, opportunities, and threats. This involves reaching out to consumers in a fashion that is inclusive and representative. Asking whoever is available to participate in a SWOT analysis is the equivalent of gathering a convenience sample.

It is also important to keep in mind that the loudest voice, regardless of the constituency group, is not necessarily the best or most accurate source of data. The organization will benefit the most from information that accurately describes internal and external conditions.

Task Environment

An examination of an organization's task environment, or ecology, identifies important relationships with funding sources, collaborators, competitors, regulators, consumers, and the general public. The intent is to depict how an organization relates to external entities.

Many planners formulate charts or maps to illustrate graphically how various social organizations relate to their agency. Coding schemes are devised. For example, solid lines might indicate intense relations, or arrows might connote flow of information. Specific symbols are used to point out coalitions, conflict, collaboration, and competition.

As with each form of strategic planning, social workers and consumers have an obligation to work to broaden the sources of input and information, especially to include the perspective of consumers. Assessing the task environment is often laden with assumptions, perceptions, and conjecture. For the sake of validity, any such assertions need to be questioned and challenged in a direct manner by consumers of services.

Again, to be effective, strategic planning needs to take place in an open (above-board) fashion. Constituency groups and stakeholders need to feel free to debate the accuracy of task environment maps and the assumptions underlining the depictions of interorganizational relationships. This can yield an accurate picture of the current state of the organization and can be a useful tool in planning for the organization's future. Be sure to note how professionals, consumers, and community leaders hold similar or differing views of the nature of interorganizational relationships.

Constructing Mission and Vision Statements

For many human service agencies, the **mission statement** constitutes a summary of the current activities and philosophical premises surrounding the work of the organization. The mission statement describes why the agency is important, who is served, and the reason for the agency's existence. A well-written mission statement reflects the unique identity and distinct attributes (competencies) of the agency and allows the reader to differentiate this agency from other, similar organizations.

A good mission statement also affirms the strengths, values, and culture of an organization. It describes what the agency stands for and why. The mission statement is a tangible opportunity to confirm the primacy and importance of consumers in the agency.

The mission statement is an important element in strategic planning. It is a document that requires ownership by major stakeholders, especially consumers. The agency mission statement sets the tone and parameters by which an agency works and commits itself to work with consumers. Refinement or development of the mission statement is an important element in strategic planning, as it defines the essence of the enterprise.

An organization's **vision statement** is a future-oriented document that is aspirational in nature. It identifies where the agency *wants* to be. Much like a compass, the vision statement serves as a guide to direct organizational activities and decision making. The vision statement can be used to show the way for organizational changes and program development.

Many people would say that a good leader provides an organization with a vision. This assertion may be valid, but the means by which a leader develops a vision merit consideration. Vision statements, like mission statements, require broad-based ownership. They need to be derived from a process that involves a collectivity of stakeholders. Vision is a product of dialogue, contemplation, and debate, not an individual creation.

In strategic planning, the vision statement becomes the driving force behind organizational behavior and decision making. It constitutes an organizational directive for the future and becomes a source of reference for every planning initiative.

Marketing

For many social workers, the term *marketing* has historically carried negative connotations. It evokes images of promoting product identification for the sake of profit. In a business sense, marketers encourage people to consider goods and services and foster a sense of desire and need.

In human services, marketing can be viewed as a comprehensive approach of discerning consumer strengths and needs in order to discern the best ways of responding to any such demands. Most important, a marketing outlook changes the planning focus from what an organization or special-interest group wants or needs to the hopes and desires of consumers.

Although marketing is of particular interest to profit-making organizations, the general tenets of a marketing perspective can also be applied to nonprofit agencies, particularly in the context of macro social work practice (Kotler, 1982). For example, marketing principles can be especially helpful in identifying the specific needs and wants of consumers. A basic assumption in marketing is that "one size *does not* fit all." In social planning, it is always useful to contemplate who is and is not being served. Marketing efforts help organizations refine their programming niches and attract and retain consumers of services, the lifeblood of human service agencies.

Marketing takes into account lifestyle, demographic information, and the developmental characteristics of consumers in order to use their strengths and respond to their needs in the formation and development of programs. Marketing recognizes that organizations serve distinct groups of people and encourages tailoring services to better address the differential strengths and needs of different groups. This is often referred to as *market segmentation* or *target marketing*. It breaks the "average customer" into "specific somebodies" (Kotler, Ferrell, & Lamb, 1987, p. 164).

Finally, marketing can be used to help secure resources and as a means of educating the public, providers of services, consumers, and professionals about important news and impending issues (Stoner, 1986). In strategic planning, it is important to keep various parties, especially those capable of giving, interested, informed, and engaged in the planning process.

BOX 7.2

Does your agency have a symbol or insignia that captures the essence of the organization? Around the world, people recognize the golden "M" of McDonald's. Contemplate with other professionals and consumers what your social service agency stands for and how this is portrayed to the public.

SOCIAL PLANNING PHASES

Whether at the societal, community, or organizational level, social planning can be viewed as a series of phases. Over the years, a number of models have been proposed to help guide social-planning processes. Traditionally, many of these approaches have deemphasized the role of consumers in social planning in favor of professionally or administratively directed and rendered assessment, planning, goal setting, implementing, and evaluation (Dudley, 1978).

The notion of consumer-driven social planning demands a slightly different way of thinking. First, full-fledged participatory social planning requires a sense of readiness on behalf of consumers as well as other members of the planning processes. Prior to initiating consumer-oriented social planning, there needs to be a determination of whether conditions are favorable for the active and meaningful involvement of consumers. In writing about readiness for participatory research, Altpeter, Schopler, Galinsky, and Pennell (1999) offer several interesting considerations for consumer-driven social planning.

1. At the individual level, are there actors ill prepared or unready to engage in participatory, democratically oriented social planning involving consumers? "Old-timers" may be skeptical about bringing new faces to the planning table. Similarly, the planning group may oppose changes in participatory behavior that threaten established ways.

2. Consumer involvement in planning efforts should be viewed as a process of empowerment. The level of commitment provided by consumers will vary over time. The goal is to find ways to enable consumers to build confidence and skills in sharing their knowledge and expertise. Social workers should expect variations in the ability of consumers to participate in social planning.

3. Over the long run, are you as a social worker ready to promote and sustain consumer involvement in social planning? Meaningful participation of consumers in social-planning processes requires encouragement and an appreciable investment of time and energy on the part of social workers.

4. Promoting and establishing a sense of equity in social planning for diverse groups of consumers is an important consideration. Does it make sense to have both primary consumers and secondary consumers (e.g., family members) involved in the planning process? How can the planning process be enriched through sensitivity to diversity on the basis of race, ethnicity, gender, age, class, disability, sexual orientation, and other factors? Optimally, the planning group will function in a democratic fashion with a commitment to free expression and a diversity of ideas and opinions from a variety of perspectives and positions.

A Three-Phase Model

Once it has been established that consumer participation in social planning is viable, social workers and consumers can move forward with a degree of self-assurance. This is with the realization that planning initiatives take time— months if not years. Indeed, the actual process of social planning can be described in terms of three distinct phases. According to Jones and Harris (1987), social planning involves being socially aware of the need for planning, taking responsibility for planning, and achieving institutional change. Each phase is important and presents distinct opportunities for consumer involve-ment and participation.

With respect to *heightening consciousness and awareness*, the tone and direction of social planning are set early. The call for social planning typically comes from a group of people or a set of powerful leaders and is framed around specific areas in need of strengthening and particular agendas. The general public is often unaware of social issues and will have to learn about the subject matter and become convinced that there are good reasons for engaging in social plan-ning. Consumers of services possess expertise that personalizes appeals for change and grounds them in real-life experience. Hearing about the impetus for social planning from the mouths of consumers makes the plea more real, more human, and aligns the planning process with the will of consumers.

Persuading people to take responsibility can be a delicate ordeal. Assuming responsibility to pursue a cause goes beyond recognition; it entails a degree of commitment of time, resources, and funding. Usually a social organization or group, private or public, believes that an important issue or cause exists, and this group legitimizes and sanctions social-planning efforts. Even when issues have a direct impact on the quality of life of citizens, people may be reluctant to invest their energies to pursue resolutions. This can be especially true for consumers who already feel disenfranchised or alienated from decision making. Indeed, it only makes sense that people are more likely to assume responsibility for social planning when they have a direct interest in an outcome, believe their involvement will make a difference, and feel there is a likelihood of success.

It is clearly a mischaracterization to describe social planning solely in terms of activities and steps associated with the actual planning group and its delib-erations. A considerable amount of "advance work" occurs in preparation for planned change. And, once formal planning begins, it often entails **incremen-tal planning,** smaller step-by-step changes that will occur over an extended time period. While many people would prefer to invest in **comprehensive planning,** attempts to bring about large-scale change quickly, this is often less practical and unrealistic.

Institutional change encompasses actions and activities in the planning process directed at creating large-scale, macro-level change (e.g., program development, policy formation, and legislative initiatives). Like community leaders, citizens, and policymakers, consumers of services should be viewed as fully endorsed partners in weighing circumstances, strategizing alternatives, and authorizing courses of action.

THE NIMBY PHENOMENON

Have you ever heard of the NIMBY phenomenon? The acronym stands for "Not In My Back Yard." It is the name devised decades ago to describe com-munity members' efforts to prevent deinstitutionalized people from living in "my backyard." People resisted the development of group homes and engaged in negative campaigns (e.g., media, petitions, door-to-door canvassing, and public meetings) to thwart housing initiatives close to their homes.

Opposition to community-based group homes was often based on misinformation, a lack of understanding, and an aura of distrust. Piat (2000) suggests that residents believed that "the development of group homes was motivated by financial considerations, either by the government or by the group home developers" (p. 131). Additionally, community members often argued that consumers did not want to integrate into a neighborhood lifestyle and, as a result, would feel "self-conscious and uncomfortable participating in routine community activities" (p. 134).

Clearly, in the cases examined by Piat (2000), ordinary citizens and policymakers differed in their beliefs concerning the value of community-based group homes. However, noticeably absent from these analyses was any consideration of consumer participation in social planning. Indeed, most studies of the NIMBY phenomenon "examine only the perceptions of administrators, staff, or group home developers, disregarding the general community's perspective" and the point of view of consumers of services (p. 128).

One can only imagine the power of an aggressive and proactive approach designed to include consumers in the very earliest phases of the social-planning process for deinstitutionalized persons. When this takes place, community leaders and citizens hear directly from the mouths of consumers about the importance and meaning of living in and belonging to a community (awareness and consciousness). For many people, this represents new information and works to dispel myths and assumptions associated with people leaving institutionalized settings.

As illustrated by the NIMBY phenomenon, community members could benefit greatly from the voices of consumers. Deinstitutionalized persons represent diversity, and they frequently make other people feel uncomfortable. Such uneasiness can be helpful, particularly when it presses citizens to think critically and reflect upon new and differing views of the world. Constructive dialogue and reflection between divergent groups of people as partners in social planning can be the stimulus for creativity and innovation that builds capacities for effecting social change.

In the instance of the NIMBY phenomenon, structured dialogue between residents, consumers, policymakers, professionals, and administrators from the outset of the planning process would likely have yielded a multitude of viewpoints and findings concerning the usefulness of establishing community-based group homes for deinstitutionalized people. Regardless of the eventual outcome, all parties, including the community as a whole, would have benefited from a thorough and comprehensive discussion of housing for deinstitutionalized people from varying experiences and perspectives.

RESOURCE CONSIDERATIONS
IN SOCIAL PLANNING

Social planning, like almost all activities, requires resources, including time, talent, and money. Resources devoted to social planning can be viewed as an investment in the health and well-being of an organization, community, or society.

In human services, resources of all kinds are notoriously short in supply. This means that agencies and organizations are forced to use their assets in wise and well-thought-out ways. Accounting for investment behavior in social planning is a valid consideration and a functional imperative. Budgeting can be divided into human costs (e.g., time, wages, salaries, and fringe benefits) and nonpersonnel commitments (e.g., meeting space, transportation, communications, and supplies).

Consumers of services need to be included in decision making with respect to the use of resources. Investment in social planning needs to be productive and fruitful, as it could divert resources from other important activities (e.g., counseling, group work, and program implementation). Any mandate to use resources for social planning needs to be shared by consumers.

SOCIAL PLANNING AS A
COOPERATIVE EDUCATIONAL PROCESS

Social planning need not be conceptualized as an authoritarian, top-down process. Instead, planning represents an opportunity for various parties and constituencies to learn from one another about common interests and concerns through structured social interaction. Healthy, evenhanded exchange of ideas is the motor that drives participatory planning. From a strengths orientation, the goal is to promote constructive dialogue and debate between citizens, leaders, and consumers, and to foster a spirit of shared governance.

If social planning is to be educational in nature, then people need to respect one another and strive for cooperation. This includes agreeing to disagree. This sounds simple, but it is often difficult for people to acknowledge and validate opposing beliefs, positions, and ideas. Humans are creatures of rational thinking and also of emotion. When passionate about a subject, even the most reasonable people can lose their perspective and temper. Indeed, the ability to learn from others presupposes a certain level of maturity—a discarding of the "I am right" philosophy.

Fruitful dialogue and collaboration necessarily involve differences of opinion. Divergent views challenge our frames of mind. Consumers can cause us to see phenomena in unique and thought-provoking ways. The ability to approach assumptions and evidence in social planning from multiple frames of mind allows us to envision change through the eyes of others.

Purposeful selection of consumers to participate in the planning process is crucial. They need to be endorsed by their peers and exhibit the aptitude, enthusiasm, maturity, confidence, and skills necessary to press forward with ideas and proposals for planned change. The ability to hold one's own is a useful barometer. Successful consumer leaders seek the backing and support of their constituency group and are careful not to stray from the will of those they represent.

PLANNING FOR
SUSTAINABLE DEVELOPMENT

All too often, social planning is nearsighted. It involves short-term thinking designed to address people's immediate needs and concerns, with little consideration given to the sustainability of proposed programs and projects.

In macro-level social work practice, the prospect of creating enduring, long-term social change should always be a consideration. As an example, in Nicaragua, social workers in association with the Center for Development in Central America (CDCA) have worked hand in hand with consumers to plan for and create several successful employment cooperatives (e.g., sewing, concrete construction materials, clay water filter, coffee, and security).

Confronted with dire poverty, natural catastrophes, and harsh (subsistence-level) living conditions, the people of Nicaragua have overcome disease, economic barriers, and political obstacles to build business cooperatives that use their interests, talents, and natural resources. The goal is sustainable development. "This is *their* challenge—to throw away the emotional shackles and tap the resourcefulness, the stubbornness, the creativity, the power inside that keeps them and their families surviving, and then use that to move towards success" (Center for Development in Central America, 2003).

SUMMARY

In this chapter, social planning is depicted as a participatory, collaborative process between consumers of services and others. In reality, this is not always the case. The impetus for social planning can come from multiple sources (e.g., elected officials, administrators, and funding sources) and may be imposed. Indeed, actors with specific vested interests often move to undermine and discredit the active participation of consumers in social planning.

Even under undesirable circumstances, however, it is the professional responsibility of social workers to work with consumers in collaborative ways to promote and advocate for social planning as an open, inclusive, and didactic process. The term *inreach* is offered with great enthusiasm. View consumers as a pool of stakeholders and encourage inreach so that their talents and expertise can be fully utilized and appreciated as a cherished resource.

In Chapter 11 ("Evaluating Macro Change"), the similarities between social planning and participatory research will become evident. Both processes seek to empower consumers as full-fledged members at all stages; both conceptualize consumers as co-learners and co-experts. In each instance, a major role of the social worker involves helping consumers identify their strengths and abilities to effect change.

A FEW KEY TERMS

social planning	strategic planning	comprehensive planning
eclectic approach	mission statement	institutional change
inclusion	vision statement	
inreach	incremental planning	

USING INFOTRAC®
COLLEGE EDITION AND INFOWRITE

InfoTrac College Edition

Social planning can be a dynamic and exciting process. Part of the excitement is in eliciting the ideas of others. The goal is to capture as many relevant perspectives as possible. This allows individuals and groups of people to claim ownership of social planning and encourages a broader view of the issue(s) at hand. Complete the following exercise:

1. Go to InfoTrac College Edition.

2. Search under the Keyword Search using "social planning consumers."

3. Browse through the articles and identify an article that focuses on consumer participation in planning processes. This can be an article examining health-related issues, business, or social welfare.

4. In one page, summarize how consumers are embraced and utilized in social planning. Indicate whether consumer participation is to facilitate profit, for quality improvement, tokenistic in nature, or for some other purposes.

5. Does the article approach social planning from a rational, political, empowerment, or strengths perspective?

InfoWrite

In the preceding exercise, you identified an example of how consumers can participate in social planning. Examples are often intended to either inform or persuade people. Careful analysis of writing style and content can help the reader to discern what type of example, informative or persuasive, is being offered. In order to refine your reading skills, do the following:

1. Go to InfoWrite.

2. Scroll to Modes of Expression.

3. Read the sections focusing on "The Goal of Example" and "Purpose: To Inform or Persuade."

4. With a critical eye, analyze your InfoTrac College Edition article with respect to the *inform* versus *persuade* distinction. Is the intent of the article mainly to inform readers about a mode of consumer participation in social planning, or does it lean more toward persuading readers that this is an admirable form of social planning?

5. On a separate sheet of paper form two columns, headed "Informative" and "Persuasive." Note specific words in the article that fall into each category. For example, informative words represent concrete observations (e.g., an open microphone, a Web page), whereas persuasive words tend to be more evaluative (e.g., *best, outstanding, inferior*).

CASE EXAMPLE: Social Planning with a Latino Consumer Group

Angela is a social worker employed at a neighborhood community center. Her time is almost evenly split between family preservation services and activities aimed at community asset building. Angela enjoys both the micro and macro elements of her practice. She finds working for planned change at multiple levels interesting and a source of professional motivation.

Over the past five years, the city's Latino population has grown, enriching the urban area with new ideas and customs. In general, people have welcomed the changing composition of the population. In fact, public officials often tout the fact that the city is becoming more diverse and now has an appreciable Latino population.

Nearly half of the recent immigrants have come from Mexico and the remainder from Guatemala, Puerto Rico, and Nicaragua. Most are poor and do not speak English. In addition, people are segregated in their living and social interaction by country of origin and social-economic status. Consumers from each group frequent the community center and receive a wide variety of services. Unfortunately, there is currently little sense of homogeneity among these groups. To the contrary, at times, there has been hostility and friction as traditions have clashed.

To her credit, Angela has built excellent working relationships with individuals from each of the Latino groups. As a result, she has been successful in working with consumers to facilitate a beginning level of awareness and appreciation of the commonalities and strengths that the various Latino groups share. Angela and representatives from each of the local Latino groups formed a planning group that includes consumers, agency administrators, professionals, and community leaders. Everyone senses a readiness for the various Latino population groups to come together and plan for change. A concerted effort was made to embrace inclusion, the desire to ensure that a wide variety of people are included. Angela and

(continued)

CASE EXAMPLE *(continued)*

others intentionally participated in "inreach" and found people able and willing to participate in social planning.

Interestingly, the first point of contention in the planning process involved language. Many people did not speak English, but not everyone spoke Spanish, and those who did speak Spanish often struggled with dialect. Although Angela speaks Spanish, she is not fluent. Ultimately, the consensus of the social-planning group was to speak in English but to hire a translator.

The second decision of the planning group was to establish itself as a formal unit. They chose the name Uno Latino as a gesture of solidarity. Rather than becoming an issue- or agency-specific planning group, Uno Latino was to be the community's collaborative entity for the Latino population.

Soon, Uno Latino developed a vision statement. It articulates the desire to promote education, safety, health, and employment for all Latinos in the city. Although Uno Latino is currently only at the "persuading people to take responsibility" phase of social planning, most agree that the organization has already been highly successful in raising consciousness about shared concerns, creating a spirit of shared leadership, and rallying people to use their strengths to contemplate planned change.

THINKING CRITICALLY
ABOUT THE CASE EXAMPLE

1. Understandably, Angela is approaching social planning with sensitivity to a variety of approaches (rational, political, strengths, and empowerment). So far, how successfully has Angela tapped the strengths of consumers in social planning? Using the strengths perspective, contemplate how her practice could be improved. Clearly, consumers are involved in decision-making processes (empowerment). But how could the strengths of individuals or specific groups of people (e.g., differentiated by country of origin) be more fully used?

2. Angela speaks some Spanish, but she is not fluent in Spanish. Clearly, in this case example, language is a barrier. Contemplate professional and organizational responsibilities with respect to cultural competencies in social work practice. Is providing a translator for meetings a reasonable solution? What would be the optimum situation? Members of Uno Latino most likely can offer insight and suggestions concerning ways to enhance communication.

3. Uno Latino has successfully formed a vision statement. This is an important first step in social planning. Consider possible subsequent steps. For example, is a more formal mission statement needed? At what point should the members of Uno Latino establish concrete short- and long-term goals? These are typical considerations in social planning.

REFLECTION EXERCISES

1. Is your agency actively involved in social planning? Identify the current phase of social planning, ascertain consumer involvement, and estimate the degree to which the views of consumers are valued. Discuss with your supervisor how and when consumer participation in social planning could have been enhanced.

2. If you have direct contact with consumers, individually or in a group context, discuss their vision for the agency's future. Contemplate how these dreams could be formalized and included in social planning.

3. How could professionals and consumers better market the essence (the "biological DNA") of your agency or program? Allow yourself to be creative and "corny." The United States Marines asks people to "be all that you can be." Is there a slogan, phrase, symbol, or image that captures the purpose of your agency and would educate people concerning organizational goals?

SUGGESTED READINGS

DiNitto, D. (2002). *Social welfare: Politics and public policy*. Boston: Allyn & Bacon.

O'Melia, M. (2002). Excavating our frames of mind: The key to dialogue and collaboration. *Social Work, 48*(3), 401–408.

Perlman, R., & Gurin, A. (1972). *Community organization and social planning*. New York: Wiley.

Stoner, M. R. (1987). Marketing of social service gains prominence in practice. *Administration in Social Work, 10*(4), 41–52.

REFERENCES

Altpeter, M., Schopler, J. H., Galinsky, M. J., & Pennell, J. (1999). Participatory research as social work practice: When is it viable? *Journal of Progressive Social Work, 10*(2), 31–53.

Center for Development in Central America. (2003). Newsletter, September.

Delgado, M. (2000). *Community social work practice in an urban context: The potential of a capacity-enhancement perspective*. New York: Oxford University Press.

DiNitto, D. (2000). *Social welfare: Politics and public policy*. Boston: Allyn & Bacon.

Dudley, J. R. (1978). Is social planning social work? *Social Work, 23*(1), 37–41.

Jones, E. R., & Harris, W. M. (1987). A conceptual scheme for analysis of the social planning process. *Journal of the Community Development Society, 18*(2), 18–41.

Kahn, S. (1991). *Organizing: A guide for grassroots leaders*. Silver Spring, MD: NASW Press.

Kotler, P. (1982). *Marketing for nonprofit organizations* (2nd ed.). Englewood Cliffs, NJ: Prentice Hall.

Kotler, P., Ferrel, O. C., & Lamb, C. (1987). *Strategic marketing for nonprofit organizations: Cases and readings.* Englewood Cliffs, NJ: Prentice Hall.

O'Melia, M. (2002). From person to context: The evolution of an empowering practice. In M. O'Melia & K. Miley (Eds.), *Pathways to power: Readings in contextual social work practice.* Boston: Allyn & Bacon.

———. (2003). Excavating our frames of mind: The key to dialogue and collaboration. *Social Work, 48*(3), 401–408.

Piat, M. (2000). The NIMBY phenomenon: Community residents' concerns about housing for deinstitutionalized people. *Health and Social Work, 25*(2), 127–138.

Ramon, S. (1999). Collective empowerment: Conceptual and practical issues. In W. Shera & L. Wells (Eds.), *Empowerment practice in social work: Developing richer conceptual foundations.* Toronto: Canadian Scholars Press.

Rapp, C. A. (1998). *The strengths model: Case management with people suffering from severe and persistent mental illness.* New York: Oxford University Press.

Saleebey, D. (2002). The *strengths perspective in social work practice.* Boston: Allyn & Bacon.

Staples, L. (1984). *Roots to power: A manual for grassroots organizing.* New York: Praeger.

Stoner, M. R. (1986). Marketing of social services gains prominence in practice. *Administration in Social Work, 10*(4), 41–52.

Whitmore, E., & Wilson, M. (1995). Accompanying the process: Principles for international development practice. *International Social Work, 40*(1), 57–74.

Zachary, E. (2000). Grassroots leadership training: A case study of an effort to integrate theory and method. *Journal of Community Practice, 7*(1), 71–93.

8

Administration from a Strengths Perspective

Chapter Content Areas

Administration

Assumptions Related to Administration

Administrative Roles

Administrative Tasks

Ethical Considerations

Administration from a Strengths Perspective

dministration is a crucial aspect of macro social work practice. Consider for a moment just how much every element of the social welfare system depends on the quality of administrative leadership. To perform administrative responsibilities effectively, social workers must have an extensive set of skills to meet the challenges presented in social welfare organizations at the local, state, and national level. Implied in this statement is the need for schools of social work to design curricula that develop administrative skills and strategies that are both consumer-centered and viable in complicated political arenas (Patti, 1977). Simultaneously, social work students must explore their professional interests and career options in light of the complexities of social administration.

In support of these efforts, this chapter broadly defines the term **administration** and several concepts associated with social workers as administrators. It also describes ethical issues that are common in organizational systems. If administrators do not deal with these dilemmas, then direct-line social workers must be prepared to initiate individual action or develop collective strategies to resolve them.

A strengths perspective for administration is introduced as a guide for social workers leading human service organizations. As in previous chapters, the focus is on consumers as the principal element associated with administration. The unique strengths and wants of consumers are the driving force in administrative decisions related to organizational goals, budget allocations, personnel issues, and program design.

WHAT IS ADMINISTRATION?

The word *administrator* comes from the Latin *ad ministrare,* meaning "to minister to" or "to serve." The word *administration* refers to the processes by which social worker administrators address social and personal needs, confront social problems, and create the conditions in which people's welfare can be improved by the efforts of a social service agency (Brueggemann, 1996). Administration, then, is a process that has to do with running an agency and that involves goals, policies, staff, management, services, and evaluation (Skidmore, 1990, p. 12).

Throughout the discussion of administration, think about administrators you've worked with in your jobs, volunteer activities, or field placement. Based on your experiences, consider the following:

- Was the administrator a professional social worker?

- From your perspective, what were the responsibilities and duties of the administrator?

- How available was the administrator to you, staff members, and consumers?

- What four adjectives would you use to describe the administrator?

Ideally, your experiences with an administrator support the notion that administrators assume several responsibilities and hold many job titles, including line supervisors, department managers, and executive directors. Whatever the title given to the administrator, assume the following:

- The social work administrator works with people based on a philosophy of practice, including an explicit value and belief system and a theoretical framework.

- Administrative practice occurs in organizations, policies, programs, and direct services.

- The social work administrator is responsible for the resources, both material and symbolic, necessary for the organization to achieve its purpose.

- The organization's structure and processes largely reflect the character of the social work administrator.

- The social work administrator influences the technical base of the organization—that is, the knowledge and skills required to maintain the program and service system.

- The method of supervision, leadership, and management mirrors the social work administrator's practice model.

An administrator's performance is intricately linked to the overall performance and public image of the organization where the administrator is employed. Administrators are deemed responsible for the functions of the entity they manage, whether it is an interdisciplinary team, a social service office, a particular program, or a complex agency. It is highly uncommon to find an outstanding administrator responsible for a dysfunctional program, or an effective team being supervised by an ineffectual administrator.

The centerpiece of agency and administrative performance are the benefits accrued by consumers. A successful administrator focuses on the outcomes that reflect improvement of the consumer's life situation or thwart the further deterioration of that situation. Consumer outcomes act as the bottom line in human services in much the same way that profits serve business (Rapp & Poertner, 1992). Consequently, administrators perform in a variety of areas, but adequate performance in these areas is neither sufficient nor a proxy for consumer outcomes. It is this notion that leads Patti (1985) to argue that effectiveness—meaningful consumer outcomes—should be the "philosophical linchpin" of human service agencies.

ADMINISTRATIVE ROLES

Any social service organization is an integral component of the entire community where it is located. As such, it is a social tool for improving the quality of life for the residents in its proximity. The organization's administrator is ultimately responsible for ensuring that this occurs through a variety of roles, including the following:

Leader

The hallmark of administration is dynamic leadership. The administrator as **leader** helps communities of individuals to take calculated risks and imagine improvements in life. Further, the administrator encourages commitment to change from staff and consumers alike and facilitates the movement of people along a path to meet their needs and wants.

The administrator as leader sometimes assumes several incongruent roles. For example, the administrator must understand the complexities of the community where the social service organization resides. Simultaneously, the administrator as leader must relate the organization's mission, goals, and value system to the community at large. Thus, the administrator is called upon to be skilled as a ceremonial figure capable of symbolizing and articulating the social service organization while also living in the community and serving its ideals. In this way, the administrator represents a bridge between the community and the organization—a leader in the public eye demonstrating how both entities can learn and grow from one another.

Consider the following questions in terms of administrative leadership:

- In what ways could an administrator of a large metropolitan child welfare agency design a delivery system to respond to the growing needs of a diverse and bilingual population?

- In what ways can the administrator convey the agency's mission and goals?
- How can the administrator involve the community with the agency?
- What can the administrator do to support the agency's staff with regard to consumers' service needs?

Decision Maker

Decision making is a crucial aspect of administration. Administrators as decision makers affect organizational goals, relationships with the community and consumers, internal harmony, organizational change, and fiscal stability (Hasenfeld & English, 1974). At all levels of the organization, administrators are required to make decisions on personnel selection, labor relations, service delivery, community relations, and budget allocations.

Although "decision making" appears at first glance to be individualistic, most administrators attempt to use a rational approach to decision making (Katz & Kahn, 1978; Neugeboren, 1996). Such an approach includes four sequential stages:

1. *Respond to immediate pressures.* Pressures that the administrator must consider may be internal or external to the social service organization. Internal pressures include opinions from upper-level administration, staff assignments and training, consumers' service needs, fiscal limitations, and space allocations. External pressures often derive from interagency relationships, public and media relations, and funding requirements.

2. *Define the problem.* Basic to decision making is problem definition. The more information the administrator has about the problem, the greater the likelihood that a successful decision will be made. It is essential that administrators assess problems holistically. This is accomplished by reviewing all available information and consulting with a variety of people, most importantly consumers. Further, the history, scope, and duration of the problem must be examined.

3. *Search for solutions.* More often than not, administrators will attempt to use existing policies and procedures to solve presenting problems. However, administrators must be prepared to initiate more innovative solutions if necessary.

4. *Evaluate alternatives.* The final stage of the approach requires that the administrator assess the cost and benefits of the decision. Although the evaluation may differ depending on perspective and organizational position, the administrator must be able to connect any proposed alternative solution to the organization's existing goals and objectives.

Although rational decision making is part of the administrator's repertoire of skills, it is always necessary to consider how nonrational features such as emotions and intuition impinge on the decision-making process. On occasion, administrators will settle for a satisfactory decision rather than an optimal one.

Mediator

It is the responsibility of the organization's administrator to mediate diverse interests, both internal and external to the organization. Mediation helps to reduce irrationality and promote rationality among the parties, provides opportunities for development, facilitates communication, explores resources, reveals alternative solutions to problems, and expands professional and personal opportunities (Hardcastle, Wenocur, & Powers, 1997). As a mediator, the administrator is the link between administrative actions and direct services, between policy formulation and policy implementation.

An essential aspect of the role of administrator as mediator involves the interdependence between the administrator and other levels and units of the organization. Specifically, it is not unusual for the administrator to serve as the mediator between supervisees and the organization's environment, including consumers and other service providers. This role requires considerable skills in decision making and conflict management, as well as sensitivity to the needs of consumers, staff, and the organization as a whole.

Administrators comment that the role of mediator sometimes places them in a no-win situation, a feeling of being caught in the middle. To avoid such a predicament, administrators must try to establish a sufficiently harmonious relationship with all parties involved in the mediation process. Administrators are successful in mediation when participants feel they have received what they wanted and when the mediation process is considered to be efficient and effective. Indeed, the dynamics of mediation are similar to those that social work counselors employ with couples and families. Administrators require the same authority and credibility that counselors need to conduct clinical sessions. The analogy with counseling can be taken a step further in that administrators often seek to show contending parties how to negotiate successfully with each other. For organizations with little experience in negotiation or conflict management, the development of effective mediating skills is a major accomplishment in itself that can have benefits beyond the immediate situation (Gummer, 1991).

Collaborator

Collaboration implies the notion of a joint venture. Administrative collaborations involve agreements in which two or more organizations within the community agree to establish common goals, such as a new program or service. When an administrator assumes the role of collaborator a partnership emerges. Partnerships may expand resources or generate new ideas. However, the collaboration necessary to foster partnerships requires administrators to relinquish a degree of power, expertise, and control to others. In this way, collaboration often alters the balance of power and authority of the administrator (Poulin et al., 2000). According to Johnson, McLaughlin, and Christenson (1998, p. 396), administrative collaboration does the following:

- It encourages and facilitates an open and honest exchange of ideas, plans, approaches, and resources across disciplines, programs and agencies.

Table 8.1 Forces for Collaboration

Individual Level	System Level
Multiple, diverse needs of individual	Multiple, diverse needs of system
Fragmented view of the individual	Fragmented agency services
Lack of responsiveness to individual needs	Lack of responsiveness to consumer needs
Lack of parental voice	Lack of consumer voice
Uncoordinated services	Uncoordinated services
Inadequate services	Gap/duplicated services
Multiple professionals	Multiple/overlapping planning bodies
Differing treatment modalities	Different program models
Multiple billing procedures	Multiple funding systems
Professional jargon	Agency jargon
Professional territoriality	Agency territoriality

SOURCE: Reprinted from "Interagency Collaboration: An Interdisciplinary Application," by Vicki C. Pappas, in H. G. Garner & F. P. Orelove, *Teamwork in Human Services: Models and Applications across the Life Span,* p. 64. Copyright 1994, with permission from Elsevier.

- It enables all participants to jointly define their separate interest by mutually identifying changes that may be needed to best achieve common purposes.
- It utilizes formal procedures to help clarify issues, define problems, and make decisions about them.

Table 8.1 identifies some of the forces associated with collaboration for an administrator based on an individual and a systems perspective. At the outset of collaboration, individual personalities, style, and readiness to collaborate certainly affect the interactions. The major issues on the collaborative agenda reflect the agencies' individual interests, resources, and ideas about the potential outcome around which collaborations will occur (Garner & Orelove, 1994). Additionally, information about policies and procedures, eligibility requirements, target populations, geographic boundaries, legislative initiatives, confidentiality policies, and funding streams need to be shared and related to the other agencies.

At any level and on any issue, administrative collaboration takes time to develop. Just as individual professionals become increasingly responsive to collaboration on consumer service plans, administrators representing agencies also experience a parallel growth process before collaboration is achieved.

Politician

Over half a century ago, Bertha Reynolds (1987/1951) offered comments on the role of political activity in social work practice:

> The philosophy of social work cannot be separated from the philosophy of a nation, as to how it values people, and what importance it sets upon their welfare. . . . [We are] faced with a choice between contradictory forces in

our society: those which are moving toward the welfare of people . . . and those which destroy human life in preventable misery and war, and relieve poverty only grudgingly to keep the privileged position they hold. (p. 45)

These words prove a guidepost for social work administrators. More specifically, administrators cannot divorce their practice from the political debates that surround social welfare organizations (Reisch & Gambrill, 1997). In fact, in many cases, administrators are in the midst of policy debates, as exemplified in public discussions on Medicaid and Medicare and welfare reform.

Organizational politics provide the administrator with an arena for making critical decisions about issues, including the establishment of agency goals and objectives, procedures for pursuing them, and distribution of resources. When there are apparently irreconcilable conflicts among organizational members over these issues, it becomes necessary for the administrator to engage in political decision making. An essential feature of decision making from a political perspective is the explicit recognition of conflict as a normal part of organizational life, and the provisions it makes for transforming potentially disruptive conflicts into negotiated settlements.

Gummer and Edwards (1985) suggest that it is incumbent on social work administrators to work at acquiring and using power in their organizations. They should do so not merely to gain power, but from the conviction that the acquisition and appropriate use of power ensures that social work principles and values are infused throughout social welfare organizations.

The administrator–as–politician assumes that consideration will be given to important elements before reaching premature conclusions about the political landscape. For example, once the relevant groups and individuals, or organizational stakeholders, have been identified, it is imperative that the administrator assess their strengths (Pfeffer, 1981). In this context, an important step for the administrator to take is to distinguish between the power and foresight of stakeholders. Some individuals are adept at forecasting what is likely to happen in an organization and then aligning themselves with the winning side. Administrators

---

CASE EXAMPLE

Amy Devine is the social work administrator of a rural mental heath agency, McDowell Outreach Program. Much like agencies across the state, McDowell Outreach Program is experiencing severe budget constraints and a consequent hiring freeze. Amy must explain the fiscal situation to the agency's advisory board, service consumers, and staff. Further, as a member of the county's Social Service Council, Amy plans to discuss budget issues at the next council meeting.

To address the budget crisis, Amy is considering staff furloughs and program retrenchment. Such decisions are significant to the immediate and long-term operation of McDowell Outreach Program. During an interdisciplinary meeting, program supervisors present their concerns to Amy, who notes increased competitiveness and anxiety among the supervisors.

© Thomson Higher Education/Heinle Image Bank.

must come to understand this power, especially in terms of organizational change efforts. In many ways, administrators can be perceived as powerful because of their association with the powerful. Thus, administrators must be mindful that the skill of foresight is a good one to develop, but it is also important to be able to recognize and develop it in others.

Read the following scenario and consider the described administrative roles that come into play. What are some additional roles you think administrators might be asked to assume in the course of their work? How do organizational settings affect the role of an administrative?

ADMINISTRATIVE TASKS

Most human service administrators are employed in public organizations, such as departments of social services, hospitals, and schools, or in nonprofit agencies that have been created to meet specific community needs, including community mental health centers. Whether social service organizations provide direct or indirect services and whether they are housed in public or private agencies, they tend to require similar administrative functions, as described in this section:

Planning

Social agencies are always in a state of change. Policies introduce new services, new problems demand attention, new contingencies emerge, the agency's environment changes, and new political and economic agendas develop. Consequently, an administrator devotes considerable time and effort to day-to-day and long-term planning. Planning is one of the major tasks of administration.

Planning is the development, expansion, and coordination of social services and social policies "utilizing rational problem solving at the local and societal level" (Lauffer, 1981, p. 583). Planning is an administrative task that provides for the welfare of society—to ensure that social programs, policies, and services meet the people's needs to the greatest extent possible. Therefore, administrators must ensure that individuals with few resources, little power, and minimal influence be given the opportunity to engage in program planning. Only through integration into the planning process can people gain the sense of empowerment and control over their lives that is a prerequisite for achieving social and economic justice.

Planning involves activities and structures that are used as tools to construct future events in organizations. Plans are usually presented in written form to guide employees and consumers in specified directions. Goals and objectives are crucial elements of planning. They provide a roadmap for accomplishing tasks within an organization and offer a system of accountability for program evaluation. Planning is also tied to the development of internal policies, procedures, programs, and budgets.

An administrator initiates the planning process with a comprehensive assessment of community and consumer needs. The administrator employs a variety of methods to determine what problems and opportunities exist within a given population and, just as important, what consumers and community members see as their most pressing priorities. Current services are also analyzed, providing the administrator with an understanding of gaps in the service system. The recognition of needs and service gaps gives the administrator a vision of a desired future state for the organization, which is eventually reflected in the agency's mission statement.

The assessment of needs and the identification of community strengths or assets provide the basis for selecting the potential goals of the agency or program (Kretzmann & McKnight, 1996). It is essential that community members, consumers, and service providers all be involved in designing service goals. These goals lead to the development of actual programs. Thus, the administrator designs programs through an integrative process that involves consumers from the outset.

Human Resource Development

Social welfare organizations are labor-intensive: an organization's plans and design are put into operation by people. Although human resource development has received considerable attention, the area still creates problems for social work administrators. Therefore, the success of services is highly dependent on the administrator's ability to make effective use of valuable human resources so as to address the immediate and long-term needs of the organization and its consumers.

To ensure desired consumer outcomes, the administrator must remain focused on staff behavior, competencies, and morale. From this perspective, staff and consumers are the anchors of the organization. Further, the development of human resources is seen as a crucial administrative task that recognizes the unique contributions staff members offer to the human service enterprise. This is especially true of the knowledge and skills that women and people of color bring to the organization (Asamoah, 1995; Bailey, 1995; Healy, Havens, & Pine, 1995).

Administrators must be as concerned about the needs, growth, and development of their staff members as they are about consumers if consumers are to receive services in an effective manner. Considering the ever-changing environment and program activities of social welfare organizations, administrators understand that ongoing staff development is essential. In other words, if consumers are to receive needed services, the professional needs of staff must be a priority to an administrator. It is difficult to imagine an instance in which a depressed and cynical social worker would be as effective in producing positive consumer outcomes as an energized social worker whose work needs are satisfied (Lewis, Lewis, Packard, & Souflée, 2001).

It should be obvious by now that securing personnel is a critical responsibility for administrators. Recruitment efforts involve not only the number of people needed but also their characteristics, qualifications, and talents. An administrator may want to recruit and hire minority staff to better match personnel with consumers being served. Or perhaps staff must have certain educational credentials in order to be reimbursed for services.

Volunteers are an important human resource of social welfare organizations, and they require the attention of administrators. Administrators need to ensure that the recruitment and assignment of volunteers are planned as carefully as the hiring of professional employees. Volunteers with creative ideas and strong ties to the community can add significant energy to a program. The community participation that comes with volunteers increases the agency's service delivery capacity when volunteer contributions are respected as highly as those of paid personnel.

Supervision

The administrator engages in **supervision** to help a staff member maximize his or her effectiveness in service delivery. Supervision has several aspects, including the following:

- *Providing support and encouragement:* Staff members need to know that administrators are both accessible and available. Such support comes by way of regular feedback and ongoing open communication.

- *Building skills and competencies:* As organizations change, the demands on staff change as well. Therefore, ongoing staff development, membership in professional organizations, attendance at conferences, and interagency collaboration are essential to maintain staff competencies. This also includes identification and nurturing of consumers as leaders and active participants in leadership roles.

- *Performance feedback:* Stated performance goals and objectives, specified methods of evaluation, and appropriate compensation all send the message that staff members are needed and respected for the contributions they offer the organization. Performance feedback should be both vertical and horizontal. In other words, administrators should expect to receive feedback on their performance from staff in much the same way that staff is evaluated by administrators. Establishing mechanisms for feedback from consumers is crucial.

When considering the elements of supervision, it is obvious that the nature of the supervisory relationship depends on the administrator's leadership style, the worker's motivation, and the organization's needs.

The supervisory role requires that the administrator perform a number of interrelated tasks. Leadership is central to all the tasks associated with the position of the supervisor, which uses formal authority to guide others in achieving organizational goals.

As a supervisor, the administrator is accorded certain powers of reward and coercion by the organization (Lewis et al., 2001). Consequently, he or she must possess knowledge and skills relevant to the day-to-day direction and control of unit operations—for example, assigning, delegating, and coordinating work. Further, the supervisory tasks of the administrator often involve mediating relationships between members of the organization and the environment (Kadushin, 1985; Shulman, 1993).

Think about a supervisor you have worked with or the supervision you have provided, and consider the following questions:

1. How did supervision assist you in your work?

2. What were the strengths of the supervisory experience you had?

3. What changes would you recommend, and why?

Resource Acquisition

In order to function, a social welfare organization needs funds, personnel, technology, consumers, and public support and influence. Understanding the operating budget and streams of funding allows an administrator to understand an organization. The administrative process of designing and monitoring the budget is closely related to organizational planning and evaluation. In fact, many would argue that a budget is fundamentally an organization in fiscal terms. The more closely related the budget is to the goals of people who hold a stake in the agency's success, the more effectively it is likely to work (Lewis et al., 2001).

A budget must be seen as the concrete documentation of the planning process, bringing ideals not reality. According to Flynn (1985), the **budget process** has four stages:

1. Define the problem and target groups to be addressed, set actual goals and objectives, and determine the program models or interventions.

2. Estimate revenues (based on available funds) and expenditures.

3. Monitor expenditures and revenues.

4. Make necessary revisions.

An annual budget can be based on recognition of program goals and the costs of activities expected to attain those goals. More specifically, a goal of program budgeting is to develop a system of accountability for programs whereby the allocation of resources is tied to the achievement of stated objectives rather than to "line items" such as supplies or personnel costs.

Budget making is definitely an exercise in decision making through which funds are allocated to one program or service rather than another. In the budget process, it is important to solicit input from key staff and consumers. At the very least, they need to be aware of how the planning process has been translated into financial terms. This will help people understand the decisions an administrator makes throughout the fiscal year and will link people to the costs of programs. Although such understanding is crucial at any time, it is essential during times of fiscal difficulty or program retrenchment.

There can be little doubt that social welfare administrators devote a vast amount of time and energy to resource acquisition activities. For example, grant writing, legislative testimony, private fund raising, and program advocacy within a larger organization are all administrative tasks associated with the budget.

Over the last two decades, the ability of an administrator to acquire funds from varying funding sources has come to be viewed as a major criterion for performance. Public agencies are highly dependent on legislative appropriations as sources of revenue. Private, nonprofit agencies tend to depend on grants, contracts, contributions, and fees paid for services, either by consumers or third parties, as sources of financial support. As one might imagine, the brand of funding has a major impact on an agency's programs because (1) the length and stipulations of funding vary, (2) some services encourage more funding support than others, (3) some populations of consumers are more likely to receive funding support than others, and (4) the community may support certain services more than others. However, administrators must maintain a balance between program goals and funding sources. In other words, funding should not dictate services or jeopardize the integrity of agency goals. At all times, administrators must remember that budgeting and funding tasks should remain subsidiary to planning.

Make a point of reviewing an agency's budget, and consider the following questions:

1. What are the agency's funding sources?

2. What does the budget tell you about the goals and services of the agency?

3. What surprises you about the budget?

4. What questions emerge after your review of the budget?

Evaluation

Tasks associated with program evaluation are used by administrators to assess whether programs and services have met stated goals and the related needs of consumers. The information generated by evaluations gives administrators a basis for making decisions about current or projected programs. For example, data related to particular services can help in decisions about resource allocation, staffing patterns, and provision of services. Simultaneously, data concerning program outcomes can support more rational decisions about the continuation, expansion, or elimination of programs. Equally important, decisions concerning the development of new programs can also be made.

Social research procedures are used in program **evaluation.** Administrators build on their liberal arts foundation to construct evaluation processes that include the following:

- *Systematic processes:* The process is well thought out and developed to measure stated goals and objectives.

- *Reviews of interventions:* Policies and programs are examined in light of meeting consumers' needs and wants, with consideration given to the efficient and effective use of resources.

- *Questions related to adequacy:* The evaluation process should reveal the extent to which identified and anticipated needs are addressed by programs and services.

- *Scanning the political environment:* The organization's stakeholders, such as community members, advisory board, politicians, and other agencies, need to be included in the evaluation to ensure their continued support and regular input into program design and implementation.

- *Scanning the internal environment:* The organization must be an integral part of the evaluation. In particular, staff morale and satisfaction should be considered (Lewis et al., 2001, p. 236).

Ethical Considerations

The values and principles of social work provide an administrator with the road map necessary to guide an organization on a course in the pursuit of organizational effectiveness. Professional values help administrators focus their technical, efficiency-oriented decisions and actions on consumers' needs rather than on production quotas or political exigencies. It is not that productivity and politics are without import, but their importance is as means of achieving the goal of quality service delivery. The values of the social work profession in turn serve to define the profession's code of ethics, which are essentially behavioral guidelines for practice. In addition to these ethical guidelines, several writers have offered specific guidance for administrators.

Table 8.2 A Hierarchy of Ethical Rights

Principle	Ethical Right: People Have the Right to:
1	Life
2	Equality
3	Autonomy
4	Least harm
5	Quality of life
6	Privacy
7	Truthfulness

SOURCE: From *Ethical Decisions for Social Work Practice*, 5th edition, by Loewenberg/Dolgoff, © 1995. Reprinted with permission of Wadsworth, a division of Thomson Learning: www.thomsonrights.com. Fax 800-730-2215.

Lewis (1987, p. 282) provides some helpful principles for administrators to consider:

1. Administrators should not advocate against the interests of the organization that employs them.

2. Administrators should not assume or accept responsibilities that they are not competent to fulfill.

3. Administrators should not allocate resources in a manner that promotes distrust of their motives among the various clientele they must serve.

Ethical dilemmas can sometimes be avoided or made easier to deal with if an organization has clearly articulated values that are used regularly to guide decision making. As depicted in Table 8.2, Loewenberg and Dolgoff (1996) propose a hierarchy based on defined ethical principles to evaluate one's possible actions when confronted with ethical dilemmas. The hierarchy, which shows how each principle takes precedence over the ones below it, gives an administrator a clear guide for thinking through perplexing situations.

It is likely that an administrator will encounter ethical issues in many areas of responsibility, including planning, resource allocation, and supervision. For example, what would you do in the following situation? Explain which principles apply to the situation:

You attend a conference for regional social agency administrators. During the conference you directly hear a colleague present misinformation to sway the vote on resource allocation to favor her agency. You are appalled by this behavior and wonder what is the appropriate response.

ADMINISTRATION FROM A STRENGTHS PERSPECTIVE

It should be clear to you at this point that administration demands a set of skills, as well as attitudes, that administrators can employ in situations with communities, consumers, and staff alike. Administrators communicate the values of a program to those who use it and to the community in which it operates. Additionally, consciously or unconsciously, social work administrators must also display in their daily actions how people should be treated in keeping with the values and principles of the social work profession.

Indeed, conceptualizing administration from a strengths perspective is crucial. Central to seeing consumers as individuals and agencies as a tool for social action is the view of strengths, growth, and change. From such a perspective, administrators value and respect an agency's ability to survive and adapt, and to complement the development of community life. How can administrators incorporate a strengths perspective into their practice? The following principles should be considered as a way for administrators to nurture the strengths, needs, and interests of people and communities involved in their agencies.

Stay Consumer Centered

The raison d'être of the social work administrator is the well-being of consumers and the quality of their life in communities. Administrators accomplish this by knowing who their consumers are, not just in terms of problems but as whole individuals who have lives beyond their needs and the services they receive. From this perspective, "individuals are valued and respected for their ability to survive and adapt, and there is a sense of hope regarding each person's capability to continue to learn and develop over time in relationship with others" (Rapp & Poertner, 1992, p. 17).

All planning and goal setting are guided by consumers' perceptions of their own needs and desires. The role of the administrator is to assist consumers and agency staff in making program and personal goals specific, to explore alternatives, and to identify resources (Saleebey, 1997). In this way, consumers experience the following:

- They are engaged in ongoing communication with agency staff.
- They are not judged by their life conditions but are congratulated for their resiliency and ability to cope with difficult situations.
- They are recognized as the experts on their lives.
- They are members of a larger community.
- They are often supported by informal systems that can be incorporated into the program plans and intervention.

As indicated, administrators are called on to focus on the strengths of people and of communities; to convey the belief that people want to be the directors of their lives, to view the entire community as a place of possibilities, and to advocate for resources to promote social justice. The administrator has a firm commitment to people as active and creative agents who form social meaning for themselves.

Conduct Holistic Assessment

Central to the strengths component is the role and place of assessment. Holistic community assessments allow an administrator to analyze what is occurring within the agency's service area. The strengths perspective assumes that an agency has the competence, in partnership with the community, to articulate the nature of social issues, identify a course of action, explore alternatives for achieving goals, and achieve those goals. Assessment for administrative practice requires (1) focused and precise data collection, (2) analysis of historical trends, and (3) a thorough understanding of qualitative elements that reflect human experiences, interactions, and relationships (Netting, Kettner, & McMurtry, 1998).

For administrators, such assessment ensures the integration of the community and its resources into the fiber of service delivery. Thus, the community in which the agency is located and which it serves has a lot to do with not only the social problems faced by an administrator but also the strengths and the resources available to consumers. Comprehensively assessing the community leads to conceptualizing it as an arena in which consumers experience hope and draw strength, as well as face oppression and frustration. Administration from a strengths perspective quickly highlights whether or not an agency's mission and goals are feasible in the context of community influences.

Know the Agency's Story

The administrator who takes the time to understand the history and development of an agency will uncover its unique characteristics, virtues, and past and current status in the service delivery system. With this information as a backdrop, the administrator has a better grasp of the agency's values, development, and traditions and the significance of these elements in either maintaining the status quo or allowing for agency change. Therefore, administration from a strengths perspective means believing that an agency has the ability to resolve difficult situations, learn from experiences, and change.

Inherent in administration from a strengths perspective is the recognition that to focus on agency possibilities is to practice with an explicit power consciousness (Cowger, 1994). Whatever else administration is, it is always political, because it encompasses power and power relationships. Indeed, exploring the agency's history with specific obstacles to empowerment and power relationships provides the administrator with guidelines to identify, secure, and sustain external and internal resources to ensure that consumers gain as much support as they need to maintain as much control over their lives as possible.

Maintain the Focus

In administration from a strengths perspective, monitoring is a continuous process that begins when agency goals are established. According to Rapp and Poertner (1992), this can be accomplished by doing the following:

1. Selecting and establishing an agency focus

2. Defining the focus in terms of consumer outcomes

3. Eliminating potentially worthwhile goals and activities that do not support the focus

4. Committing, through a preoccupation or obsession, to achieving that focus (p. 19)

To maintain a focus, the administrator frequently contacts and collaborates with not only staff and other agencies, but also consumers, their family members, and informal systems of support. Ongoing contacts with the network of service providers enable the administrator to influence agency strategies and cost-effectiveness by increasing, decreasing, or terminating programs or services expeditiously.

Rapid responsiveness to consumers and community changes can have a dramatic impact on service costs. Reductions in costs can be expected in administration from a strengths perspective because services are reduced and shifted to consumers on the basis of their needs and regained levels of self-sufficiency.

SUMMARY

In light of recent trends on the national and state levels, it appears likely that administrators will be given greater discretion regarding the organization, funding, and delivery of services to consumers. Consequently, it becomes imperative for administrators to develop consumer-centered practices that ensure efficient responses to needs.

This chapter's description and examples demonstrate how administrators can affect social programs through a process of interactions with consumers, staff, and the community. A strengths perspective for administration that supports self-determination, maximizes consumer choice, and supports empowerment is highlighted. It is hoped that administrators will better discover their own strengths as they implement a consumer- and strengths-oriented approach to leadership and supervision.

A FEW KEY TERMS

administration	supervision	evaluation
leader	budget process	

USING INFOTRAC®
COLLEGE EDITION AND INFOWRITE

InfoTrac College Edition

This chapter highlights the complex role of a social work administrator. The following exercise places the administrator in the context of an actual social service agency. As you complete the exercise, ask yourself if you would enjoy being an administrator. Be prepared to explain why or why not administration might be a career path you will follow.

1. Go to InfoTrac College Edition.

2. Under the Subject Guide, search for "agency administrator."

3. Examine the articles that describe the work of administrators in various agency settings.

4. Select an article that draws your attention in terms of the agency setting.

5. Read the article and define the roles of the administrator.

6. List the roles that you think address your professional strengths, such as technical writing or decision making.

7. Consider what professional areas you need to develop or enhance to be an effective administrator.

8. How important is it that the strengths orientation is to be used in an agency setting where you seek employment?

InfoWrite

If social work administration is a career goal, it is important to design a résumé to reflect such an aspiration. The following exercise will be helpful:

1. Go to InfoWrite.

2. Scroll to Special Kinds of Writing.

3. Click on "Business and Technical Writing."

4. Read the material that discusses writing for the business world.

5. Focus on the content entitled "Résumé."

6. Take a moment to reflect how to market oneself as a social work administrator. Then write a concise paragraph that provides a clear statement describing the position sought in administration. What key terms would you use? Which of your professional strengths would you highlight in the description?

CASE EXAMPLE: The Group of 20

Helen is the top administrator at The Women's Center, a service organization dedicated to providing services for women and promoting women's rights. Helen's original appointment at The Women's Center was as a social advocate, and she worked her way up through the administrative chain of command to become director. During her time as a frontline worker, Helen developed a profound appreciation for keeping her practice activities consumer-centered and -directed. This philosophy has extended into her administrative approach.

Within weeks of assuming her position as director, Helen organized what is called "the group of 20" (GO20). Each program and constituent group at The Women's Center was asked to put forward the name of a consumer representative for appointment to the GO20. Members serve one-year terms, with a term limit of three years.

The GO20 meets with Helen on a monthly basis. Its charge is to give Helen information and feedback with respect to organizational performance (goals, policies, programming, staff, management, services, budget, and evaluation). In addition, the GO20 completes an annual evaluation of Helen's ability to supervise, manage resources, and provide organizational leadership.

Helen uses the GO20 as a sounding board with respect to decision making. This has allowed for various perspectives, including the consumer viewpoint, to gain prominence. On several occasions the GO20 has made recommendations concerning policy and program initiatives. The group is politically astute. Because of their influence and close working relationship with Helen, membership in the GO20 is sought after and seen as prestigious at The Women's Center.

The GO20 is a reflection of Helen's and the organization's commitment to reaching out and tapping into the strengths of consumers in administration. Employees and consumers at the agency believe that The Women's Center is a stronger, more effective organization as a result of the value placed on consumer involvement and participation in leadership. For Helen, the GO20 is an exceptional asset in her attempts to balance competing interests and demands for resources.

THINKING CRITICALLY
ABOUT THE CASE EXAMPLE

1. While members of "the group of 20" (GO20) represent programs and constituency groups, how are people selected for membership? Potentially, people in the GO20 could be handpicked by Helen. Devise a system for selecting members of the GO20 that reflects a strengths perspective and promotes active, impartial voices.

2. Helen worked her way from being a frontline social worker to a position as the top administrator of the agency. Although she exemplifies many of the virtues of the organization (e.g., hard work, advocacy, and consumer-centeredness), identify some of the pitfalls associated with promoting people from within an organization.

3. The GO2O is described as a "sounding board" for decision making at the agency. How could the role of the GO2O be strengthened? Is the sounding-board approach sufficient from the empowerment or strengths perspective?

REFLECTION EXERCISES

1. Interview an administrator at a social service agency. Ask about her or his philosophy with respect to management, leadership, and supervision. How does she or he embrace consumer input and feed-back in administrative style? Who participates in completing admin-istrative evaluations, and why?

2. Enter a conversation with a classmate. Ask for his or her perceptions concerning your potential for leadership. Why does this person think you would be a good administrator? What would be some of your challenges in assuming an administrative role?

Consider entering a similar discussion with your academic advisor.

3. Ask a faculty member in your program for the program's or school's administrative story. Who founded social work? Identify the basic values and theoretical underpinnings of social work at your university. How does the administration of your school or program embrace the strengths perspective or empowerment theory?

SUGGESTED READINGS

Gutierrez, L., GlenMaye, L., & DeLois, K. (1995). The organizational contest of empowerment practice: Implications for social work administration. *Social Work, 40,* 249–258.

Iglehart, A., & Beccra, R. (1995). *Social services and the ethnic community.* Boston: Allyn & Bacon.

Lubove, R. (1959). The New York Association for improving the conditions of the poor: The formative years. *New York Historical Society Quarterly, 11,* 307–327.

Shin, J., & Corbin, J. (1998). Top exec-utive leadership and organizational innovation: An empirical investigation of nonprofit human service organiza-tions. *Administration in Social Work, 22*(3), 1–21.

REFERENCES

Asamoah, Y. (1995). Managing the new multicultural workforce. In L. Ginsberg & P. Keys (Eds.), *New management in human services.* (2nd ed.). Washington, DC: NASW Press.

Bailey, D. (1995). Management: Diverse workplaces. In R. Edwards (Ed.), *Encyclopedia of social work* (19th ed.). Washington, DC: NASW Press.

Brueggemann, W. G. (1996). *The practice of macro social work.* Chicago: Nelson-Hall.

Cowger, C. D. (1994). Assessing client strengths: Clinical assessment for client empowerment. *Social Work, 39*(3), 262–268.

Flynn, J. P. (1985). *Social agency policy: Analysis and presentation for community practice.* Chicago: Nelson-Hall.

Garner, H. G., & Orelove, F. P. (1994). *Teamwork in human services: Models and applications across the life span.* Boston: Butterworth-Heineman.

Gummer, B. (1991). *The politics of social administration: Managing organizational politics in social agencies.* Englewood Cliffs, NJ: Prentice Hall.

Gummer, B., & Edwards, R. L. (1985). The enfeebled middle: Emerging issues in education and social administration. *Administration in Social Work, 12*(3), 13–23.

Hardcastle, D. A., Wenocur, S., & Powers, P. R. (1997). *Community practice: Theories and skills for social workers.* New York: Oxford University Press.

Hasenfeld, Y., & English, R. A. (1974). *Human services organizations.* Ann Arbor: University of Michigan Press.

Healy, L., Havens, C., & Pine, B. (1995). Women and social work management. In L. Ginsberg & P. Keys (Eds.), *New management in human services* (2nd ed.). Washington, DC: NASW Press.

Johnson, H. W., McLaughlin, J. A., & Christenson, M. (1982). Interagency collaboration: Driving and restraining forces. *Exceptional Children, 48,* 395–399.

Kadushin, A. (1985). *Supervision in social work* (2nd ed.) New York: Columbia University Press.

Katz, D., & Kahn, R. (1978). *Social psychology of organizations* (rev. ed.). New York: Wiley.

Kretzmann, J., & McKnight, J. (1996). Assets-based community development. *National Civic Review, 85*(4), 23–27.

Lauffer, A. (1981). The practice of social planning. In N. Gilbert & H. Specht (Eds.), *Handbook for social services.* Englewood Cliffs, NJ: Prentice Hall.

Lewis, H. (1987). Ethics and the managing of service effectiveness in social welfare. *Administration in Social Work, 11,* 271–284.

Lewis, J. A., Lewis, M. D., Packard, T., & Souflée, F. (2001). *Management of human service programs.* Pacific Grove, CA: Brooks/Cole.

Loewenberg, F. M., & Dolgoff, R. (1996). *Ethical issues for social work practice* (5th ed.). Itasca, IL: F. E. Peacock.

Netting, F. E., Kettner, P. M., & McMurtry, S. L. (1998). *Social work macro practice* (2nd ed.). New York: Longman.

Neugeboren, B. (1991). *Organization, policy, and practice in human services.* New York: Haworth Press.

Patti, R. (1977). Patterns of management activity in social welfare agencies. *Administration in Social Work, 1*(1), 5–18.

———. (1985). In search of the purpose for social welfare. *Administration in Social Work, 9*(3), 1–14.

Pfeffer, J. (1981). *Power in organizations.* Boston: Pitman.

Poulin, J. (Ed.). (2000). *Collaborative social work: Strengths-based generalist practice.* Itasca, IL: F. E. Peacock.

Rapp, C. A., & Poertner, J. (1992). *Social administration: A client-centered approach.* New York: Longman.

Reisch, M., & Gambrill, E. (1997). *Social work in the 21st century.* Thousand Oaks, CA: Pine Forge Press.

Reynolds, B. (1987). *Social work and social living.* Silver Spring, MD: National Association of Social Workers. (Originally published in 1951.)

Saleebey, D. (1997). *The strengths perspective in social work practice.* New York: Longman.

Shulman, L. (1993). *Interactional supervision.* Washington, DC: NASW Press.

Skidmore, R. A. (1990). *Social work administration: Dynamic management and human services* (2nd ed.). Englewood Cliffs, NJ: Prentice Hall.

9

Accentuating Strengths in Policy Practice and Political Persuasion

Chapter Content Areas

Defining Social Policy

The Problem-Centered Approach

The Strengths Approach

A Policy Analysis Framework

Influencing the Political Process

The Legislative Process

Lobbying

Professional Skills in Policy Practice

Social work has always had a dual focus: individuals/families *and* the environment within which they live. An essential concern of the profession is improving the conditions that affect individuals and families. This dual focus is often summarized as *person in environment*. This connection demonstrates that policy practice, which affects the environment, in turn has a direct effect on individuals. Policy practice is not just a desirable activity for social work; it is an essential activity if social work is to achieve its historic mission.

One of the early social work leaders, Porter Lee, described social work as "cause and function," where the *function* of social work might typically be seen as individual work and the *cause* as the social advocacy role. In his presidential address at the National Conference in 1929, Lee concluded:

> In the last analysis, I am not sure that the greatest service of social work
> as a cause is contributed though those whose genius it is to light and
> hand on the torch. I am inclined to think that in the capacity of the
> social worker, whatever his/her rank, to administer a routine functional

responsibility in the spirit of the servant in a cause is the explanation of the great service of social work. (p. 20)

Later formulations have described "the cause in function," shifting the focus to a more substantiated type of advocacy that is derived from and pertinent to the individual (Porter, 1929).

Policy practice and political persuasion have always been central themes in macro practice. An early example was the settlement house movement at the beginning of the 1900s, which was closely connected with the Progressive Era, a time of intense social reform activity. Jane Addams and others from Hull House intervened at multiple levels of government to promote social justice (Levine, 1971; Lundblad, 1995). They were heavily involved with the Chicago Civic Federation, an influential local political advocacy organization (Linhorst, 2002). Through involvement in this organization and other activities, Hull House participants supported the establishment of the Cook County Juvenile Court, which served as a model for the nation. Furthermore, their advocacy efforts at the federal level led to passage of national child labor legislation (Linhorst, 2002).

This chapter explores policy practice, the political process, and advocacy skills. Of particular interest is the promotion of social change through policy analysis, formulation, and development, using a strengths perspective. Consumer empowerment via political involvement is explored in relationship to the population group or groups being served by the social worker. Various forms of legislative and political participation are examined, including testifying, lobbying, promoting ordinances and laws, connecting with political action committees (including PACE), electing social workers to political office, serving as staff members for officeholders, and networking with politicians.

DEFINING SOCIAL POLICY

Social policy defines what services will be delivered, who consumers are, and what roles social workers will assume. As principles of action, policies translate a government's sense of responsibility to citizens and the world at large (Tice & Perkins, 2002). According to DiNitto (2000), social welfare policy is "anything a government chooses to do, or not do, that affects the quality of life of its people" (p. 2). The dynamics of policy include broad categories ranging from taxation to health care and environmental protection. Indeed, the boundaries of social policy are unclear; however, policies encompass a core of ideologies that tend to polarize us (Axinn & Levin, 1992). For example, priorities regarding children are often juxtaposed to those associated with people who are older, or the needs of the poor are presented as being in conflict with those of the middle class.

Contextual factors and an array of political processes shape specific policies in each historical era (Jannson, 2001). Such processes are influenced by laws, rules, regulations, and budgets. Aspects of social policies can be found in:

- Constitutions that define social policy powers of the local, state, and federal governments

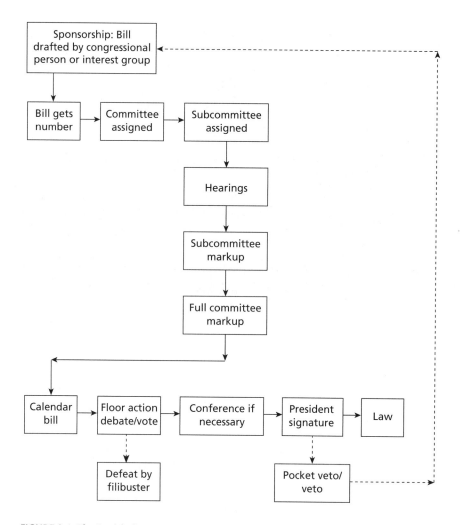

FIGURE 9.1 The Legislative Process

SOURCE: From *Faces of Social Policy: A Strengths Perspective,* 1st edition, by C. Tice/K. Perkins, © 2002. Reprinted with permission of Wadsworth, a division of Thomson Learning: www.thomsonrights.com. Fax: 800-730-2215.

- Public policies or laws enacted in local, state, or federal legislatures
- Court decisions that overrule, uphold, and interpret statutes
- Budgets and funding allocations that demonstrate societal values and priorities
- Stated objectives that specify missions and goals
- Rules and procedures that define how policies will be implemented at the local, state, and federal levels (Jannson, 2001, pp. 18–19).

Social policy development occurs on many levels. Most social policy is the result of government decisions. This point is demonstrated in Figure 9.1, which displays the legislative pathway that a bill travels to become a social policy and law. Two primary groups participate in the passage of policy into law: the legislature and special-interest groups. Much of the policy work is completed by legislators who are appointed to committees and subcommittees on the basis of their particular interests. Committees are the loci of testimony on issues, and legislative hearings provide for official testimony from the public.

Special-interest groups fall into two broad categories based on their activities. Political action committees (PACs) influence the composition of legislatures before elections. Lobbyists exert pressure between elections to gain legislative actions for their interests (Tice & Perkins, 2002). The National Education Association (NEA) and the American Medical Association (AMA) are examples of powerful special-interest groups that influence policies relevant to their membership.

THE PROBLEM-CENTERED APPROACH

To understand the implications and effects of social welfare policies and to influence the development of those decisions, social workers must be familiar with the policymaking process from the problem-centered approach. Social workers involved in macro practice operate in both the political and the policy arena. The

provision of benefits and services to people to meet basic needs, including housing, income, food, and health care, is regulated by social policy. Thus, society's
response to social problems often comes by means of social policy. The traditional
approach to policy development involves unraveling a problem in a series of
processes. In problem-centered policy development, problem definition is the
cornerstone of policy design (Chapin, 1995; Tice & Perkins, 2002).

To demonstrate the problem-centered approach to policy development,
follow these steps:

1. Consider at least six social issues facing our nation, such as access to health
   care, drug legalization, or homelessness.
2. Decide on the "real" or "root" cause of the issues.
3. Explore societal responses to these issues.
4. Define the services designed to address the issues.
5. Consider how people and their communities are labeled in order to
   receive the services.

As this exercise illustrates, the problem-centered approach involves a series of
processes intended to address an entanglement of problems, issues, and values that
combine to make policy development a complex web of activities. Thus, social
policy occurs on many levels and reflects government choices and decisions.

Although social policy is often developed in response to social problems, the
relationship between problems and policies is not simple. For instance, a social
issue is labeled as a problem only when it affects a significant number of people
or gains the attention of influential, powerful people. Consequently, social policies reflect the social and personal values of those with decision-making capabilities (Tice & Perkins, 2002). To illustrate this point, attend a neighborhood,
residential life, or residents' council meeting. During and after the meeting:

1. Review the meeting agenda, listen
   to the meeting's discussion, and
   read previous meeting minutes.
2. List at least three issues that were
   labeled as problems for the
   membership.
3. Investigate what measures were
   taken to address these problems.
   Did policy statements result from
   the identified problems?

Problem identification is a basic aspect of the process of understanding
human needs and priorities. Problem definition creates a source of knowledge
that can be used in assessing current policy trends and implementing new policies and programs. Finally, problem definition reflects commonly held beliefs
and values about our environments (Karger & Stoesz, 1998). Expanding on
problem identification, consider a number of steps:

1. *Identify the policy or program goal and needed change.* What is wrong with
   the current policy? How does this affect communities? Organizations?

Groups? Individuals? How can it be improved? It is an important first step to know as much as possible about the current policy. Find out what needs it addressed at the time of its inception and how those needs may have changed. Who advocated for the implementation of the policy? What would they say about the proposed change?

2. *Identify the values related to the problem/human need.* Why is this change desirable? Have various levels of society that might be affected been consulted? Is it ethical? Have diverse populations been considered?

3. *Analyze the current situation or operation—"the actual."* What is currently in place? Who is affected? How can it be improved? Investigate the situation from the perspectives of communities, organizations, groups, and individuals. Notice the impact at the different levels. Who benefits from the situation? Does anyone suffer from it?

4. *Determine "the ideal" policy program or service provision.* How does the proposed change improve the system? Why is it better? What are the elements of this program or provision that make it ideal? Are the effects of this policy program or provision beneficial to all? How so?

5. *Identify options.* Can this policy be implemented in different ways? What are the fundamental principles? Are there many plans or courses of action, or is it more restrictive? Who supports the change? Who are the opponents of the change? What are the points of opposition?

6. *Choose the best or most feasible option or alternative.* What is most likely to be implemented at this time? Are there any future changes that might affect this policy? How can this policy have the most crucial impact?

7. *Implement the modified policy or program through an action plan.* What steps need to be taken to implement the change? What groups or organizations would be advocates in this process? How will the public know about the proposed change?

8. *Evaluate the change.* What is different as a result of the change? Were there unexpected implications? Were any problems created by the change? Has it been accepted? Criticized? Have the benefits been reaped?

THE POLICY PROCESS
FROM A STRENGTHS APPROACH

With the problem-centered approach to policy development as a backdrop, it is time to shift attention to a strengths perspective for policy design. In essence, the strengths perspective suggests that many of the barriers that confront people "come from educational, political, and economic exclusion based on demographics rather than individual characteristics" (Tice & Perkins, 2002, p. 5; Rappaport, Davidson, Wilson, & Mitchell, 1975). The task for social workers is to identify and create opportunities that nurture the growth and capabilities of people in their environments. Thus, policy development from a strengths perspective highlights the potential for community and large-scale change rather than perceived deficits or weakness.

If social policy is to reflect the reality of its intended recipients and if self-determination is paramount, consumers must be included in the strengths approach to policy. What are the responsibilities of social workers? According to Chapin (1995), social workers must ensure that the voices of clients are both heard and understood by policymakers and must focus on the common needs and strengths of people rather than their deficits.

A FRAMEWORK FOR ANALYSIS

The strengths approach demands a framework of analysis that incorporates the unique strengths of individuals and communities while addressing human needs. Charlotte Towle's (1945/1987) *Common Human Needs* provides a foundation for the framework by suggesting that social policy is a tool for helping people meet their basic needs. As Tice and Perkins conclude (2002, p. 12), an emphasis on human need suggests that social workers should recognize:

- People with similar needs are nevertheless confronted with different barriers to meeting their needs.

- Highlighting common needs instead of social problems eliminates labels based on deficiencies or pathologies.

- With human needs as the basic criteria, people do not have to be described as deficient to justify receiving benefits and services.

- The social work values of self-determination and respect for worth and dignity are operationalized by a focus on human needs.

- Recognizing common human needs supports the conceptual core of the strengths perspective whereby social workers collaborate with people as opposed to exerting the power of knowledge or institutions.

- Human needs involve communities as a resource that offers opportunities for growth and development (Chapin, 1995; Saleebey, 1992; Tice & Perkins, 1996, 2002; Towle, 1945/1987).

As designed by Tice and Perkins (2002, p. 13), Table 9.1 integrates the traditional problem-centered approach to policy development with the strengths perspective. Saleebey (1992) describes the strengths perspective as a collaboration of ideas and techniques rather than a theory or paradigm. It "seeks to develop abilities and capabilities in clients" and assumes that "clients already have a number of competencies and resources that may improve their situations" (Saleebey, 1992, p. 15; Tice & Perkins, 2002, p. 11). When applied to policy and macro practice, the strengths perspective addresses common human needs and barriers to meeting such needs rather than community or individual deficits, weaknesses, or pathologies.

Policy development from a strengths perspective negotiates needs and barriers by soliciting input from people, the eventual consumers of services. This is

Table 9.1 Comparison of the Problem-Centered and Strengths Approaches to Policy Development

Policy Process	Problem-Centered Approach	Strengths Approach
Identify the problem	■ A condition or situation is labeled as a "problem" to be corrected. ■ "Problem" impacts the quality of life for a large group of the economically/socially powerless ■ Definition of problem is shared by sets of values ■ Political ideology affects problem identification	■ Identifies barriers associated with meeting common needs ■ Problem definition is negotiated with all parties involved ■ Stories and observation of ordinary people are included in the definition ■ Recognition given to peoples' methods of coping and confronting barriers
Formulate policy alternatives	■ Knowledge accumulation is essential ■ Federal departments/ agencies compile data ■ Professional associations provide sources of data ■ Professional policymaker is considered the expert ■ Involves organized activities on legislatures and elected officials	■ Knowledge accumulation focuses on the strengths of the individuals ■ Alternatives are considered as tools to assist people to meet their needs ■ Consumers of services are collaborators in policy development ■ Environment is scanned for support of policy that supports individuals in their environments ■ Program consumers introduce formal and informal resources into policy implementation. ■ Considers if consumer needs are met.
Legitimize policy	■ Special-interest groups influence the process of passing bills into law ■ Social welfare advocacy groups endorse or confront issues/programs ■ Involves relatively scientific methods ■ Provides a pool of information	
Evaluate policy	■ Universities and government entities conduct and evaluate studies	

SOURCE: From *Faces of Social Policy: A Strengths Perspective*, 1st edition, by C. Tice/K. Perkins, © 2002. Reprinted with permission of Wadsworth, a division of Thomson Learning: www.thomsonrights.com. Fax: 800-730-2215.

primarily accomplished through the worker–consumer relationship, collaborative knowledge building, linking people with existing resources and services, and advocating for services when they do not exist. Consequently, the process of social policy development becomes more inclusive by considering problems ranging from the personal through the external environment, and interweaving these two dimensions in a circular fashion (Gutierrez, Parsons, & Cox, 1998; Tice & Perkins, 2002, pp. 12–13).

The strengths perspective can be used to conceive a new understanding of the relationship between social workers, consumers, and policy development. When policymakers move beyond seeing themselves as the experts, more attention is paid to community outreach to give voice to diverse groups. Policy developed from a strengths perspective should be evaluated according to the extent to which policies reflect the ideas and needs of people in their communities. Thus, as social workers, we are challenged to develop strengths not only in individuals but in communities.

It is at this juncture that empowerment comes into play. Empowerment represents a means of accomplishing policy and community development by conceptualizing two key elements: giving community members the authority to make decisions and choices and facilitating the development of the knowledge and resources necessary to exercise these choices (Zippay, 1995, p. 266).

Read the following case study and apply the strengths perspective framework to its analysis. How did the analysis support empowerment? What aspects of the analysis were most difficult for you?

CASE EXAMPLE: Forming a Coalition

Betty James works at a local domestic violence shelter that receives significant funding from the state human services agency. A bill has been introduced in the state legislature that would require domestic violence shelters to share all of their records with the state agency. After discussions with staff and client representatives, many concerns have been raised about the purpose of such disclosure and the ability to maintain client confidentiality. The state government has experienced a shortfall in income in this fiscal year because of a financial downturn and resultant reduction in income from taxes. Despite a 5 percent increase in the number of clients this year, the state has informed Betty's agency that it can expect a reduction in the state allocation. Consider the following questions:

1. How would Betty help develop a coalition with other agencies?
2. How could clients be involved?
3. How could Betty contact legislators? What could she present?
4. Should discussions be held with the state agency? If so, how should this be accomplished?
5. How could support from the community, from groups associated with the agency, or from churches be secured?
6. What should Betty's group prepare for testimony before legislative hearings?

INFLUENCING THE POLITICAL PROCESS

If social workers are to engage in policy practice, they need to have a general knowledge of practice and specific training in advocacy techniques. The political knowledge base should include political institutions, the policy process, current economic and social conditions, the positions of political players, and related areas (Delli Carpini & Keeter, 1996). Unfortunately, "politics" is often viewed negatively. The public conception often is that politics is manipulative and dishonest. Politicians are perceived as untrustworthy. The news media launch investigations into the moral character of politicians and often expose unsavory aspects of their past. The term *politics* is also used to describe the manipulation of interpersonal relationships involving influence and power, particularly in the workplace.

This type of negative thinking about politics tends to limit our interest in becoming part of the political process. Whatever we think of politics, however, the political process influences everyday life for social workers and clients alike. Public policy and funding are part of the political process. Social workers need to be aware of politics and participate in the political process to maximize their effectiveness. To opt out of political processes is to turn important decisions over to other people who may have less knowledge or a lesser commitment.

Although politics is often viewed negatively, most politicians in fact are honest and struggle to reconcile competing interests. They want to achieve the best results in difficult situations. As Reisch (2000) notes:

> If we continue to regard electoral politics as choosing between the "lesser of two evils," if we continue to see electoral participation as an "either/or" strategic decision, it is inevitable that we will become disheartened and drop out of the dialogue over the future of our society. . . . Making effective choices, however, requires us to assess the current political climate carefully, affirm our commitment to the values we profess, and ally ourselves with other forces, locally and globally, that share our vision and goals. (p. 293)

THINKING AND ACTING POLITICALLY

For social workers to have maximum impact on behalf of consumers and communities, it is important to think politically. Most policies have come about as a result of political processes. When social workers neglect to engage in **thinking politically** about the politics of social welfare policy, the needs of consumers and their communities are left out of the policy development process. Social workers, according to Domanski (1998), are in a unique position to increase the political salience of social issues. To make a difference, it is important that social workers be aware of social issues, their political implications, and the political process. Reisch (2000, p. 294) suggests that social workers consider several crucial questions to launch their political thinking:

- What political strategies can create change in the era of globalization?

- How can politics confront the isolation experienced by urban and rural communities and the marginalization of their populations?

- What will be the roles of the public, private, and nonprofit sectors in the provision of income maintenance and social services?

- What roles will social workers play in the social welfare nexus as the relationships among the government, nonprofit, and for-profit organizations change dramatically?

- Who should bear the economic and social costs of rapid economic and technological changes?

- Can a welfare state exist if all of the essential services are not provided or if services are provided by nongovernmental organizations?

As these queries suggest, it is important that social workers stay abreast of the political climate in their jurisdiction, the state, and the nation. Often the election of a new politician to a key position can have a major impact on funding allocations. This may also be the catalyst for new initiatives and opportunities to explore new areas of interest. A politician's agenda may focus on an area of social service that has been neglected in the past, opening up opportunities for funding and new programs. This shift in spending may have an impact on current programs, which may see a loss in available funds. Whether political change threatens funding or broadens possibilities, social workers should be aware of the possibility of future changes.

There are a number of things that social workers can do to become part of the political process. The most basic act is simply to *register and vote*. This is a very simple process and has become easier in recent years. Not to vote is to opt out of the political process and one's role in a democracy. Most social workers get involved by voting, advocating, and keeping informed of political issues, while only a few consider themselves activists or attend public hearings (Domanski, 1998).

Getting involved in political activities on behalf of a party or a particular candidate is another way to support the political process. Campaigns depend on the support of staff and volunteers for success in elections and implementation of political agendas. Tasks may range from answering phones and distributing flyers to assisting in speech preparation and hosting events. Some restrictions may be placed on federal workers by the Hatch Act, which limits certain political activities for individuals whose salaries are supported by federal funds, but most agencies do not restrict political activities (Thompson, 1996).

Helping consumers to get involved and to increase their political awareness is one way of empowering individuals. Encouraging consumers to register and vote, emphasizing their potential to contribute to their community, invites feelings of importance and connectedness. Social workers should further develop consumers' connection to their community by emphasizing the political context in which they live and offering suggestions to get consumers involved in political activities.

INFLUENCING THE
LEGISLATIVE PROCESS

Social workers possess the knowledge and skills needed to influence legislation. Strategies that can be used by social workers include advocacy, networking, lobbying, coalition building, using the media, using technology, participating in political action committees, and taking part in campaigning efforts.

To be effective, social workers should be aware of the basics of the legislative process and of the groups that influence legislation. Some of these are briefly discussed next:

Getting Information about Legislative Proposals

Sources of legislative information include the following:

- Web-based resources such as NASW legislative alerts, the National Priorities Project (www.nationalpriorities.org), and the Electronic Policy Network (www.movingideas.org)
- Web sites such as www.politicalinformation.com and www.policylibrary.com
- Periodicals such as the *Congressional Quarterly Weekly Report*
- Newsletters from organizations that deal with specific issues
- Social advocacy groups
- Trade associations or coalitions of service agencies, which are interested in policy proposals that will impact their member organizations, including groups that are concerned with, for example, the collective needs of voluntary child welfare agencies or those of hospitals
- Coalitions interested in policy developments
- Newspaper indexes

Using Information from Policy Groups

In every state and nationally there are organizations that study current policy and make recommendations for modification of policies to better serve clients. These groups issue position statements and advocate for changes. Frequently these groups have Web sites or issue newsletters. A comprehensive list of advocacy groups can be found on the Electronic Policy Network Web site at www. movingideas.org. Membership in such groups is beneficial for fueling initiatives to change legislation, gaining information, and networking.

Tracking Proposed Legislation

It is useful to know how a particular piece of legislation is moving through the **legislative process.** A bill, once introduced by a member, will be referred to a committee, which, it is hoped, will schedule hearings on the bill. Once the committee votes the bill out, it will be dealt with by the legislative body in which it was introduced. At each step, there are opportunities to influence the process. By tracking the legislation, a social worker or groups of social workers can target their efforts more effectively.

Building Relationships with Legislators and Their Staff

An agency should develop and maintain contacts with legislators to gain their support. These relationships are significant in times of crisis, when a legislator's support could benefit the agency or when the need arises for letters of support. Agency leaders should strive to maintain contacts by calling legislators regularly and sending them letters, agency newsletters, and newspaper clippings about agency successes or events. Legislators should receive invitations to agency functions, such as annual meetings. Some agencies gear regular meetings toward legislators to inform them of current social issues that affect the agency and its clients and that pertain to legislative proposals. When asking for help, it is advisable to have developed an established relationship with a legislator.

Obtaining Funding

When legislation is passed that will potentially benefit a cause, the budget is the next crucial issue of concern. Funding is typically handled separately from the regular passage of bills. The allocation of funding will contribute to determining how the effort will be implemented.

Lobbying

Lobbying is the process of influencing legislation. It encourages leaders to consider issues of great importance to individuals and organizations. The late Sheldon Goldstein, who served as the executive director of the National Association of Social Workers, described a number of principles he learned while involved in legislative advocacy in Illinois:

- Legislators want to say "yes" to constituents, all things being equal.

- On the other hand, legislators hate controversial proposals. Individuals and groups have long memories if a legislator has voted against their proposals. As legislators have said, "Friends come and go but enemies accumulate."

- Voters, not dollars, vote. Letters and calls from a legislator's constituents are taken very seriously—much more seriously than efforts of paid lobbyists. Often a few letters or calls will determine a legislator's vote.

- Bills are most easily killed in committee.

- Choose a bill's sponsors carefully.

- Tell the truth (Goldstein, 1990).

When meeting with an elected official in person, keep in mind that representatives need both *opinions* and *information*. Two issues are of primary importance to legislators: (1) the *cost* of the proposed bill and subsequent services and (2) the intended *outcome* or social impact of the policy (Brueggemann, 1996, p. 359). Written material, consumer comments, and other supportive material should be made available to legislators whenever possible.

Dear and Patti (1981) suggest a number of "empirically based tactics," which include introducing the bill early or before the session, getting multiple sponsors (particularly influential legislators), securing majority-party support and support of the governor, and trying to get open committee hearings and testimony at these hearings. Not surprisingly, bills that have low fiscal impact, have the support of the majority party, and are not controversial will generally have the best chance of passage.

As you become more familiar with the state legislative processes, there are a number of things that you may find striking. One is the sheer volume of legislation. Many legislators deal with thousands of bills in a session. It is impossible for any legislator to have detailed knowledge about either the subject matter of all the bills or the specific provisions of the bills themselves. In practice, this means that legislators have to rely on other members or on outsiders to provide guidance on how to act on specific proposals. Second, many lobbyists try to influence legislative decisions in ways that are favorable to their group's interests. Third, legislative committees are crucial to the outcome of bills because many bills are modified in—or never emerge from—committee. The final vote on a bill may be largely a formality, as decisions about bills are largely made in committee, by lobbying, or by recommendations of legislative leaders.

PROFESSIONAL SKILLS
IN POLICY PRACTICE

At this point, the importance of social workers engaging in the broad range of activities considered "political" should be obvious. What skills are necessary to participate in the political process of policy development?

Communication

Communication skills are crucial to the effect social work discussions will have on consumers and on public- and private-sector policymakers. As stated by Gummer (1990):

> The first step in any policy process is to see the issues one is concerned with are placed on the public or private agenda. The capacity to determine which items go on, and which are excluded from, the policy maker's agenda is an important and much sought-after source of power. (p. 107)

Communication also plays an essential role in correcting errors in policy thinking (Burch, 1991). Social workers can frame social welfare issues in ways that reflect social work's professional interests. Further, social workers may have opportunities to testify at legislative hearings. Should this opportunity arise, the following may be useful to consider:

- Know your audience. Who are the actors? What arguments will appeal to each?

- Do not argue for your position from a moral standpoint alone. Present your recommendations as being reasonable and responsible. Deal frankly with fiscal considerations: Why does this proposal make good fiscal or business sense?

- Use human interest stories in addition to statistics and other factual information. Be aware that overuse of statistics or "facts" may be boring.

- Do not use academic language or professional jargon. Do not talk down to legislators.

- Anticipate counterarguments. Be ready to answer critical questions or include responses to potential concerns in your presentation.

- Role-play and critique your presentation before an official meeting. Have someone play the role of devil's advocate, using potential counter-arguments or questions.

- Prepare a written presentation, but do not read it word for word. Have a brief handout for distribution to officials.

- Be prepared to modify your presentation. Hearings may fall behind schedule, and you may have to shorten or change your presentation to fit conditions.

- The hearing setting may be rather hectic, with several things going on at the same time. Be prepared and stay focused.

- Be clear about what you want the legislators to do. If you are seeking support of a particular bill, this should be stated at the outset of your presentation and again in the conclusion.

Collaboration

Domanski (1998) suggests that collaboration demonstrates the importance of power in numbers while diversifying the support for social welfare programs. When collaborating with consumers, community members, and other policy stakeholders, "skills of negotiation, a willingness to compromise, and an under-standing of the incremental nature of the U.S. social welfare policy reform are important tools" (p. 161). Social workers acting as collaborators encourage and facilitate open and honest exchange of ideas, plans, and resources, and they enable consumers and community members to jointly define their separate interests by mutually identifying changes that may be needed to achieve common purposes (Garner & Orelove, 1994, p. 63).

Assessment

For policy development from a strengths perspective, social workers must conduct a holistic rather than a diagnosis assessment. Consumer knowledge and motivation are the basis of such an assessment, as opposed to professional expertise. Strengths assessment focuses on optimizing community resources. As stated by Saleebey (1997), "acquisition of natural community resources is predicated on the belief that including consumers in the decision about who or what entity provides the service will promote adherence to the form and direction of the help received" (p. 125).

Three principles define an assets-based approach to assessment (Saleebey, 1997, pp. 205–206). First, social workers begin with the resources that are present in the community rather than what lacking or what a community and its citizens need. Second, the assessment is internally focused. It is essential that social workers know what is going on in the community and with its residents, and what individual and group capabilities exist. Finally, the process is relationship-driven.

Critical Thinking

Critical thinking involves the dual process of "identifying and challenging assumptions" and "imaging and exploring alternatives." Policy development requires thinking rationally to address social issues by building on unique strengths. However, social workers must be reminded that there is more to policy development than calculated rationality. In other words, efficiency does not always result in the best social policy.

Policy development from a strengths perspective requires synthesis: the integration of various needs and values. This means first seeking to *understand*. Too often, social workers' own agendas and need to be heard make it extremely difficult to give undivided attention to the needs and wants of others (Timpson, 2002).

SUMMARY

The better social workers understand the functioning of government and the process of policy development, the greater the likelihood of exerting influence over social programs and services. This chapter examines policy development from a strengths perspective designed to empower individuals and their communities.

Ideally, this framework of policy analysis will encourage macro social workers to envision themselves and consumers as political actors with the capacity to change the United States' course of action. Only within such a framework will the unique human needs and social issues of individuals, groups, and communities be effectively addressed.

A FEW KEY TERMS

social policy   legislative process   critical thinking

thinking politically   lobbying

USING INFOTRAC®
COLLEGE EDITION AND INFOWRITE

InfoTrac College Edition

At the federal, state, and local level, policy proposals and recommendations are made with the goal of modifying policies to better serve consumers. There are a number of sources of legislative information, as described in this chapter. To track a particular piece of legislation through the legislative process, do the following:

1. Go to InfoTrac College Edition.

2. Under Keyword Search, search for "pending legislation."

3. Select an article that describes a policy of interest to you.

4. Read the article.

5. Use InfoTrac College Edition online resources and other articles linked to this subject to answer the following questions:

   a. What social issues does the policy address?

b. What is the goal of the policy?

c. Who supports the policy? Why?

d. Who opposes the policy? Why?

e. What are the social programs implemented as a result of the policies?

f. How have the voices and perspectives of consumers been expressed?

InfoWrite

As stated in this chapter, policy development requires thinking rationally to address social issues by building on strengths. To engage in this rational thinking process:

1. Go to InfoWrite.

2. Scroll to Critical Thinking.

3. Read under the bullet "Distinguishing Fact from Opinion and Bias from Reason."

4. Using the policy selected from the InfoTrac College Edition exercise,

describe what types of deceptive arguments have been used to influence the public's opinion regarding the policy.

5. To what degree have your opinions of the policy been influenced by deceptive arguments?

CASE EXAMPLE: Police Profiling of Persons of Color

Ken is a social worker at St. Peter's social service agency. His primary role is to assist consumers in securing meaningful employment. Most of the people served by St. Peter's live within a two-mile radius of the agency. St. Peter's is located in an urban area plagued by poverty, crime, and unemployment.

In the past few weeks, several of Ken's male consumers have expressed concern about racial profiling. In particular, it appears that police officers are routinely stopping and questioning African American males. The mayor and chief of police have publicly stated that the area surrounding St. Peter's needs to be "cleaned up." Merchants and store owners have been complaining to politicians about vagrancy. Indeed, police patrols have been stepped up, and in recent weeks there has been an appreciable increase in the number of misdemeanor violations given to local residents of color.

Consumers of services are livid. They seek an immediate end to racial profiling. Consumers of color can barely walk or drive down streets without being harassed, let alone look for employment. In their zeal to satisfy local businesspeople, it appears that the mayor and police chief have created an unofficial campaign to rid the streets of racial minorities.

Ken has facilitated two community meetings in reaction to the present situation. Consumers agree that police actions constitute an affront to their human dignity and believe that it is time to start thinking politically and to get involved in local politics. There is a general concern that many people do not realize or understand what is happening. Additional information and documentation are needed, and consumers have begun the process of making contacts with community leaders and elected officials to raise consciousness and better assess the situation. Consumers have begun seeking ways to place the issue of racial profiling on various public agendas. The official name of this new group is Citizens Committed to Dignity for Persons of Color.

THINKING CRITICALLY
ABOUT THE CASE EXAMPLE

1. Racial profiling by police officers is a complex, multifaceted phenomenon. For example, profiling could involve citations of a number of types—arrests for traffic violations, vagrancy, and other violations of the law. Specificity is often an ally in police practice. Contemplate ways to differentiate perception from social facts in documenting racial profiling. How might consumers of services shed light on the techniques, practices, and ploys used in racial profiling in their community?

2. Given the limited information from the case example, create a sixty-second narrative capsule of the situation. How could consumers and Ken present their

concerns to a politician or community leader in a brief, succinct (sixty-second) statement?

3. In this case example, the mayor and chief of police have been depicted as potential barriers to reform and change. Using the strengths perspective, how might these individuals and their offices or departments be viewed as potential assets?

REFLECTION EXERCISES

1. Research a legislative proposal through the use of the Web, newspapers, and newsletters. Eventually, identify and read the original legislative bill and any subsequent amendments. Track the progress of the legislative initiative and its support. Was the bill ever enacted? Why or why not?

2. Join an e-mail list, message board, or online discussion group dedicated to social advocacy. Assess the involvement and participation of consumers of services. How could the system be improved (e.g., Web site development)?

3. Write to one of your legislators in support of or opposition to a pending bill that you have researched. Ask the legislator about the possibility of your making a presentation or talking with her or him about the merits of the bill. How could consumers be involved in any such effort?

SUGGESTED READINGS

Lindblom, C. E. (1959). The science of muddling through. *Public Administration Review, 19,* 79–88.

Seccombe, K. (1999). *So you think I drive a Cadillac? Welfare recipients' perspectives on the system and its reform.* Boston: Allyn & Bacon.

Weick, A. (1992). Building on the strengths perspective for social work. In D. Saleebey (Ed.), *The strengths perspective in social work.* New York: Longman.

Wildavsky, A. (1979). *The art and craft of policy analysis.* Boston: Little, Brown.

REFERENCES

Axinn, J., & Levin, H. (1992). *Social welfare: A history of the American response to need.* New York: Longman.

Brueggemann, W. G. (1996). *The practice of macro social work.* Chicago: Nelson-Hall.

Burch, H. (1991). *The whys of social policy: Perspective on policy preferences.* New York: Praeger.

Chapin, R. K. (1995). Social policy development: The strengths perspective. *Social Work, 40*(4), 506–514.

Dear, R., & Patti, J. (1981). Legislative advocacy: Seven effective tactics. *Social Work, 26,* 289–296.

Delli Carpini, M. X., & Keeter, S. (1996). *What Americans know about politics and why it matters*. New Haven, CT: Yale University Press.

DiNitto, D. M. (2000). *Social welfare: Politics and public policy* (5th ed.). Boston: Allyn & Bacon.

Domanski, M. D. (1998). Prototypes of social work political participation: An empirical model. *Social Work, 43*(2), 156–168.

Garner, H., & Orelove, F. P. (1994). *Teamwork in human services*. Boston: Butterworth-Heinemann.

Goldstein, H. (1990). Strengths or pathology: Ethical and rhetorical contrasts in approaches to practice. *Families in Society, 71*(5), 267–275.

Gummer, B. (1990). *The politics of social administration: Managing organizational politics in social agencies*. Englewood Cliffs, NJ: Prentice Hall.

Gutierrez, L., Parsons, R. J., & Cox, E. O. (1998). *Empowerment in social work practice: A sourcebook*. Pacific Grove, CA: Brooks/Cole.

Jannson, B. S. (2001). *The reluctant welfare state: American social welfare policies— past, present, and future*. Pacific Grove, CA: Brooks/Cole.

Karger, H. J., & Stoesz, D. (1998). *American social welfare policy.* New York: Longman.

Levine, D. (1971). *Jane Addams and the liberal tradition*. Madison: State Historical Society of Wisconsin.

Linhorst, D. M. (2002). Federalism and social justice: Implications for social work. *Social Work, 47,* 201–222.

Lundblad, K. S. (1995). Jane Addams and social reform: A role model for the 1990s. *Social Work, 40,* 661–669.

Porter, L. R. (1929). Social work: Cause and function. *Proceedings, National Conference on Social Work.*

Rappaport, J., Davidson, W., Wilson, M., & Mitchell, A. (1975). Alternatives to blaming the victim or environment: Our places to stand have moved the earth. *American Psychologist, 30,* 525–528.

Reisch, M. (2000). Social workers and politics in the new century. *Social Work, 45*(4), 293–297.

Saleebey, D. (1992). *The strengths perspective in social work practice*. New York: Longman.

———. (1997). *The strengths perspective in social work practice* (2nd ed.). New York: Longman.

Tice, C. J., & Perkins, K. (1996). *Mental health issues and aging: Building on the strengths of older people*. Pacific Grove, CA: Brooks/Cole.

———. (2002). *The faces of social policy: A strengths perspective*. Pacific Grove, CA: Brooks/Cole.

Thompson, J. J. (1996). Social workers and politics: Beyond the Hatch Act. *Social Work, 39*(4), 457–465.

Timpson, W. M. (2002). *Teaching and learning peace*. Madison, WI: Atwood Publishing.

Towle, C. (1987). *Common human needs*. Silver Spring, MD: National Association of Social Workers. (Original work published 1945.)

Zippay, A. (1995). The politics of empowerment. *Social Work, 40*(2), 263–268.

10

Promoting a Just Society

Chapter Content Areas

Relationship between Social
Work and Social Justice

Ideological Differences between
Social Workers and Consumers

Defining Social Justice

A Just Society

Reflection, Discernment, and
Questioning

Distributive Justice

Relational (Processual) Justice

Social Justice at the Societal
Level

Social Reductionism

Parity Laws for Mental Health
and Social Justice

Respecting Consumers and Their
Images of Reality

Social Justice and
Understandable Language

Preserving Rights and
Strengthening Voices

Practical Considerations for
Promoting Social Justice

How Far Can We Go?

Hate Crime and Sexual
Orientation

SOCIAL JUSTICE AND SOCIAL WORK

Many people enter the social work profession with lofty goals. For the most part, their intentions are admirable. Social workers often hope to promote **social justice**—to help create a more equitable world. They take pride in championing various causes and promoting the rights of vulnerable and oppressed population groups. Social workers are rarely satisfied with services and programs aimed at helping consumers merely to cope with or survive their woes. Instead, as the NASW *Code of Ethics* describes it, social workers encourage and facilitate activities "to ensure access to needed information, services, and resources; equality of opportunity; and meaningful participation in decision making for all people" (NASW, 1996, p. 5).

If you are experiencing personal difficulty in accepting the ethical principle that social workers challenge social and economic injustice, this chapter should provide an opportunity for personal reflection and contemplation. Other professions, such as psychology and counseling, do not require the same level of commitment to social justice. Indeed, in these professions, social change, social advocacy, and social justice are not valued as explicit professional expectations or mandates. The belief that promoting social justice is integral to helping others succeed is a unique and defining attribute of social work.

Although few social workers would question the profession's commitment to social justice, identifying a commonly held, shared definition of the concept is more difficult. Longres and Scanlon (2001) contend that when social work educators were asked to explain the meaning of justice, "respondents often found themselves at a loss . . . faculty members did not provide formal definitions of justice nor did they usually demonstrate familiarity with the literature on justice" (p. 453). To complicate matters, justice was frequently referenced "both in social and economic terms [and] in macro as well as in micro terms" (p. 453).

Although it is clear that social workers assign importance to the quest for social justice, this enthusiasm is not always widely shared—particularly in a capitalistic society. Indeed, social justice, to some scholars, is neither a useful nor a relevant concept, but "wholly devoid of meaning and content" (Hayek, 1976, p. 96). Social workers need to recognize that for a segment of our citizenry, unencumbered and unimpaired pursuit and accumulation of resources is part and parcel of a free society. For many people, social-economic inequalities and distinctions are viewed as natural, functional, and justifiable.

When considering social work's ethical stance and the vested interest of the rich, one might expect social workers and affluent members of our society to disagree on the relevance of social justice. For wealthier Americans, the ability to amass possessions and privileges is accompanied by justifications for class differences and differential ability to exert power. Hard work, fortitude, persistence, superior intellect, capability, aptitude, and motivation are often earmarked as reasons for favored status in American society.

Interestingly, there is also an emerging literature describing ideological differences between social workers and members of the working and middle classes. Hodge (2003) suggests that the values of social workers are far more liberal concerning many political, economic, and social issues than those of working- and middle-class consumers of services. Furthermore, "conservative populations, who are disproportionately working class are, in aggregate, cognizant of the discrepancy in values between themselves and social workers, do not believe that social workers understand or respect their values" (Hodge, 2003, p. 116).

The potential for real and profound discrepancies between social workers and consumers concerning the conceptualization of social justice is an important consideration for macro social work practice. As noted in earlier chapters, strengths-based macro change relies heavily on the narratives, perspectives, and will of consumers. Indeed, it is likely that consumers would think about and embark upon social justice in ways far less radical than those of the social worker. In these instances, social workers "may have difficulty deconstructing left-wing values and engendering a strengths-based, empathic understanding of worldviews outside the purview of the knowledge class" (Hodge, 2003, p. 116).

As social justice is examined more closely, it is important to keep the perspectives of consumers as the focal point. In a very practical manner, consumers of services could often care little about philosophical, ideological, legalistic, or social work's definition of social justice. Although these notions can be helpful for us as practitioners in considering larger-scale social change, consumers are confronted with more pragmatic considerations than professionals. Consumers are blessed with their own, often unique, expertise on topics. Indeed, the insight of consumers concerning social justice may be as important as—or even more important than—wisdom from social workers, members of Hodge's "knowledge class."

DEFINING SOCIAL JUSTICE

Given that the definition of social justice is somewhat vague, often blurred, and subject to interpretation, it is helpful to identify important meanings and connotations commonly associated with justice. The work of Rawls (1999) represents a comprehensive analysis of the notion of justice and what constitutes a "just society." Although this is a complex subject, two distinct themes emerge from his work. First, a just society promotes the liberties of equal citizenship. Second, justice emphasizes equality of opportunity—that opportunity is open to all.

The crux of Rawls's argument concerning social justice involves "the basic structure of society, or more exactly, the way in which major social institutions distribute fundamental rights and duties and determine the division of advantages from social cooperation" and how "the major institutions define [women's and] men's rights and duties and influence their life prospects, what they can expect to be and how well they hope to do" (Rawls, 1999, pp. 6–7).

For macro–level social work practice, this conceptualization of social justice has profound implications. Foremost, it suggests distinguishing social justice from charity. Charity offers consumers basic assistance (goods and resources) in times of hardship. Social justice, too, involves the distribution of resources (physical and otherwise), but it is a broader and more encompassing notion: *Social justice involves promoting and establishing equal liberties, rights, duties, and opportunities in the social institutions (economy, polity, family, religion, education, etc.) of a society for all citizens.* Justice, by this definition, is both social and economic. Justice encompasses many dimensions and becomes embedded in the very fabric and structures (institutions, laws, policies, and programs) of a social system or society.

The "social" of social justice has a second meaning. It references "inspiring, working with, and organizing others to accomplish together a work of justice" (Novak, 2000, p. 11). In this connection, social justice can be viewed as being as much process as product, involving actions carried out with others to promote, affect, or help design just systems and practices (p. 11). This usage seems particularly relevant to strengths-based macro practice, as it highlights the need for consumers, professionals, and other interested parties to "come together" and inspire various works and practices of justice through collaboration.

The struggle for social justice is a social process, not an individual endeavor. People approaching social justice alone, as individuals, will experience frustration over their limited potential for success. Thorough examination of a complex issue such as social justice necessitates thoughtful reflection with others. The vantage point of any individual, including people in positions of leadership, is restricted. Hence, the ability to promote liberties, opportunities, and rights is as much socially as intellectually derived.

The process of coming to know (intellectually) with others about issues of social justice also requires that participants be open to questioning existing practices, entertaining new ideas, and advancing change. How often have you attended meetings where differing or opposing ideas and positions were neither solicited nor valued? You probably asked yourself, "Why was I invited or required to be present?" If people had been allowed to participate fully and critically in the meeting, the group could have reached a comprehensive and richer understanding of the issues. Indeed, the capacity to question stances, practices, policies, programs, and positions in a social forum is fundamental when approaching issues of social justice.

Distributive and Relational (Processual) Justice

The ability to identify specific types of social justice is helpful for practitioners and consumers alike. Social justice is an abstract concept that can seem overwhelming—more of an ideal or utopian state than a practical goal. Whenever possible, social justice needs to be demystified and captured in terms that are understandable by consumers and other segments of the population.

In a concrete fashion, social justice can be broken into two meanings. **Distributive justice** refers to the manner in which social and economic goods and services are distributed or spread throughout a society. A second, related but distinguishable orientation involves **relational justice** or processual justice—focusing on "decision making processes that lead to decisions about distribution and to the relationships between dominant and subordinate groups" (Longres & Scanlon, 2001, p. 448).

For experienced social workers, it goes without saying that consumers of services routinely contend with distributive justice—the actual (often disparate) distribution of goods and services in an organization, community, or society. This is particularly evident in a prosperous nation like the United States, where there are noticeable differences in the division of goods and services and associated lifestyles across groups of people and segments of society. In everyday practice, social workers devote a considerable amount of their time to helping consumers identify and seek strategies to procure needed resources—basic, desired, or otherwise.

Of equal or greater importance for consumers is the way decisions are made concerning the distribution of goods and services—relational or processual justice. Careful, thorough analysis of decision-making processes is crucial for consumers. It allows for and can yield opportunities for consumers, both individually and collectively, to affect the distribution of societal resources. The ability to influence decision making can take place in a number of ways in a variety of social institutions (economics, social welfare education, religion, the family, and politics). Alignment with relational or processual justice encourages consumers to focus on how resources, liberties, rights, duties, and opportunities are "divvied up."

Suffice it to say that the notion of social justice transcends simple distributive references to fairness, equity, and equality. Instead, *social justice*, particularly in a macro sense, also references the ability of consumers to affect decision-making processes governing the distribution of social and economic resources, liberties, duties, rights, and opportunities for their own (the consumers') good. In this sense, social justice is both dynamic and action-oriented. Efforts of social workers and consumers alike become directed toward empowerment. There is heightened awareness and concern for establishing ways to actively reach out and influence policy and program decisions in the name of social justice.

BOX 10.1

When consumers feel powerless and alienated from decision making, they say (collectively or individually):

- There is nothing that we can do.
- What we say or think does not matter.
- There is no place for us here.
- No one is listening.

- No one understands or feels like we do.
- Nothing will change, so why should we try?
- Decisions are made elsewhere.
- Why pretend our ideas make a difference?

When social justice prevails, people are not only respected and consulted, but their opinions are valued and they are able to exert power and take control over their own lives. A "just society" acknowledges the potential for contributions from all of its members and engages people in decision-making processes that affect their lives. Cohen, de la Vega, and Watson (2001) offer the following suggestions to enhance consumer participation in decision-making processes. Consumers should:

- Introduce, endorse, and ratify decisions, both formally or informally.
- Engage in visioning and plan solutions to issues affecting their (consumers') lives.
- Assess and provide feedback concerning existing and prospective programs and services.
- Secure public space, support, and procedures to challenge unjust behaviors and actions. (p. 8)

BOX 10.2

When consumers feel engaged in decision-making processes, they (collectively or individually) ask:

- Are our rights or liberties being violated or infringed upon?
- How can we more closely examine this (e.g., law, policy, or program)?
- What can we do to make things better?

- Why does this have to stay the same?
- What is our first (or next) step?
- Where and when we can meet?
- Who among us has the passion, time, and abilities to address this issue?
- How can we question and challenge this policy or practice?
- Are we getting a fair deal?

WHY PROMOTE SOCIAL JUSTICE
AT THE SOCIETAL LEVEL?

Interestingly, social workers have historically viewed macro social work practice as intervening with groups of people, organizations, and communities.
Societal change has often been seen as less do-able. Social work practitioners
and educators belabor these questions: How much can we really affect society?
Who has time to advance societal change? Society is too big and complex a target for change. Consumers can feel the impact of society, but society is difficult
to see and analyze.

American society is complex—diverse, geographically spread out, urbanized,
scientifically and technologically advanced, industrialized, and filled with special-
interest groups vying for resources. Accordingly, living conditions and the ability
to influence life circumstances at the societal level often seem too complicated
and unwieldy for each of us. Yet, it is important for us to conceptualize society as
a separate, real, and potentially powerful unit of analysis for change.

Sociologists tell us that societies grow, change, adapt, and are susceptible
to social influences. When a society experiences change, the ramifications
can be wide-ranging and often stimulate advances at smaller system levels—
communities, organizations, and families. And, "For those people who are living
in a state of oppression or deprivation, and for those who are morally outraged by
some aspect of society, neither individual nor organizational change is sufficiently wide-ranging. It is necessary to bring about change at a larger level, in
the power structure of the society or its laws or culture or institutions" (Lauer,
1991, pp. 412–413).

Accordingly, consumers need to be realistically encouraged, not dissuaded,
from seeing societal mandates, beliefs, and values as possible spheres for engagement and advancement. Although there is often disagreement in the United
States over the role of federalism and "big government," particularly in relation
to social welfare, it is clear to many that "to reduce the federal role through
decentralizing opens up the door to even greater diversity among the states"
(Morris, 1986, p. 235). Indeed, it may be "that only greater federal involvement
can assure fair treatment of those in need" (DiNitto, 1995, p. 162).

The tendency to push decision making over liberties, rights, duties, opportunities and the distribution of goods and services to smaller system sizes represents **social reductionism.** As you will recall from our overview of the
historical development of macro social work practice in Chapter 1, societies
often experience significant shifts in the political and public mandates for exercising social responsibility. Under certain social-economic circumstances, the
federal government assumes accountability for promoting social justice. At
other times, the states and local governments are delegated greater authority to
monitor and influence distributive and relational justice. Economic conditions,
international conflict, crisis, technological advances, and ideological shifts, as
well as a variety of other factors, can trigger changes in public sentiment with
respect to the role of federalism.

Linhorst (2002) argues the importance of advocacy for social justice at multiple levels—federal, state, and local. He also suggests "the need for social workers to adapt their approaches for promoting social justice to the particular phase of federalism" (p. 204). For example, if state and local governments are unable or unwilling to support efforts to promote justice (laws, policies, funding, and programs), then pressure for the federal government to be more assertive is necessary. Conversely, "although changes at the federal level are the most efficient for enacting social justice policies, lobbying each state to achieve social justice for all Americans becomes a necessity during times of federal inaction" (p. 203).

You will find that many consumer-oriented voluntary organizations and professional organizations have organized themselves in order to promote justice at all levels—local, state, and national. As an example, the National Alliance for the Mentally Ill (NAMI; www.nami.org) is the nation's largest organization working to improve the lives of people affected by mental illness. In addition to its national prominence, NAMI is a comprehensive system of more than 1,200 state and local affiliates with over 200,000 members.

NAMI provides an important and powerful consumer voice in advancing the rights and liberties of persons experiencing mental illness. For example, state and federal parity legislation is a current priority for consumers of mental health services. Parity laws would require health care insurers to provide comparable coverage and benefits for mental health and physical health services. Currently, many insurers focus almost exclusively on physical medical needs.

Parity legislation is a matter of social justice. It involves rights and liberties for persons with mental illness. Thus, organizations like NAMI act to educate and influence decision-making processes concerning the creation and enactment of parity legislation at both state and federal levels.

NAMI is a highly visible and recognized leader, both nationally and locally, in advocacy, research, education, and supportive services for people experiencing mental illness. If your intention is to practice in the area of mental health, you will quickly get to know the local NAMI representatives. Conversation and discourse with members of NAMI is just one way that social workers can better hear the voices of consumers on issues of mental health. Be attentive to seeking and nurturing various means of consumer engagement (e.g., community forums, consumer councils, and social action groups).

Similarly, the National Organization for Women (NOW; www.now.org) is the largest organization of feminist activists in the United States, with chapters in all fifty states and the District of Columbia. Dedicated to bringing about equality for women, NOW provides a valuable and powerful voice for women in advancing rights and seeking liberties.

NOW has been a major force in advocating for social change (e.g., supporting women in the workplace, advocating for an equal rights amendment for women, ending violence against women, promoting diversity, and supporting abortion rights, reproductive freedom, and lesbian rights) both nationally and locally. NOW members organize marches and rallies, participate in nonviolent civil disobedience, file lawsuits, and use a variety of traditional and nontraditional means to promote social justice for women.

Whatever the unit of analysis (society, community, or local area), active engagement of consumers in dialogue concerning issues of social justice is exciting work. It requires knowledge of rights, freedoms, laws, policies, and practices affecting a population group. Concerning this type of information, consumers are highly motivated, self-educated, and rich in everyday wisdom with respect to their rights and limitations. Although professionals are genuinely interested in the population groups they serve, consumers are confronted with their conditions on a regular, even a daily basis. Issues of social justice for consumers surround them.

As suggested in Chapters 3 and 4, social workers can readily call upon the passion of consumers to educate and inform others of their situation. And although professionals, administrators, and policymakers may believe they are experts concerning themes of justice for a particular group of people, the perspective of the consumer is often the most enlightening and grounded in reality of all. The social worker's role is to capture, harness, and direct these energies for the deliberate and thoughtful examination of decision-making processes affecting social justice for consumers.

In preparation for this type of intense dialogue and discourse, Gil (2002) warns that social workers "need to be sensitive to the thoughts, feelings, and circumstances of people . . . positions people hold do make sense to them in terms of their life experiences and frames of reference" (p. 49). Respect for differing perspectives is paramount "even when their [consumers'] positions and values conflict with those of the activist" (p. 49). After all, it is the consumers' images of social reality that social workers hope to discover and help portray to other segments of the population and the majority of the U.S. public.

In many respects, societal change hinges on the ability of consumers and professionals "to develop impressive sound bites, not only to capture major policy issues, but also to define where we [consumers] are and how we [consumers] got that way" and what can be done about conditions affecting consumers (Wilson, 1999, p. 24). "Impressive sound bites" does not mean glib, oversimplified depictions of complex issues. Instead, the phrase suggests an ability to translate matters of justice into understandable and acceptable terminology that a wide range of people can readily relate to and embrace.

For example, when examining issues of social justice for the poor, the following slogans could be persuasive: "If people work, they ought not to be poor," or "Your ZIP code and who your parents are shouldn't determine the quality of education you have" (Wilson, 1999, p. 24). These sayings invite thought and discussion and would appeal to many people in the United States.

Brawley and Martinez-Brawley (1999) are well known in the social work profession for their scholarship examining the promotion of social justice through partnerships with mass media. They suggest that "[a]dvocates for social justice need to become more media-literate and active participants in these public agenda setting, opinion making, and policy formulation processes" (p. 64).

Working with the media is a multifaceted undertaking. It involves establishing relationships with members of the press and other media personnel in order to better inform the public. In particular, newspapers, radio, and television represent means of communication to enhance "the public's understanding of critical social justice civil rights issues and appropriate responses to these issues" (Brawley & Martinez-Brawley, 1999, p. 82).

Educating the public through the media can take many forms. Brawley (1988) suggests that appropriate activities for social workers would include providing accurate information, articulating the activities of social workers, educating people about the merits of services, communicating supportive messages that are helpful to consumer groups, and encouraging the creation of mutual-aid groups (pp. 15–16). In the context of strengths-based macro practice, activities (e.g., portrayals and depictions) presented to the media facilitating the public's understanding of social justice issues also appear appropriate. However, special care is required to assure that professional obligations to consumers (e.g., confidentiality and privacy of information) are maintained.

"THE POWER OF SOCIAL WORK: PRESERVING RIGHTS. STRENGTHENING VOICES"

"Preserving rights. Strengthening voices" was the National Association of Social Workers' theme for 2003. NASW President Terry Mizrahi and Executive Director Elizabeth Clark suggest that this subject "focuses on an essential tenet of social work practice—many people thinking, working and acting together to empower those who are frequently unheard" (NASW, 2003, p. 1).

Although March is the month each year that Americans celebrate the work of more than 500,000 social workers, "preserving rights and strengthening voices" accurately reflects an ongoing commitment of our profession. Social workers have historically been dedicated to the promotion of "children's rights, civil rights, disability rights, lesbian and gay rights, crime victims' rights, labor rights, women's rights, human rights, among many other movements. The profession began, and continues to lead, many efforts that enhance human well-being" (NASW, 2003, p. 11). Social work's emphasis on achieving a just society has embraced, and continues to take, many forms.

How do social workers engage in preserving rights and **strengthening voices**? This is an important but difficult question, because engagement in social work practice is consumer-centered and consumer-driven. Typically practicing in the context of a social service agency, social workers are charged by their profession to follow the will and passion of the people they serve. Thus, consumers determine which domain deserves attention for preserving rights and strengthening voices. Similarly, it is through healthy conversation and discourse with consumers that the most appropriate means of preserving rights and strengthening voices concerning an issue are determined.

Social workers should be wary of standardized, cookie-cutter approaches to eliciting consumer engagement. No single methodology can be used to effectively capture the spirit of consumers. Instead, social workers need to be flexible and creative in encouraging consumers to assume ownership in determining the best and most appropriate means for preserving *their* rights and strengthening *their* voices.

You can be sure that on issues involving rights and resources there will be individuals, groups, and organizations competing and vying for their vested interests and voices to be heard. Indeed, it is not uncommon for social service agencies and voluntary organizations to develop their own special-interest associations. Ask about special-interest groups, provider councils, and other associations that are recognized as effective lobbying entities in your community.

To help us think about macro-level change, social workers have identified several domains of engagement that have been traditionally applicable to the many faces and forms of social work practice. Regardless of the population group you serve, these are potential areas for consumer and professional involvement. In the spirit of promoting social justice, social workers do the following:

1. Advocate for improved health care coverage and access
2. Promote global human rights
3. Promote justice for all
4. Advocate for improvements in educational systems
5. Build partnerships with others
6. Support economic and social equity
7. Create social change through grassroots organizing (NASW, 2003, pp. 7–16).

Be advised: social workers cannot, and are not expected to, do or be all things for all people. There are many people who have left the profession of social work as a result of overextending themselves in the name of social justice. Call it "burnout," a lack of balance in life, or a lapse in setting professional–personal boundaries—it is not difficult to become overly consumed with a social cause. As passionate as a social worker might feel about an issue of social justice while working with consumers, special care needs to be given not to compromise anyone's personal, social, or mental well-being. Social workers and consumers alike can alienate family and friends when they become obsessed with the pursuit of social justice.

PRACTICAL CONSIDERATIONS
FOR PROMOTING SOCIAL JUSTICE

From a strengths-based approach, several points are provided for consideration by professionals and consumers when addressing issues of social justice. These suggestions are appropriate both for affecting the decision-making process (relational justice) and in procuring resources (distributive justice). They are also suitable for application in practice with a multitude of population groups.

1. *Pursue social justice with intended (specific) outcomes.* Social workers often conceptualize empowerment and the quest for social justice "as important in and of itself, without any connection to the outcome . . . [where] consumers emphasized tangible outcomes that achieved concrete results" (Boehm & Staples, 2002, pp. 452–453). Although process and outcomes are connected, it is clear that social workers can become overly focused on process (e.g., strengthening consumer skills, capacities, and control), while consumers continue to experience concrete forms of social injustice (e.g., oppression and discrimination).

2. *Promote consumer leadership as a joint (social) enterprise.* Leadership involves the ability to equip consumers to create an environment of sharing and questioning. "You become a leader as you contribute your perceptions, understanding, intuition, and values to the group. Macro social work is committed to help all engage in leadership, not just 'the best and brightest' or those who are most skilled in impersonal rational problem-solving" (Brueggemann, 2002, p. 88). Leadership concerning issues of social justice needs to be socially derived, defined, and owned.

3. *Prosper from coalition building.* Examine the benefit(s) of forming coalitions with those who hold different philosophical perspectives but support common goals for social justice—the "strange bedfellows" phenomenon. Many people share a common view with respect to human needs, rights, opportunities, and liberties. **Coalition building**—the pooling of thought, dialogue, and resources—can be beneficial to all concerned. Work to "gain as much understanding as possible about the social justice perspective held by individuals and groups with whom a coalition is sought," and try to "use language and arguments that are consistent with the social justice perspective held by those with whom you are communicating" (Van Soest, 1994, p. 716).

4. *Construct a clear, understandable message that appeals to many segments.* We do live in a "sound bite" society. Consumers and social workers must appeal to and educate segments of the population who are not experiencing a particular form of injustice. For example, "if you don't address the concerns of the non-poor segments of the population who are struggling, they [the more fortunate] are not going to be real interested" in poverty or joining in the quest to combat poverty (Wilson, 1999, p. 24).

5. *Seek power.* Social justice, regardless of its form, involves "processes and outcomes whereby less powerful individuals and groups move to reduce discrepancies in power relationships" (Boehm & Staples, 2002, p. 450). The procurement of rights, opportunities, liberties, and responsibilities means the acquisition of power to control one's life. People do not live, function, or play on "equal playing fields." Acquiring social justice is directly related to the ability of any group of people to claim and exert power and control over their lives.

HOW FAR DARE WE GO?

It would be wonderful to say that the quest for social justice in strengths-based practice is boundless, and many would agree that social justice should be viewed as limitless. But idealism must be tempered by realism. The process of seeking and securing resources, liberties, rights, and opportunities with consumers is filled with "contradictions, quandaries, and questions, such as . . . [w]hat if being true to my empowerment principles will get me fired?" (Cohen, 2002, p. 143). It prompts the question, "How far can social workers and consumers push boundaries in the context of macro practice, especially when social justice involves examining and confronting sources of power?"

As mentioned earlier, social workers usually practice as paid employees in social service organizations. As a consequence, the practice of social work is defined in the context of organizational rules and policies as well as an administrative chain of command. For the social worker, a thorough examination of the various terms and conditions of employment is very important and can lead to insights on several levels. It can illuminate the potential of one's social service organization to support consumer efforts for social justice. It can also identify organizational constraints and barriers that work to impede progress in the pursuit of social justice for consumers.

Organizational control that regulates the activities of the social worker should be expected and respected. In addition to ethical obligations to consumers, the

---

BOX 10.3　Social Service Agencies as Resources and Allies in Promoting Social Justice

Here are a few helpful tips for creating, building, and securing opportunities for working with consumers on issues of social justice at your agency:

- Know your policies and procedures manual, and seek ways to include or improve language that supports the ability of social workers and consumers to engage actively in activities concerning social justice.
- Be aware of and follow the administrative chain of command at your place of employment. In an appropriate fashion, consult with and advise supervisors of your actions involving themes of social justice. Embrace administrators as allies in the quest for social justice.

- Educate agency personnel and employers as to the NASW *Code of Ethics* and your professional obligations and responsibilities (e.g., social and political action) in social work practice in relation to the pursuit of social justice (NASW, 1996, p. 21).
- Whenever possible, be a role model of professional behavior by advocating for fair and open resource allocation procedures and decision-making processes that include consumer input, both within and outside your agency (NASW, 1996, p. 20).
- Provide information and research to administrators concerning relevant issues of social justice.

NASW *Code of Ethics* (1996) delineates many important responsibilities for social workers in relation to their practice settings. This includes a commitment to employers to "adhere to commitments made to employers and employing organizations" while working "to improve employing agencies' policies and procedures" (p. 21).

This clearly places social workers in difficult and, at times, perilous positions. Indeed, "Acting as an agent of social change may require combating the power of agencies' hierarchies, funding sources, accrediting bodies, and even our own power as professionals" (Cohen, 2002, p. 153). Working for social justice, particularly procuring resources and affecting decision making at the societal level, can be risky business. It is not unusual to have both one's professional and personal motivations challenged when acting with consumers for collective empowerment and structural change.

SUMMARY

The issue of social justice lies at the heart and soul of the social work profession. Social justice has many dimensions, including rights, liberties, responsibilities, resources, and opportunities. It involves both the just distribution of power and resources and the ability to affect decision-making processes concerning these elements.

Macro practice from a strengths perspective, in this domain, can amply be summarized by the professional call to "preserve rights and strengthen voices." This chapter has identified and examined practical considerations to assist practitioners as they engage in efforts to promote a just society. The emphasis has clearly been on empowering consumers to question and enter into productive conversations to challenge injustices and secure rights and liberties. Readers are also asked to contemplate the pursuit of social justice at multiple levels (national, state, and local), as dictated by the position and will of consumers. Finally, consumers and social workers need to ask one another, both idealistically and realistically, "How far dare we go?" in the search for social justice—remembering that consumers are often interested in specific outcomes, not just process.

A FEW KEY TERMS

social justice	relational justice	strengthening voices
distributive justice	social reductionism	coalition building

USING INFOTRAC®
COLLEGE EDITION AND INFOWRITE

InfoTrac College Edition

Social justice at the societal level often requires the coming together of various groups of people to brainstorm ideas, identify common interests, and pool resources. Hence, efforts to promote social justice prosper from coalition building and the ability to form healthy partnerships among concerned parties. Before attempting to pull together and unite groups of people, it is helpful to read about the successes of others in coalition building. Complete the following exercise:

1. Go to InfoTrac College Edition.

2. Under the Keyword Search, search using "social justice coalitions" or "social justice partnerships."

3. Browse through the articles and identify one that focuses on promoting social justice at the societal level through the use of coalitions.

4. Wilson (1999) suggests that we live in a "sound bite" society. Construct several one-sentence slogans, jingles, or phrases that capture the spirit of your article. Strive for both substance and creativity. You want people to remember the sentence as well as its message.

5. Do your article and one-sentence description involve distributive justice, relational justice, or both?

InfoWrite

In the preceding exercise, you were asked to summarize an article involving social justice in one sentence. This requires focus, brevity, and the ability to express thoughts in a succinct fashion. It represents a unique ability in writing. In order to refine your writing skills:

1. Go to InfoWrite.

2. Scroll to Modes of Expression.

3. Read the sections focusing on Narration.

4. Pay special attention to Developing Focus and Selecting Topics for Narrative Essays.

It is good to practice the ability to reduce long, narrative works to a clear thesis or a specific topic. This particular section of InfoWrite provides useful tips for writing brief papers or narrative pieces. The Narrative Checklist is a handy tool for reviewing your work and encourages this style of writing. Many agencies and organizations produce newsletters and Web sites to inform their constituency groups and promote participation. Contributors should consider the suggestions offered in this section in preparing pieces for these types of publications.

CASE EXAMPLE: Hate Crimes and Sexual Orientation

At first glance, the newspaper article appeared to read like so many others in the past, a holiday shooting in an entertainment district of a big city. Bad things sometimes happen over the holidays. New Year's Eve is a particularly vulnerable night for crime—excessive drinking, drunk driving, and parties of all sorts. People are prone to do irrational things in moments of drug-induced impairment, excitement, and passion.

A closer examination of the news article revealed that this murder was quite different from most killings. Two young men holding hands were walking down a street in a trendy bar district when people in a passing car began to shout antigay epithets. Moments later, a shot rang out, and one of the two young pedestrians was dead. The city's forty-seventh homicide of the year was a hate crime targeted against two thirty-year-old men on the basis of their sexual orientation.

The assailants will be tried for murder. In this particular state, however, hate crime law does not include sexual orientation. And, although there are several city ordinances against hate crimes, criminalizing misdemeanors involving assault, menacing, telephone harassment, and vandalism, local law also does not include sexual orientation as a basis for prosecution.

As you might expect, the gay, lesbian, bisexual, and transsexual (GLBT) community has provided an outpouring of concern and support to the survivor and the victims' families and friends. This has been very important in helping those affected most directly by the shooting to cope with this tragedy. But all agree that much more needs to be done.

Given the politically conservative mood of the federal government, those closest to the deceased have chosen to introduce city and state legislation to extend protective status against hate crimes to people on the basis of sexual orientation. Currently, city hate crime law applies only to race, color, religion, and national origin. Along with sexual orientation, activists are also proposing that protection against hate crimes be provided to people on the basis of gender, age, and disability.

For the GLBT community, hate crimes constitute a violation of basic human rights and a matter of social justice. Communities and states need to send a clear message that threats or violence of any kind that targets people on the basis of their sexual orientation will not be tolerated. In particular, hate crimes work to strike fear in the hearts of identifiable groups of people who have not done anything wrong. These threats and actions inhibit participation in many social and civic activities, impairing the ability of gays and lesbians to share in community-based functions and decision-making processes.

As fundamental as the right of protection from violence may seem, the expansion of the hate crime laws to include sexual orientation will not be easy in this community or this state. Efforts have already met resistance from conservative groups espousing "community values." Indeed, several years ago these same groups opposed the passage of local ordinances designed to ban various forms of discrimination against gays and lesbians.

Fortunately, local organizers from the GLBT community are not in this battle alone. Organizations such as the National Gay and Lesbian Task Force (NGLTF) have been working for years to organize people, identify and train leaders, equip activists, build

(continued)

CASE EXAMPLE   (continued)

grassroots movements, and form coalitions to develop a social justice movement linking progressive ideas to action. One of the NGLTF's current campaigns involves addressing the needs of state and local organizers in promoting legislation against anti-GLBT hate crimes.

The NGLTF is a national organization that offers a number of supportive services and programs (e.g., research, policy analysis, strategy development, public education, and coalition building) to assist local efforts in promoting rights, liberties, and opportunities for this constituency group. The NGLTF respects and celebrates the dignity and diversity of all people. Hence, it encourages and promotes linkages and partnerships with a number of groups and organizations fighting hate crimes as well as other forms of oppression (e.g., on the basis of race, class, and gender). A comprehensive examination of the mission and services of the NGLTF, as well as an overview of current issues and news, can be found on their Web site (www.ngltf.org).

Legislation against hate crimes is a specific, concrete outcome that has been identified both by the people victimized by this particular heinous shooting and, more generally, by members of the GLBT community. The clear message is that communities and states should not tolerate people being targeted for violence and crime as a result of their sexual orientation. And, although some professionals and activists would argue that hate crime

legislation does not go far enough in protecting the rights of gays and lesbians, it is clear that the perceptions and understanding of consumers have been given primary consideration.

For Kevin, a social worker employed by a community-based victims' rights organization, this has been an extremely difficult case. His consumer is the sole survivor of the hate crime. And, although his agency has been very supportive of his participation in micro-level interventions (e.g., grief counseling), his employer has been less than enthusiastic about the pursuit of hate crime legislation on the basis of sexual orientation.

It appears that Kevin's employer receives city funds and monies from the county. Local leaders reflect the conservative nature of the community and are not in favor of increasing the rights and liberties of the GLBT community. Nearly a decade ago, these same politicians and businesspeople successfully passed legislation prohibiting city law from giving protection to people on the basis of sexual orientation. To Kevin's credit, he has kept his supervisor and other agency administrators aware of activities with regard to hate crime legislation. He has reviewed his agency's policies, which support his active involvement in this type of macro-practice endeavor. Kevin has also consulted with leadership from his local and state NASW chapters to keep them informed of his actions and to be proactive with respect to any ethical considerations.

THINKING CRITICALLY
ABOUT THE CASE EXAMPLE

1. This case example rests on an underlying assumption. Because of similar interests and concerns, is it reasonable to believe that the National Gay and Lesbian Task Force (NGLTF) and local gay, lesbian, bisexual, and transsexual (GLBT) groups are destined to work together in a seamless and concerted fashion? Because of vested interests, are strategic and tactical differences inevitable when national and local organizations are called upon to coordinate their activities? Contemplate whether divisiveness between groups is more likely to occur for issues involving basic human rights (e.g., protection from physical and mental harm). Think about how potential conflict between organizations can be reframed and redirected into sources of strength.

2. Can social justice, distributive or relational, for groups of people be attained state by state and city by city? In this case example, given the federal mood toward progressive legislation, protection from hate crimes is being sought at the local level. Although legislative initiatives at the city level may be most realistic, how would federal legislation be more effective? Identify ways that community-level energy can be converted or channeled into momentum to promote federal legislation.

3. Activists have broadened their efforts to include protection against hate crimes for people on the basis of gender, age, and disability. Is this a good strategy? Identify the strengths and limitations of using this kind of approach.

REFLECTION EXERCISES

1. Secure a list of student organizations and clubs sponsored by your college or university. Identify organizations that advocate for rights, liberties, and opportunities of constituents at the national level. Are there any organizations whose causes you either *disagree with* or *do not find interesting*? If so, consider making arrangements to attend one of their meetings. Listen carefully to the dialogue and materials presented at such a gathering. Strive to understand the positions, perspectives, and passions of the members. Ask yourself if you could work with this group of people as consumers. What might be difficult for you? Why? Is it better to align yourself with issues of social justice for which you have enthusiasm? Is this always possible or practical?

2. Consumers are interested in pursuing concrete objectives when working for social justice. Surf the Web and find an Internet site that is dedicated to an issue of social justice in our society. Does the organization delineate specific goals and desired outcomes for its constituency? Are the goals and outcomes specific and open to

operationalization? What kind of a time framework is offered for achieving these gains? How much of the Web site is devoted to affecting decision-making processes? Assess the Web site's ability to share information among consumers. Can you identify from the site any viable organizations for coalition-building efforts?

3. Enter a conversation or structure opportunities for one or more dialogues with students majoring in psychology, sociology, counseling, and/or other helping professions at your school. Do students from these disciplines hold a professional commitment to promote a just society? What is their reaction to your professional responsibilities with respect to social justice? Do they have a commitment to large-scale structural change? Do the other students know anything about the strengths orientation? How does your professional orientation to promote social justice differentiate you from others?

SUGGESTED READINGS

Allen, J. A. (1997). Social justice, social change, and baccalaureate degree generalist social work practice. *Journal of Baccalaureate Social Work, 3*(1), 14–16.

Brawley, E. A., & Martinez-Brawley, E. E. (1999). Promoting social justice in partnership with the mass media. *Journal of Sociology and Social Welfare, 16*(2), 63–86.

Finn, J. L., & Jacobson, M. (2003). *Just practice: A social justice approach to social work.* Peosta, IA: Eddie Bowers.

Rawls, J. (1999). *A theory of justice.* Cambridge, MA: The Belknap Press of Harvard University Press.

REFERENCES

Boehm, A., & Staples, L. H. (2002). The functions of the social worker in empowering: The voices of consumers and professionals. *Social Work, 47,* 449–460.

Brawley, E. A. (1988). Promoting human well-being through the mass media. *Arete, 12*(1), 11–20.

Brawley, E. A., & Martinez-Brawley, E. E. (1999). Promoting social justice in partnership with the mass media. *Journal of Sociology and Social Welfare, 16*(2), 63–86.

Brueggemann, W. G. (2002). *The practice of macro social work.* Belmont, CA: Brooks/Cole.

Cohen, D., de la Vega, R., & Watson, G. (2001). *Advocacy for social justice: A global action and reflection guide.* Bloomfield, CT: Kumarian Press.

Cohen, M. B. (2002). Pushing the boundaries in empowerment-oriented social work practice. In M. O'Melia & K. Miley (Eds.), *Pathways to power: Readings in contextual social work practice.* Boston: Allyn & Bacon.

DiNitto, D. M. (1995). *Social welfare: Politics and public policy.* Boston: Allyn & Bacon.

Gil, D. (2002). Challenging injustice and oppression. In M. O'Melia & K. Miley

(Eds.), *Pathways to power: Readings in contextual social work practice*. Boston: Allyn & Bacon.

Hayek, F. A. (1976). *Law, legislation, and liberty, Vol. 2: The mirage of social justice*. London: Routledge & Kegan Paul.

Hodge, D. R. (2003). Value differences between social workers and members of the working and middle classes. *Social Work, 48,* 107–119.

Lauer, R. H. (1991). *Perspectives on social change*. Boston: Allyn & Bacon.

Linhorst, D. (2002). Federalism and social justice: Implications for social work. *Social Work, 47,* 201–208.

Longres, J. F., & Scanlon, E. (2001). Social justice and the research curriculum. *Journal of Social Work Education, 37,* 447–463.

Morris, R. (1986). *Rethinking social welfare: Why care for the stranger?* New York: Longman.

National Association of Social Workers. (1996). *Code of ethics.* Washington, DC: NASW Press.

————. (2003). *NASW Social Work Month 2003: Preserving rights. Strengthening voices.* Washington, DC: NASW Press.

Novak, M. (2000). Defining social justice. *First Things, 108,* 11–13.

Rawls, J. (1999). *A theory of justice.* Cambridge, MA: The Belknap Press of Harvard University Press.

Van Soest, D. (1997). Strange bedfellows: A call for reordering national priorities from three social justice perspectives. *Social Work, 39,* 710–717.

Wilson, W. J. (1999). A coalition of power and hope. *Sojourners, 28,* 24.

11

Evaluating
Macro Change

Chapter Content Areas

Understanding Reality

Logic of Scientific Inquiry

Decision Making in Research

Descriptive Research

Exploratory Research

Explanatory Research

Evaluation Research

Stakeholders

Program Monitoring

Participatory Research

Grounded Research

Action Research

Awareness Contexts

Criticisms of Participatory Research

Strengths-Based Principles in Participatory Research

Strengths-Based Measures of Macro Change

Examples of Participatory Research

Participatory Research and Welfare Reform

THE QUEST TO UNDERSTAND REALITY

"A researcher cannot easily see through the eyes of those being studied" (Newman, 1997, p. 391). This is a profound, yet humbling, assertion that many social workers and scientists come to appreciate during their lifetime of work. Guided by professional education and advanced degrees and armed with the logic of scientific inquiry, social scientists possess a degree of expertise in relationship to investigations of the social world. Concepts are defined and theories postulated with varying degrees of consideration given to the ideas, thinking, and perspectives of the very people being studied. To complicate matters, some

© Thomson Higher Education/Heinle Image Bank.

researchers would interpret inviting consumer participation in the research process as introducing a source of contamination, bias, or subjectivity.

Social scientists are much like historians and others who seek knowledge in that they do "not even include in his [or her] account all the material with which he [or she] is either directly or indirectly acquainted. He [or she] selects certain aspects of the event which he [or she] describes, ignoring other aspects" (Mandelbaum, 1938, p. 23). In this sense, the perspective of the scientist is by definition constrained and limited. The thinking of scientists is confined intellectually, by professional discipline, and experientially, by the individual scientist's life experiences.

It is relatively easy to see that in a purely scientific sense, adherence to one's professional expertise or scientific discipline results in a "selected perspective on the material in question" that can serve to hinder or limit discovery (Mandelbaum, 1938, p. 23). In the social sciences, psychologists seek to explain social change through the thoughts, accomplishments, and actions of individuals. Sociologists concentrate on the influence of social forces in creating social change. Meanwhile, social workers are educated and trained to focus on the relationship and interaction between the person and the social environment.

Yet, complex issues involving change in large social systems (e.g., organizations, communities, and society) are usually attributable to many factors, biological, psychological, cultural, political, and social, some of which fall well beyond the professional realm and understanding of any single discipline or set of disciplines. And, although collaboration among scientists enriches and broadens the perspective pool, it is safe to say that a concerted effort to understand the point of view of the persons being studied or affected is often an underemphasized or missing component of social research.

THE LOGIC OF SCIENTIFIC INQUIRY

Scientific research is predicated on specific tenets that distinguish it from other forms of inquiry (e.g., theological or philosophical). Scientific pursuit of knowledge involves a rational and systematic process for pursuing knowledge involving a topic, a comprehensive review of literature, the formulation of a hypothesis or theory for testing, a specified methodology, and an analysis and reporting of findings. Social scientists build upon previous research in a cumulative fashion in an attempt to replicate previous research findings and advance knowledge.

At the heart of research is the struggle for objectivity, an attempt to eliminate bias and influence in the research process. Although objectivity is an ideal state, social scientists approach research in a manner designed to thwart subjectivity and pressure from others. Objectivity is sought through adherence to formulated rules and procedures that guide research and by the provision of checks and balances (e.g., entertaining divergent perspectives). Indeed, skepticism is deemed a desirable and healthy attribute to the extent that researchers question and challenge one another with respect to their adherence to scientific principles in research.

DECISIONS IN RESEARCH

When examining macro-level change, it is important to acknowledge, up front, that research is a process inundated with decisions. While scientists strive for objectivity, each determination in the research process is influenced by one's position, past experiences, and current outlook on life. Definition of concepts, formulation of theories and hypotheses, selection of variables, and decisions concerning the means of analysis involve an act of will by someone, traditionally the researcher(s).

The more visionary (progressive) thinker "seeks to understand and interpret particular insights from an ever more inclusive context" [in the hope of] "bring[ing] the conceptual system and empirical reality into closer contact with one another" (Mannheim, 1936, pp. 105, 200). In social work terminology, this means that it is important for researchers to seek the active involvement of consumers throughout the research process. This somewhat nontraditional view is a crucial step in enabling researchers to conceptualize the world through the eyes of the people being studied and to use the insights, talents, and abilities of consumers of services in social research.

A primary goal in this chapter is to examine ways to empower consumers to become full-fledged participants "in all stages of the research project, which includes education, reflection, research, and action . . . [where] academic and professional researchers serve not only as experts, but as co-learners who share their research skills and also recognize and benefit from the skills and knowledge of the other group members [including consumers]" (McNicoll, 2001, p. 91). Although this may seem ambitious, many researchers believe that it is time to confront long-established hierarchical models that have hindered practice-oriented research in the social sciences.

BOX 11.1 Assessing Stakeholders and Influences on Research

Stakeholders: When conducting research, take time to identify major stakeholders in the process. The following checklist will get you started. As you proceed in the research process, note how these stakeholders have acted or have attempted to act to influence methodological decisions.

Checklist:	Stakeholder	Influence on Research
_____	Funding source	
_____	Sponsoring organization	
_____	Research team	
_____	Administrators	
_____	Politicians	
_____	Special-interest group	
_____	Other:	
_____	Other:	
_____	Other:	

TRADITIONAL APPROACHES
TO SOCIAL RESEARCH

Social research is usually categorized as one of four kinds. Schutt (1996) summarizes these types of research as follows:

- *Descriptive research:* At first, researchers simply want to define what they are studying and describe the social phenomena of interest.

- *Exploratory research:* Some researchers seek to find out how people get along in the settings in question, what meanings they give to their actions, and what issues concern them.

- *Explanatory research:* The focus gradually shifts to the causes and effects of the phenomenon.

■ *Evaluation research:* Special attention is given to whether particular policies
and programs help to alleviate the problem (p. 13).

People conducting **descriptive research** collect data with the intent of better describing social phenomena. In macro social work practice, this could involve
collecting data describing a community, an organization, a service population
(e.g., teenagers or older adults), social conditions (e.g., poverty, opportunity or
lack of opportunity, or homelessness), and social actions (e.g., discrimination,
collaboration, and kinds of support). When considering specific kinds of social
phenomena, consumers of services often find themselves uniquely equipped to
facilitate an advanced understanding and description of influences and occurrences. For example, who better to "brainstorm" and identify factors related to
economic opportunity in a community than consumers of services who have
experienced a degree of upward mobility?

It should also be noted that social workers have a rich tradition of documenting needs, opportunities, and characteristics of people being served via
descriptive research. Funding sources often require such information (e.g., community needs assessments and consumer profiles). For social workers and consumers alike, descriptive data facilitate the identification of population groups at
risk and allow for a differential assessment of the availability of resources, barriers, and opportunities by consumer groups.

In **exploratory research,** the primary focus is on formulating or refining
definitions of concepts, issues, actions, and conditions. To initiate a preliminary
grasp of a phenomenon, situation, or circumstance, a beginning characteriza-
tion of what is occurring is needed. Consumers of services possess expertise in
providing these kinds of understandings and conceptual breakthroughs.

If you are interested in learning about the unique culture and areas of
strength of a particular social service agency, ask for a depiction of this organization from the perspective of consumers. They will often be able to identify
specific qualities and characteristics that differentiate a given human service
organization from its social counterparts. Without consumer insight, the sense
of discovery in exploratory research is often compromised.

One of the most difficult and complicated types of research is **explanatory
research.** Examining the causes and effects of social phenomena is a complex
matter, as causality likely involves multiple factors. For example, communities
typically change as a result of technological innovation, changes in leadership,
variations in the availability of resources, and population shifts. Understanding
the relevance, time order, and relationship among these and other relevant factors
in producing community-level change is greatly enhanced when incorporating
the views of consumers.

While social workers regularly engage in many forms of research, **evaluation research** is especially important in macro social work practice. Program
and policy development are common forms of macro-level intervention in
social work practice. Hence, the ability to weigh and measure the successes and
limitations associated with social programs and policies is fundamental to documenting macro-level change.

Particularly in the current age of accountability; administrators, professionals, and consumers alike are very interested in evaluating the effectiveness of social programs and services and policy initiatives. Americans want to know "how much bang for the buck." Politicians, government watchdog organizations, and special-interest groups often place intense pressure on administrators and service providers to demonstrate the efficacy of programs and policies.

Royse (1999) suggests that program evaluation has traditionally sought to address the following kinds of issues:

1. Are clients being helped?

2. Is there a better (i.e., cheaper, easier) way of doing this?

3. How does this effort or level of activity compare with what was produced or accomplished last year? (Did we achieve our objectives?)

4. How does our success rate compare with those of other agencies?

5. Should this program be continued?

6. How can we improve our program?

SOURCE: From *Research Methods in Social Work*, 3rd edition, by Royse, p. 255.
© 1999. Reprinted with permission of Wadsworth, a division of Thomson Learning:
www.thomsonrights.com. Fax: 800-730-2216.

Royse provides useful and important questions for study. For the social worker interested in implementing a strengths perspective, however, additional consideration should be given to identifying concrete mechanisms for including the insights and perspectives of consumers in evaluating social change. For example, how best could consumers be involved in defining criteria for program continuation? How can consumers give narrative (qualitative) feedback to improve programming?

Indeed, the effectiveness of any program, service, law, or policy needs to be contemplated and approached from multiple vantage points, but especially that of the consumer. Granted, this is a potentially unpopular and politically charged stance. Yet, measuring the success of any program or policy through the eyes and perceptions of the consumer—using the ideas of consumers concerning process and criteria for evaluating success—is an imperative in macro social work practice. Indeed, consumer-directed research represents as valuable and worthy a source of discovery as any other scientific endeavor.

FUNDING SOURCES AND RESEARCH

The interests of administrators, board members, legislators, and politicians are routinely imposed on helping professionals when evaluating program delivery and policy implementation. In these instances, social workers are required to produce documentation and statistics describing how consumers use service delivery (e.g., units of service by type and number of minutes). This information typically involves a detailed analysis of consumer characteristics (e.g., gender, age, social-economic status, and race) and the ability of consumers to meet or maintain eligibility requirements. Administrators are highly invested in identifying and tracking measures of consumer usage and worker production. This kind of information is used to demonstrate staff utilization and to justify the deployment of resources in the delivery of services.

Research emphasizing consumer attributes and units of service tends to emphasize cost efficiency and can be accounting-oriented. This type of data collection is typically time-consuming and is frequently viewed by practitioners as an accountability requirement dictated by funding sources. In fact, in conjunction with the expectations of funding sources, cost analyses by type of consumer group are often used by administrators as a basis for pinpointing allocation or reallocation of resources.

BOX 11.2   Program Evaluation

A stipulation of program funding is program evaluation. Here are the ABCs of program evaluation:

Always expect funding sources to mandate program evaluation.

Be prepared to advocate for consumer participation in program evaluation.

Care needs to be taken to ensure that evaluation is approached in a participatory fashion.

Unfortunately, program evaluation driven by the requirements of government and funding sources often neglects a primary question: How do consumers define quality programming? Consumer perspectives concerning the effectiveness of program delivery, services, organizational practices, and policies are particularly valuable when considering evaluative processes and procedures.

Royse (1999) suggests the need for **program monitoring:** "measuring the extent to which a program reaches its target population with the intended interventions" (p. 259). Of course, program monitoring is not meant to be the sole prerogative of directors and managers. Guidance can be derived from multiple sources, especially from consumer groups: "There is no assumption that staff or the administration know best" (p. 263). To the contrary, consumer input and feedback are essential components of comprehensive, high-quality program monitoring.

In social work research, the "basic desire to know has been intensified [at times, compromised] by the pressure for more accountability in the human services" (Monette, Sullivan, & DeJong, 2002, p. 298). Single-subject designs and other empirical-practice models give social workers and consumers a structure for evaluating and documenting consumer improvement and achievement, especially on a micro level (case by case). Although these techniques have been valuable sources of empowerment for many consumers, it is important for consumers and social workers to continue to raise the standard concerning consumer participation in research. This is especially true in assessing conditions and evaluating planned change in relation to large-scale change and larger social systems. Indeed, it should be anticipated that consumers and community leaders will differ in their assessments of the merits of macro-level change.

EVALUATING OUTCOMES

With respect to macro-level change, social workers need to be knowledgeable and skilled in "establishing ongoing systems and mechanisms to monitor and improve outcomes . . . the planned or unplanned end result of an intervention, treatment and/or process" (Neuman, 2003, pp. 8–9). In its most basic form, this involves helping to create a strategy and process for evaluating the effectiveness of efforts to create social change.

In human services, many professionals are familiar with the work of the United Way of America (UWA) in promoting outcome measurement in nonprofit agencies. For the UWA, a major emphasis has involved promoting "the use of outcome measurement as an aid to communicating results and funding decisions within its network of member United Ways" (Fischer, 2001, p. 562). Although many human service agencies continue to struggle to identify resources to fund outcome evaluation, a number of helpful publications are available to assist practitioners (see, for example, Rossi, Freeman, & Lipsey, 1999, and Chelimsky & Shadish, 1977). In addition, the UWA produced its own guide to assist agencies in managing the task of outcome evaluation (Hatry, Van Houten, Plantz, & Greenway, 1996).

It is important to note that there is no single model for developing a comprehensive outcomes management program to measure the effectiveness and impact of social intervention. Instead, think of outcome evaluation as a process whereby professionals and consumers form outcomes, develop a strategy or plan, review internal data sources, review external data sources, design a framework and finalize outcomes, standardize terms and collection procedures, determine a report format, develop guidelines for data management, present the evaluation program for support, implement the evaluation program, and evaluate the results (Neuman, 2003, pp. 10–17).

It is vital that specific outcome measures be viewed by both consumers of services and professionals as acceptable indicators of impact and change. Cheetam (1992) differentiates between "service-based measures" focusing on quality of service and "client-based services" emphasizing the effects of service (or social intervention) on quality of life. Hence, the perspective of the consumer is crucial in determining both outcomes and measures.

Concerning empowerment and strengths-oriented outcome evaluation, Jonson-Reid (2000) suggests that community-based research can be improved in the following ways. Professionals should consider: "(1) researching how a project defines community empowerment; (2) using a theory-based framework to connect program definitions, components, and measures; and (3) understanding the

relationship of time to the use of the program outcome" (p. 57). These suggestions seem appropriate both for designing a process of outcome evaluation and
with respect to the nuts and bolts of operationalizing concepts into measures.
Thoughtful consideration needs to be given to the role of consumers and other
stakeholders in shaping outcome evaluation, deeming the appropriateness of theoretical frameworks, and judging the relevance of time.

In the case of community-building efforts, special attention needs to be
given to what residents and consumers of services believe constitute the purposes of projects or programs and agreed-on gauges for success. Jonson-Reid
(2000) indicates that "[c]lear definitions and theory-based connections between program components, outcomes, and measures should be accompanied
by realistic time frames" (p. 74).

A PARTICIPATORY APPROACH
TO EVALUATION AND RESEARCH

The converse of authoritative (expert-based) approaches, conceived by administrators, politicians, and research consultants, is **participatory research.** This
is a process wherein "all participants [especially consumers] are afforded opportunities to reflect on programs, projects, and policies, the mission and aims of
the organization and their own and others' involvement in change efforts. Evaluation is something done with people, not *on* people" (Finn & Jacobson, 2003,
p. 335).

Participatory research directly challenges traditional beliefs and practices
concerning authority and power in the research process. It elevates consumers
to a co-researcher or co-evaluator status. Credence and legitimacy are given to
the capacities of consumers to conceptualize and develop measures to assess
their social circumstances and conditions.

Participatory research is closely aligned with both the strengths perspective
and empowerment theory. Emphasis on the abilities and talents of consumers
to understand their own lives and to shape research in a fashion that accurately
evaluates and assesses their realities employs a strengths-oriented approach. Promoting consumers as active participants in research processes and securing consumer ownership in decision making in research as "co-investigators" are
illustrations of empowerment.

One way of thinking about some of the virtues of participatory research is
to view it as a particular form of **grounded research.** Glaser and Strauss
(1967) describe grounded research as an inductive process where conceptual
distinctions, hypothesis, and theory formulations are derived from data. From
their perspective, important insight for decision making in research comes from
"grounded" sources—the experiences and perceptions of humans (consumers)
in everyday life.

Glaser and Strauss (1967) explain how "awareness contexts" exist in the
social world (p. 83). **Awareness contexts** can be thought of as situations or

circumstances in which people experience varied degrees of visibility and understanding of what is going on. Here, the ability to know is contingent on one's consciousness and ability to comprehend the meaning of actions, language, gestures, and behavior.

As an example, have you ever experienced a social situation—a gathering, party, meeting, or event—where you engaged in interaction or conversation with others and struggled to comprehend what was taking place? You may have felt like an outsider as others seemed able to follow and abide by the rules, terms, and conditions surrounding social interaction and discourse. Your first experience at a professional conference, political rally, board meeting, or protest demonstration may have produced a sense of uneasiness or a feeling of not being "in the know."

In social research, decision makers are confronted with the difficult task of posing questions, hypotheses, and theories in conjunction with specific social contexts. This constitutes a challenge at every stage of the research process. Consider the complexity of trying to identify the attributes of any single concept or measure in a research project without a keen awareness of social context.

For example, geographic communities and neighborhoods are often defined by corporation limits. Particularly in rural areas, however, community identity is frequently a matter of township or county affiliation. These types of distinctions are relevant for researchers to contemplate. Yet, to understand the meaning of belonging to a specific township or county will necessitate special insight and thought from people who actually reside in the area.

There are many good and rational reasons why consumers of services should be fully vested in research processes. Their insight and expertise concerning contextual awareness and understanding in relation to specific communities, neighborhoods, and organizations constitute such a justification. But, even more important, the integrity of social research rests on analytical thought, critical reflection, and the ability to entertain states of being from a variety of vantage points. This broader, more encompassing form of thinking relies on the ability to embrace participatory research and to use thinking that extends beyond professional expertise and the intellectual origins and imagination of social scientists.

CRITICISMS OF
PARTICIPATORY RESEARCH

Many criticisms have been leveled against participatory research. Most center on the idea that the involvement of laypeople in the research process interjects subjectivity and bias, thereby compromising a major tenet of logic scientific inquiry—objectivity. Traditionalists believe that in the quest to more fully understand the relevance of culture and context, consumer participation in research can taint findings and, knowingly or unknowingly, push a project in a particular direction. Participatory research provides an avenue for persuasion and influence.

Some social scientists argue that participatory research is just another name for action research, where there is a specific intent to engage consumers in research as a means of improving social conditions. In **action research,** a major goal of consumer participation is to guide or structure research in a manner that leads to practical outcomes for improving circumstances or overcoming oppressive conditions for people (Baker, 1999, p. 241). Because action research is aimed at remedying social problems and/or enhancing people's lives, acquisition of knowledge is not intended to be the sole intent of the research. Instead, consciousness raising and persuading others to adopt a particular way of thinking are often implicit, if not explicit, goals.

It is important to note that participatory research need not be action research. Participatory research allows for the talents and abilities of consumers to come forward in the research process. The primary goal of having consumers participate as co-researchers is to offer their expertise, based on experience and knowledge. Participatory research can (but does not necessarily) mean that participants are engaged in an attempt to create social change that favors their interests.

STRENGTHS-BASED PRINCIPLES
IN PARTICIPATORY RESEARCH

Some of Saleebey's (2002) basic tenets concerning the strengths perspective seem particularly appropriate when considering participatory research involving consumers of services.

- *Membership:* In order to be a full-fledged participant in the research process, people need to be recognized as legitimate members in the research process. The roles of consumers need to be specified, particularly in relation to responsibilities, rights, and ability to affect decision making. These parameters become established through conversation with consumers, with respect given to the wishes of consumers and to consumer self-determination.

- *Dialogue and collaboration:* Consumer views, knowledge, experiences, and aspirations are important ingredients in the research process. The voices of consumers are best expressed when the organizational culture illuminates a spirit of dialogue and collaboration. Evaluation of programs, policies, practices, and the strengths of larger social systems requires multiple points of view. Discovery and acquisition of knowledge are advanced when the strengths of others are acknowledged, appreciated, and confirmed.

- *Strengths of systems of various sizes:* Consider all social systems (e.g., community, society, family, group) as having a potentially positive and enriching effect on the research process. The social environment is rich with possibilities. Examine with consumers how various social systems could offer interesting insight and perspective in research.

■ *Helping consumers discover their abilities and resources:* Think of the role of the social worker as assisting consumers in their quest to identify their own abilities and available resources. Consumers can participate in many ways in research (e.g., concept formation, information, perception, data collection, and data processing). They have knowledge and access to resources (e.g., people and organizations) that are beyond the reach of others, including professionals.

STRENGTHS-ORIENTED MEASURES
IN MACRO-LEVEL CHANGE

When approaching research in a strengths-based manner, several types of measures can be identified. In each of these cases, emphasis is given to building the abilities and capacities of larger systems. Although the following is not an exhaustive list, it provides several themes for discussion among research team members when conceptualizing the evaluation of large-scale change.

■ *Assets:* Groups of people, organizations, communities, and societies consist of assets. These are positive features or resources that help to sustain and promote the well-being of a social system. For a group of people, it could be a sense of cohesiveness or "we-ness." Communities often possess a degree of pride. For a society, an asset could be adaptability. When evaluating social change, attention should be given to the potential for strengthening salient assets.

■ *Capabilities:* Larger social systems also possess abilities and potentials. These often go unrecognized or unrealized. Saleebey (2002) suggests this to be "especially true of marginalized communities where individuals and groups have had to learn to survive under difficult and often rapidly changing conditions" (p. 236). When studying social change, the research team needs to weigh the degree to which human and social capacity is actualized. This includes both formal entities (e.g., churches, agencies, and schools) and informal associations (e.g., neighborhood groups).

■ *Rights:* One indicator of macro-level change involves the formation or development of laws and policies that advance or protect the rights of people. For example, many Americans have been disappointed that an equal rights amendment for women has never been passed in United States. Such a piece of national legislation could have established guidelines and standards for the fair and equitable treatment of women. Such a law could have been a source of inspiration for women, as the Americans with Disabilities Act (ADA) has been for persons experiencing disabilities.

■ *Opportunities:* When conceptualizing structural change, think in terms of the creation of widespread opportunities for groups of people. These can be thought of as opportunity pathways or highways, where large numbers of people experience newfound access to information, power, resources, and decision-making processes. At the organizational level, opportunity could be measured by such things as recognized membership, participation on leadership committees, and the ability to vote on issues. At the community and societal levels, opportunity might involve access to education, employment, health services, day care, housing, and transportation.

- *Accomplishments and goal attainment:* Larger social systems (e.g., groups, organizations, and communities) often set goals for themselves. This could involve reducing absenteeism and truancy in schools or creating additional jobs or businesses in an area. Many times, state and national competitions establish measurable criteria for evaluating organizational or community progress and recognizing accomplishments. These can be useful markers of large-scale social change.

ARE THERE LIMITATIONS ON WHO CAN PARTICIPATE IN RESEARCH?

With law and the NASW *Code of Ethics* as basic parameters, it is advantageous to think about the involvement of people in participatory research in a limitless manner. For example, participatory research can include the involvement of youth. Finn and Checkoway (1998) ponder, "What would happen if society viewed young people as competent community builders? . . . [A]dults often view young people as victims or problems, rather than as competent citizens capable of meaningful participation" (p. 335).

Viewing various consumers of services as victims or people awaiting treatment and incompetent to contribute to the research process is a mistake. Instead, consumers of services are often ready, able, and willing to participate in research that has the potential to affect their lives. Finn and Checkoway (1998) suggest that consumers of all kinds can be skillful in exchanging ideas, refining research methodology, and challenging basic assumptions underlying theory formation and development on the basis of their personal and cultural knowledge and awareness.

It is important to note that participation in research has many positive returns for consumers. As co-investigators, consumers learn from others and build their abilities. There is a potential for consumers to enhance their prominence, nurture professional ties, and be acknowledged as contributors. Finn and Checkoway (1998) suggest that "[t]hrough participation in youth-initiated projects, young people stretch their limits, learn from people of different backgrounds, and strengthen their community" (p. 339).

TYPES OF PARTICIPATORY RESEARCH

Participatory research can take various forms. The following is a list of different types of participatory research, accompanied by some ideas for how consumers can become involved. Of course, the key to true participatory research is for consumers to assess and make informed decisions concerning their level of involvement and potential for making contributions in the research process. This is very different from having scientific experts delegate duties to consumers or allowing scientists to make unilateral decisions about how consumers can best contribute to research.

Participatory research is particularly important and challenging when examining large-scale (macro) change. Policy, legislative, and program changes will affect many people and various constituencies. This means that various special-interest groups will be positioning themselves and vying to affect decision making. To help ensure adequate consumer participation, consumers need to be involved in every phase of a research project.

The notion of a **research team** needs to be embraced in a broad and inclusive fashion with each of the following types of participatory research. The basic assumption is that the team approach extends to consumers and offers a mechanism for critical reflection and contemplation. This allows for the experiences and awareness of consumers to come forward in evaluating the impact, or potential impact, of large-scale social change. "Critical reflection is a structured, analytic, and emotional process that helps us examine the ways in which we make meaning of circumstances, events, and situations. . . . Posing critical questions is key to critical reflection" (Finn & Jacobson, 2003, p. 355).

- *Advisory groups:* It is not unusual to have an advisory group attached to research projects. Advisory groups can help guide research processes, be a helpful resource in decision making, and serve in a consultative role. Although these groups are typically loaded with experts and professionals, it is important to recruit consumers who show interest in research and evaluation and who feel comfortable speaking out in an advisory group context.

- *Focus groups:* Scientists often struggle with developing and refining the research question. "The focus group helps develop the question by making suggestions about the definitions of the question, ways of collecting the data, and other issues related to planning the research. A focus group can be particularly useful in the designing stage of a program evaluation or needs assessment" (Marlow, 1993, p. 55). The focus group format is a somewhat flexible strategy for collecting information and data from a group of people at one time and place. Facilitators initiate discussion on a subject to elicit insights, perspectives, and data from consumers of services. Anticipate high levels of participation and strong reactions from consumers when examining important topics.

- *Social-historical analyses:* Societies, communities, programs, services, and agencies function in a social-historical context. In assessing and evaluating strengths and areas to be strengthened, it is often important to document and collect data with respect to historical information and events. In any form of social-historical analysis, digging up the social remains of the past, a key question involves who is asked to remember and describe the factual events and provide documents (e.g., letters, memos, records, minutes, and photographs). Consumers provide an enlightened and unique vantage point for describing the past (Williams, Unrau, & Grinnell, 2003, pp. 271–273).

- *Surveys:* Survey research is typically conducted to collect information concerning beliefs, attitudes, and behaviors. Surveys provide leaders and politicians with a gauge of public sentiment and the opinions of various constituency groups. Deciding which questions are to be asked, how, and to whom will have a pronounced effect upon findings. The validity of measures—the extent to which they measure what they purport to measure—is of the essence. Surveys can be especially helpful in conducting program or project evaluation. Consumers can be important team members by providing contextual awareness for questionnaire construction and in refining data collection techniques. In addition, they are a crucial population to poll concerning program or policy effectiveness.

- *Program evaluations:* Royse (1999) identifies several distinct types of program evaluation. They include: patterns of use (Who is being served?), formative evaluation (How can the program be improved?), consumer satisfaction (How satisfied are consumers with the program?), outcome evaluation (Does the program reach its goals?), and cost-effectiveness (Is the program cost-effective in helping consumers?) (pp. 258–268). It is difficult to imagine devising a system for evaluating social service programming without significant ownership and buy-in from consumers. Consumers need to be active participants in determining program goals and evaluative outcomes, as well as in the process of completing program evaluation. Again, a research team with significant consumer participation would seem to be a promising format.

- *Policy and legislative analyses:* Social workers often work with consumers to assess the need for policy formulation and development. Two examples of this are community needs assessments and agency (organizational) profiles. In these instances, information is gathered to advise and influence policymakers and legislators. Additionally, consumers can serve as catalysts for evaluating the effectiveness (both successes and detrimental effects) of legislative and policy initiatives. In both cases, consumers are important participants in developing the process and criteria and adding a unique perspective for use in policy/legislative analysis.

- *Case studies:* It is often useful to analyze and describe a particular community, organization, event, program, or social unit in great depth. Although case studies are notorious for their weaknesses with respect to generalizability, they provide important information in flushing out the how, where, why, and when of social phenomenon. Consumers constitute a valuable source of information for determining the nature of programs, organizations, and communities. Consumers can also provide valuable leads concerning data sources.

- *Field studies:* Some social processes need to be studied as they happen and in a relatively undisturbed fashion. In these instances, researchers seek to understand how events and actions unfold in their natural settings. This kind of research involves acquiring a sense of social context, an understanding of how actions develop and take place. Hence, if a social worker seeks to understand a particular community, then she or he needs to know how it really functions. This will necessitate direct observation and a level of immersion in the community. This often requires the involvement of consumers. It is their expertise that often allows researchers access to the everyday workings and activities of a community that may be invisible to the casual eye.

PARTICIPATORY RESEARCH AND WELFARE REFORM

A case in point for the relevance of participatory research involves the Personal Responsibility and Work Opportunity Reconciliation (welfare reform) Act of 1996. This historic piece of social legislation resulted in significant changes in the ways communities address the needs of the poor. Enacted in a spirit of "new federalism," with the intention of promoting self-sufficiency and reducing federal spending on public assistance, this law shifted social responsibility from the federal government to the states and local communities. Additionally, time restrictions were placed on receipt of aid—hence, the change of title from Aid for Dependent Children (AFDC) to Temporary Assistance to Needy Families (TANF).

In a nutshell, states were directed to

> develop strategic plans for using TANF block grant monies that are consistent with federal guidelines and mandates concerning work requirements and payment levels. States, in turn, ask local areas (often counties) to create service delivery plans compatible with federal and state regulations, to address the needs of local constituents. The net result is a proliferation of state and local initiative, each unique in name and substance, that reinforce the two main federal directives emphasizing employment and time limits of financial assistance.
> (Long, 2000, p. 63)

It is important to note that this type of service delivery has profound implications for policy and program evaluation. The creation of customized programs by state and county produced a myriad of programs (frequently called "family or children come first" initiatives) across our nation. Each program was unique in its specific goals and objectives. Decentralization and local control allowed states and counties appreciable latitude in assessing the success of welfare reform.

Consequently, counties were challenged to develop individualized strategies for evaluating their program goals and desired outcomes.

As a result of federal mandates and prevailing belief systems (e.g., fiscal responsibility, self-sufficiency, the work ethic, and pressures for state or local control), many programs approached evaluation in terms of budgetary relief, cost-effective utilization of services, reduction in the number of people on welfare rolls, and various back-to-work ratios (Kilty & Meenaghan, 1995). These "accounting" types of criteria fit nicely with public and political concerns for reducing spending on welfare and for encouraging work. Meanwhile, consumer-oriented interests—such things as self-actualization, quality family time, and basic needs (e.g., food, medical care, and utilities)—were often overlooked or overshadowed in community-based research plans.

For many counties, it became relatively simple to rely on traditional measures of success, focusing on reducing welfare rolls and transitioning people toward available forms of employment. Although many counties developed advisory or planning boards to monitor TANF programs, political appointees and administrators were often overrepresented on these boards. The idea of embracing and including the voices of consumers in developing program goals, objectives, and measures of success was not always fashionable.

Long (2000) suggests that a comprehensive study of the effects of welfare reform would include consumer-driven criteria. From the perspective of TANF recipients, factors to be considered in an analysis of the success of welfare reform would likely include the employment market (e.g., the kinds of jobs available and their wages and benefits), the prospect of worker satisfaction, the availability of affordable child care, the presence of social support (e.g., family, friends, and groups), the availability of affordable and efficient transportation to and from work, the existence of safe housing, the effects on family preservation, options for medical insurance, and support from local organizations (e.g., social services, churches, and employers).

A thorough examination of how the lives of consumers have changed as a result of welfare reform would also include the use of multiple research methodologies, both quantitative and qualitative. Consumers could assist in the design and implementation of focus groups, case studies, surveys, and field research. Indeed, it is difficult to imagine how one could effectively describe and document the impact of welfare reform without the active participation of recipients.

Interestingly, one descriptive analysis of the impact of welfare sanctions found that only 10 percent of former recipients felt they were better off as a result of welfare reform (Lindhorst, Mancoske, & Kemp, 2000). As one might have anticipated, consumers in this study pointed to the disruptive effect of welfare reform on family life. When asked, consumers described the following kinds of struggles: changes in living arrangements, inability to pay rent, disruption in phone service, reliance on food banks or kitchens, separation of children from their caregiver, homelessness, and involvement with foster care (p. 195).

As you can see, looking at welfare reform form a consumer's perspective means considering factors that are very different from those posed by politicians and government leaders. People who are sanctioned as a result of welfare reform know firsthand the consequences of the legislation. Thoughtful reflection by consumers should be considered a source of enlightenment and discovery in research.

SUMMARY

Understanding social change with larger systems is a multifaceted proposition. The unit of analysis could be a characteristic or attribute of a group of people, organization, community, or society. The composition of the research team, including their backgrounds, expertise, and predispositions, will have a powerful effect on the research process and subsequent findings.

In this chapter, the reader is challenged to embrace a somewhat nontraditional view of research. The primary focus has been on finding ways to use the strengths of consumers to become participants and team members in research involving macro-level change. This is true of all kinds of research, including descriptive, exploratory, explanatory, and evaluative.

A participatory approach to research demands the active participation of consumers in methodological decisions as well as throughout the research process. Consumers are viewed as experts in their own right, as they possess unparalleled knowledge, direct experience, and a unique orientation to issues and problems. Grounded information is often crucial to the formation of concepts, hypotheses, and theories in the research process. Consumers need not be viewed merely as subjects for study but as potential co-investigators and valued members of a research team. This is true regardless of the methodology employed (e.g., case study, survey, or field research).

A FEW KEY TERMS

descriptive research	program monitoring	action research
exploratory research	participatory research	research team
explanatory research	grounded research	
evaluation research	awareness contexts	

USING INFOTRAC®

COLLEGE EDITION AND INFOWRITE

InfoTrac College Edition

Finding ways to involve consumers of services in the research process can be both challenging and fulfilling. Recognizing consumers as stakeholders and allowing their strengths to emerge in the planning, implementation, and evaluation of research projects requires forethought and a commitment at multiple levels (e.g., the research group, funding sources, the host organization, and consumers). Yet, many good examples exist of the enriching effect of participatory research in scientific inquiry. Complete the following exercise:

1. Go to InfoTrac College Edition.
2. Under the Keyword Search, search using "participatory research."
3. Browse through the articles and identify two articles that embrace participatory research and the active use of some form of consumer group.
4. Compare and contrast the manner in which these articles approach the involvement of consumers in research. Were consumers ever conceptualized as "co-investigators" and were consumers able to participate in decision-making processes?
5. Apply the distinction offered by Finn and Jacobson (2003, p. 335): Is research conducted *with* consumers or *on* consumers?

InfoWrite

In order to refine your writing skills, do the following:

1. Go to InfoWrite.
2. Scroll to Research and the Research Paper.
3. Read all of the sections.
4. Pay special attention to Periodicals.

It is important to be able to differentiate between legitimate research articles from professional, refereed journals that follow scientific guidelines and articles written in magazines designed to appeal to readers. The notion of welfare reform, examined earlier in this chapter, is often a value-laden and controversial subject. Using InfoTrac College Edition, conduct a search to identify recent articles examining the consequence of welfare reform for consumers of services. Using the information provided in "Research and the Research Paper," sort publications according to whether they are research or magazine articles. Is this a difficult task? Why? How do the two writing styles differ? Do any of these articles embrace strengths-based principles in conducting participatory research?

CASE EXAMPLE: Evaluating Medicare Fraud

Wanda Peterson is a social worker at a skilled nursing facility in a large city in the Midwest. She has belonged to an association of long-term skilled nursing home social workers in her metropolitan area for the past five years. This group of social workers meets on a monthly basis to discuss current topics and trends. Wanda has found her colleagues to be a source of support, enlightenment, and encouragement. They routinely share and discuss important issues involving their consumers. Over the years, this association has worked to effect policy and legislative change at local, state, and national levels.

Most recently, Wanda has become increasingly concerned about allegations of Medicare fraud at local skilled nursing facilities for older adults, including her own place of employment. She has received numerous complaints from consumers and their family members that various providers (e.g., physicians, therapists, and providers of durable medical equipment) are billing for products and/or services that are either not provided or are poorly rendered. Consumers believe they are being "ripped off" and taken advantage of as a result of their diminished physical or mental capabilities.

Reporting these types of problems to administrators has failed to produce change. In addition, filing complaints with the overworked and understaffed state regulatory commission seldom results in full investigations. When state officials visit facilities to inspect conditions and records, consumers believe administrators at the skilled nursing facilities are tipped off to visits and scurry to complete paperwork and temporarily address issues in anticipation of site visitors inquiries.

To address the situation, consumers and their families are calling for an independent evaluation of the provision of Medicare services and billing at each of the skilled nursing facilities in the area. Consumers are demanding change and are distrustful of administrators as well as state and federal regulators and auditors. They have called on the association of skilled nursing home social workers and the local Pro-Seniors organization to help them better identify and document Medicare fraud at these facilities.

Members of the association of skilled nursing home social workers are enthusiastic about this initiative and have agreed to facilitate and assist efforts as prescribed by consumers. This includes organizing meetings and coordinating meeting space and time. Two meetings have already taken place. Consumers have

asked Wanda and others to ascertain whether there is a national effort or other community efforts underway to assess Medicare fraud in skilled nursing facilities. Consumers are also interested in preparing a questionnaire for distribution to either current or recent consumers of services to assess problems with the delivery of Medicare services by contract providers.

Wanda and her colleagues in the association and from Pro-Seniors have been reading and discussing ways to implement "participatory" forms of research. One subgroup of social workers is working with consumers to identify and review current literature. A second group of social workers and consumers is exploring ethical issues associated with this type of research and ways of coordinating efforts with pertinent institutional review boards. Meanwhile, a third group of social workers and consumers is refining the kinds of issues to be considered in survey research. As an example, consumers frequently voice concern about "stop and go" visits by health professionals—where a contracted professional pays a cursory visit to a consumer and then charges for a full call, including undelivered services.

At this point, consumers and social workers view themselves as engaged in a form of descriptive (survey) research at the community level. The intent of the research is to better describe the occurrence of Medicare fraud in skilled nursing facilities. Wanda and her colleagues have relied on and attempted to bring out the strengths of consumers in evaluating Medicare fraud. Consumers are viewed as co-investigators in the research process and have been particularly valuable in providing contextual awareness and understanding of fraud.

THINKING CRITICALLY
ABOUT THE CASE EXAMPLE

1. In this particular case example, consumers of Medicare services sense fraud and want to do something about it! There is a sense of anger associated with collecting information about service providers that are taking advantage of older adults and federal reimbursements. Anger can be a source of strength in providing motivation and impetus for change. Specifically, how can the passion of consumers about a topic be viewed either as a strength or as empowering with respect to participatory research? When and how does emotion become problematic in the research process?

2. If this line of research, examining Medicare fraud in skilled nursing facilities, proceeds, is it conceivable that social workers will feel pressure from administrators and others to act in ways that might disenfranchise or dissuade consumers? How can social workers call upon their strengths, individually and collectively, to prevent this from happening?

3. The example states that "Wanda and her colleagues in the association and from Pro-Seniors have been reading and discussing ways to implement 'participatory' forms of research." Shouldn't consumers of services also be evaluating this literature? Do you believe that it is appropriate to ask consumers to read professional, research-oriented articles and materials? Why or why not? If you were to pursue this form of participation, what might be some precautionary notes?

REFLECTION EXERCISES

1. Ask a social scientist for her or his views of participatory research and the use of consumers of services as co-investigators. What types of arguments are provided for or against the utilization of consumers in the research process? Does this represent a strengths orientation or a more traditional stance?

2. Request a copy of an agency's program evaluation standards as prescribed by a funding source (e.g., United Way, grant funder, or allocation board). What kind of information is mandated? Are the standards geared toward effectiveness or efficiency? Does this constitute exploratory, explanatory, descriptive, or evaluative research? How are consumers included in decision making with respect to the research process? Do consumers serve a program-monitoring function? Are consumers considered in any fashion as members of the evaluation team?

3. Contact your local county department of human services and inquire about efforts in your county to evaluate the success of TANF. What kind of research strategy has been employed? What criteria have been used to measure the success of welfare reform at the

local level, and who determined such criteria? Was insight solicited from consumers in order to acquire contextual awareness of the consequences of welfare reform? Why or why not?

4. Identify a recent policy or legislative initiative that has been undertaken in your community.

Was a community assessment completed to gather relevant data and to gauge public sentiment? Were consumers of services in your community involved in designing or conducting any of this research (e.g., focus groups, surveys, and/or social–historical analysis)?

SUGGESTED READINGS

De Poy, E. (2003). *Evaluation practice: Thinking and action principles for social work practice.* Pacific Grove, CA: Brooks/Cole.

Ginsberg, L. H. (2001). *Social work evaluation: Principles and methods.* Boston: Allyn & Bacon.

Glasser, B., & Strauss, A. (1967). *The discovery of grounded research:*

Strategies for qualitative research. Chicago: Aldine.

Newman, W. L. (2003). Developing a comprehensive outcomes management program: A ten step process. *Administration in Social Work, 27*(1), 5–23.

REFERENCES

Baker, T. L. (1999). *Doing social research.* New York: McGraw-Hill.

Cheetam, J. (1992). Evaluating social work effectiveness. *Research on Social Work Practice, 2*(3), 265–287.

Chelimsky, E., & Shadish, W. (Eds.). (1977). *Evaluation for the 21st century.* Beverly Hills, CA: Sage.

Finn, J. L., & Checkoway, B. (1998). Young people as competent community builders: A challenge to social work. *Social Work, 43,* 335–345.

Finn, J. L., & Jacobson, M. (2003). *Just practice: A social justice approach to social work.* Peosta, IA: Eddie Bowers.

Fischer, R. L. (2001). The sea change in nonprofit human services: A critical assessment of outcome measurement. *Journal of Contemporary Human Services, 82*(6), 561–569.

Glaser, B., & Strauss, A. (1967). *The discovery of grounded research: Strategies for qualitative research.* Chicago: Aldine.

Hatry, H., Van Houten, T., Plantz, M., & Greenway, M. (1996). *Measuring program outcomes: A practical approach.* Alexandria, VA: United Way of America.

Jonson-Reid, M. (2000). Evaluating empowerment in a community-based child abuse prevention program: Lessons learned. *Journal of Community Practice, 7*(4), 57–76.

Kilty, K. M., & Meenaghan, T. M. (1995). Social work and the convergence of politics science. *Social Work, 40,* 445–453.

Lindhorst, T., Mancoske, R. J., & Kemp, A. A. (2000). Is welfare reform working? A study of effects of sanctions on families receiving Temporary Assistance to Needy Families. *Journal of Sociology and Social Welfare, 27,* 185–201.

Long, D. D. (2000). Welfare reform: A social work perspective for assessing success. *Journal of Sociology and Social Welfare, 27,* 61–78.

Mandelbaum, M. (1938). *The problem of historical knowledge.* New York: Liveright.

Mannheim, K. (1936). *Ideology and utopia.* New York: Harcourt, Brace, and World.

Marlow, C. (1993). *Research methods for generalist social work.* Pacific Grove, CA: Brooks/Cole.

McNicoll, P. (2001). Issues in teaching participatory action research. In M. Jalongo, G. Gerlach, & W. Yan (Eds.), *Annual editions research methods 01/02.* Guilford, CT: McGraw-Hill/Dushkin.

Monette, D. R., Sullivan, T. J., & DeJong, C. R. (2002). *Applied social research.* Fort Worth, TX: Harcourt College Publishers.

Neuman, K. M. (2003). Developing a comprehensive outcomes management program: A ten-step process. *Administration in Social Work, 27*(1), 5–23.

Newman, W. L. (1997). *Social research methods: Qualitative and quantitative approaches.* Boston: Allyn & Bacon.

Rossi, P. H., Freeman, H. E., & Lipsey, M. W. (1999). *Evaluation: A systematic approach* (6th ed.). Beverly Hills, CA: Sage.

Royse, D. (1999). *Research methods in social work.* Belmont, CA: Wadsworth/Thomson Learning.

Saleebey, D. (2002). *The strengths perspective in social work practice.* Boston: Allyn & Bacon.

Schutt, R. K. (1996). *Investigating the social world.* Thousand Oaks, CA: Pine Forge Press.

Williams, M., Unrau, Y., & Grinnell, R. M. (2003). *Research methods for social workers: A generalist approach for BSW students.* Peosta, IA: Eddie Bowers.

12

Promoting a
Social Justice and
Ideological Outlook

Course Content Areas

Values	**Power Elite**
Social Justice	**Code of Ethics**
Equality	**Ethical Dilemmas**
Professional Power	**Ethical Decision Making**
Social Conscience	

The current wave of neoconservatism that has washed across the United States challenges social work to remain true to the values and ethical considerations that are central to the profession. These values—a commitment to human dignity, human welfare, and social justice—remain essential characteristics of the practice of social work, much as they have been throughout the history of the profession.

This chapter considers the core values and ethics of social work in relation to consumer participation, empowerment, and dominant American values, including individualism, self-interest, work, and materialism. The strengths perspective is considered in light of social work's values and the prevailing political conservatism. Students are encouraged to embrace a strong sense of social-political activism as a personal value system.

VALUES BASE OF SOCIAL WORK

As illustrated throughout this book, social work is a values-based profession committed to enhancing positive life conditions across consumer systems (Reamer, 1990). Defined as the qualities, meanings, and intentions by which we order our lives, **values** are the premises and assumptions on the basis of which we make decisions (Brueggemann, 1996, p. 373). Values provide the foundation for social work practice and establish a course of action for the profession (Loewenberg & Dolgoff, 1992). As demonstrated by its history, social work has a long-standing commitment to values that imply that people have the right to be respected and that social workers should not discriminate against people and communities because of race, ethnicity, gender, sexual orientation, religion, country of original, or socioeconomic class.

As stated by Rapp and Poertner (1992), the collective philosophy of social work, coupled with individual philosophies, and the broader social context are all important sources of values. Compton and Galaway (1979) suggest that two core social work values are respect for the dignity and uniqueness of the individual and client self-determination. Hepworth and Larsen (1982) suggest four cardinal values:

1. People should have access to resources.

2. Every person is unique and has inherent worth.

3. People have a right to freedom.

4. Society and the individual citizen have mutual responsibility for the realization of these values.

Given the work of Hepworth and Larsen, one can see that consumer participation, self-determination, and confidentiality lie at the heart of social work practice. It is important to note, however, that the implementation of these values may vary on the basis of priorities and objectives. In consideration of this, Perlman (1976) concluded that "a value has small worth, except as it is moved, or is moveable, from believing into doing, from verbal affirmation into action" (p. 381).

In a similar manner, social workers do not expect the same behavior of their consumers that they expect of themselves. One of social work's virtues is that it has advocated allowing others to do and say certain things that social workers might not say or do. In social work practice, values are often seen as affecting the choice of objectives and goals. Values surface when purpose is addressed. The tradition speaks of the profession as value-laden but sees the ethical "oughts" as separate from the "knowns." Consequently, *values* and *ethics* are not interchangeable terms. Values are concerned with what is good and desirable, whereas **ethics** address what is right and correct (Loewenberg & Dolgoff, 1992). The paradigm of value-free propositions, providing informed, research-affirmed guidelines for action, is generally viewed as the scientific basis on which the profession's claim to competence rests (Lewis, 1984, pp. 203–204).

If "doing the right thing" on behalf of consumers is indeed a distinguishing feature between effective social workers and those who are ineffective, it is important to examine what "doing the right thing" means (Lewis, Lewis, Packard, & Soufflé, 2001). In this book, doing the right thing involves making judgments within a framework of professional values. Professional values give social workers a direction in pursuit of effectiveness. They provide a steady direction for the pursuit of social work interventions.

As stated by Reamer (1998), Pumphrey (1959) provided one of the earliest and most influential categorizations of social work's core values, placing them in three groups of values-based objectives. The first group emphasized the relationship between the values operating in the culture at large. This group was concerned with the compatibility between struggling for **social justice** and social change, and addressing basic human needs and the broader culture's values. The second category dealt more narrowly with social work's perception of its own values, particularly the ways the profession interpreted and implemented its values and encouraged ethical behavior. The final category emphasized social workers' relationships with specific groups and individuals served by social workers, particularly understanding and responding to clients' values. Of specific importance was the potential for conflict among competing values.

This book suggests that the strengths perspective embraces social work values by incorporating consumers' strengths, knowledge, and skills in the helping process. Said another way, regardless of their level of functioning, the severity of their life circumstances, and the magnitude of the problems that need to be overcome, consumers and their communities need to be seen as having the ability to resolve their problems. As social workers, we support the empowerment of consumers by expecting and recognizing their strengths and facilitating the necessary change efforts. Thus, practicing from a strengths perspective supports empowerment for individuals' well-being and the environmental factors that influence it. In this way, social work's understanding of the interaction between people and their environment is directly guided by the values defined in Table 12.1.

Underpinning social work values is the sense that people have certain basic needs related to housing, food, education, and medical care. In other words, services and the environment help to shape the opportunities and privileges available to people. During the Progressive Era, the era of the settlement movement, and the Great Depression, social workers saw all too often that social and economic problems were linked to the hardship faced by individuals and families. Today, people's suffering may be less visible, but misery remains part of daily life for segments of our society. Unfortunately, the link between environmental factors and individual and community opportunities is often less apparent, but the relationship exists even in this time of unprecedented consumerism. How can the social worker in the following scenario exemplify the value base of social work in today's environment?

Hannah Rose, a social worker, works in a community center and organizes both advocacy efforts and community-based educational programs for older people. The center is located in an upper-middle-class neighborhood consisting primarily of professionals. Hannah has been asked to begin integrative programming for older people with psychiatric conditions, including depression and schizophrenia. Her current program consumers are resistant to the idea, as are many of the community residents; however, her board of directors is supportive of the new venture.

What social work values appear to have a bearing on this case? How might the social worker empower the current consumers while taking advantage of a much needed program opportunity for people with mental illness?

Table 12.1 Values and Ethical Principles

The following broad ethical principles are based on social work's core values of service, social justice, dignity and worth of the person, importance of human relationships, integrity, and competence. These principles set forth ideals to which all social workers should aspire.

Value	Ethical Principle	
Service	Social workers' primary goal is to help people in need and to address social problems.	Social workers elevate service to others above self-interest. Social workers draw on their knowledge, values, and skills to help people in need and to address social problems. Social workers are encouraged to volunteer some portion of their professional skills with no expectation of significant financial return (pro bono service).
Social justice	Social workers challenge social injustice.	Social workers pursue social change, particularly with and on behalf of vulnerable and oppressed individuals and groups of people. Social workers' social change efforts are focused primarily on issues of poverty, unemployment, discrimination, and other forms of social injustice. These activities seek to promote sensitivity to and knowledge about oppression and cultural and ethnic diversity. Social workers strive to ensure access to needed information, services, and resources; equality of opportunity; and meaningful participation in decision making by all people.
Dignity and worth of the person	Social workers respect the inherent dignity and worth of the person.	Social workers treat each person in a caring and respectful fashion, mindful of individual differences and cultural and ethnic diversity. Social workers promote clients' socially responsible self-determination. Social workers seek to enhance clients' capacity and opportunity to change and to address their own needs. Social workers are cognizant of their dual responsibility to clients and to the

Value	Ethical Principle	
		broader society. They seek to resolve conflicts between clients' interest and the broader society's interests in a socially responsible manner consistent with the values, ethical principles, and ethical standards of the profession.
Importance of human relationships	Social workers recognize the central importance of human relationships.	Social workers understand that relationships between and among people are an important vehicle for change. Social workers engage people as partners in the helping process. Social workers seek to strengthen relationships among people in a purposeful effort to promote, restore, maintain, and enhance the well-being of individuals, families, social groups, organizations, and communities.
Integrity	Social workers behave in a trustworthy manner.	Social workers are continually aware of the profession's mission, values, ethical principles, and ethical standards and practice in a manner consistent with them. Social workers act honestly and responsibly and promote ethical practices on the part of the organizations with which they are affiliated.
Competence	Social workers practice within their area of competence and develop and enhance their professional expertise.	Social workers continually strive to increase their professional knowledge and skills and to apply them in practice. Social workers should aspire to contribute to the knowledge base of the profession.

Approved by the 1996 NASW Delegate Assembly and revised by the 1999 NASW Delegate Assembly.

SOURCE: Adapted from the NASW *Code of Ethics,* pp. 5–6. Copyright 1996, National Association of Social Workers, Inc., NASW *Code of Ethics.*

THE CODE OF ETHICS

Professions such as nursing, law, business, medicine, and psychology have ethical standards that establish their accountability to service consumers as well as the general public. How do we define ethics? In our discussion, ethics are considered statements of value related to action (Hugman & Smith, 1995). According to Levy (1993, p. 1) ethics are the application of values to human relationships and transactions. Ethics guide how social work is practiced, organized, planned, and managed. For example, if we accept that an ethical principle social workers should demonstrate is "respect for persons," then we must be able to demonstrate how respect occurs in practice (Butrym, 1976). This example leads to a series of questions for consideration:

1. In macro social work practice, how are you demonstrating your values and ethics to consumers?

2. Are your values open to modification?

3. When do you feel the need to disclose your values to consumers?

4. What are the mechanisms that help you be accountable to your consumers?

5. What are the rules under which you operate?

6. In the final analysis, where does your loyalty lie, with your consumers or with your employer?

As noted by these questions, social workers are ethically accountable, not only for what we do in the professional relationship with consumers, but for what we do *not* pursue given available opportunities and responsibilities.

Croxton-Smith's (1965) comments provide further insight into the importance of ethics in relation to a profession and to society:

> I have sometimes been asked why a profession should have a code of ethics which its members are required to observe above any requirements laid on them by law and commercial usage. . . .
>
> Members of professions enjoy a standing in the community which comes from a sense of service, if need be at times with little or no reward, from maintenance of a standard of competence in professional work, as well as from a standard of behavior in public and private life. . . . We are as human as anybody else, and a code of conduct is a help and not a hindrance provided that it is reasonable and applied with understanding and forbearance. . . . (p. 749)

As with most professions, Reamer (1983) concludes that social work's initial focus on ethics had to do with the creation of schools of thought, skills, and techniques. Ethical issues experienced by social workers involved confidentiality in relationships, conflicts in the laws, policies, and services, and obligations of social workers to employers and consumers. Therefore, codes of ethics serve as guides to ethical social work practice, criteria for the evaluation of the ethics of actual practice, and benchmarks for the enforcement of social work ethics and the adjudication of unethical conduct complaints.

EXERCISE 12.1

Ethical statements reflect personal and professional values. Ask the listed professionals to identify the relevant ethic principle for each of the following societal values. How do your findings compare to the ethics for social work practice? What are the similarities between professionals?

Professions:	Lawyer	Physician	Clergy	Psychologist	Banker
Social justice					
Freedom					
Life orientation					
Privacy					
Individual choice					
Equality					

Social work has a long-standing commitment to ethical practice. As early as 1919, attempts were made to draft a professional code of ethics. Specifically, Mary Richmond is credited with formulating an experimental draft code of ethics (Elliott, 1931). In 1922 the Family Welfare Association of America appointed an ethics committee in response to ethical questions about social work (Reamer, 1998). In addition, there is evidence that at least some schools of social work were teaching discrete courses on values and ethics in the 1920s (Elliott, 1931). It was not until 1947 that the American Association of Social Workers adopted a formal code of ethics.

In 1960 the National Association of Social Workers (NASW) adopted its first code of ethics, five years after the association was formed (Reamer, 1998). Comprising fourteen proclamations concerning the duties and responsibilities of social work, the code was preceded by a preamble that embraced the philosophical and skill base of the profession. In 1967 the fifteenth proclamation was added, describing the profession's commitment to nondiscrimination.

Revisions to the code were made in 1977, 1979, 1990, and 1993, in part because of the exponential growth of ethics-related knowledge and the research done in the area. At present, the best known statement of values and ethics to which social workers currently subscribe is the *Code of Ethics,* as approved by the NASW Delegate Assembly in 1996 and revised by the 1999 NASW Delegate Assembly.

What is important to note about the revisions to the code is the shift in orientation toward the profession. As described by Reid and Popple (1992), the paternalistic orientation that was evident in the late nineteenth and early twentieth centuries "is based on the assumption that the profession's public mission is to enhance the rectitude of its clients, enabling them to lead virtuous lives, wholesome, and gainful lives, independent of support from public or private coffers" (p. 18). In contrast, Reid and Popple (1992) point out that the social justice orientation associated with the settlement movement, the New Deal, the War on Poverty, and the Great Society supports the view that capitalism, discrimination, and oppression have produced an underclass. Thus, through primarily macro interventions, social work serves as a change agent in the nation's complex systems of power and services.

As described in the social work *Code of Ethics* provided in Table 12.2 on page 258, the wide range of principles included in the NASW *Code of Ethics* indicate that it was designed to serve several purposes. On the one hand, abstract, idealistic principles concerning social justice and general social welfare provide social workers with important aspirations, as opposed to enforceable standards. Other principles set forth specific rules with which practitioners are expected to comply, and violations of which would provide grounds for the filing of a formal grievance. In addition, a major purpose of the code is to provide social workers with principles to help them resolve ethical dilemmas encountered in practice, a topic that has received considerable attention.

The *Code of Ethics* enables social workers to expand the opportunities and choices available to all people. Read the following scenarios and consider what ethical principles apply to the situation.

The small town in which you live and work provides no after-school program for children and youth. On the basis of your work with various community groups, you have learned that many children have few activities after school and tend to hang out in the park after school with little if any supervision or organized activities. Your employment as a community mental administrator does not encompass after-school programs and your agency does not have funds for such a program.

As a social worker, what would you do in these situations? How would ethics guide your course of action?

Although professions tend to look to their respective codes of ethics for guidance, most would acknowledge that any code of ethics is necessarily limited in its ability to provide full and detailed answers. Codes of ethics are written in general terms and at a relatively high level of abstraction in order to address a broad range of issues. This is certainly the case with social work's *Code of Ethics*. Specifically, as stated by Croxton and Jayaratne (1999) much of the code is articulated within the context of a social worker–consumer relationship. Consequently, professionals in macro practice or international social work often will not find specific guidelines that address the ethical dilemmas that arise in practice. Ideally, this is a challenge that will be addressed in time.

EXERCISE 12.2

Read a national newspaper for several days and collect at least two articles that highlight a professional who has acted in accordance with the rules of professional ethics.

Consider the situation, the particular values and ethics involved in the situation, and the actions of the professional. What would you do in a similar situation?

"Ethical dilemma" was defined by Abramson (1984) as follows:

An ethical dilemma or moral quandary is one in which there are conflicts and tensions concerning the right and the good, when choosing one course of action will uphold one moral principle while violating another. (p. 129)

Ethical dilemmas can sometimes be avoided or resolved if values are clearly articulated and used in decision making. Further, Loewenberg and Dolgoff (1995) suggest that ethical decisions can be made by answering the following questions at each step of dealing with an ethical issue:

A. What are the ethical issues involved? What are the principles, rights, and obligations that have an impact on the ethical question?

B. What additional information is needed to properly identify the ethical implications?

C. What are the relevant ethical rules that can be applied? Which ethical criteria are relevant in this situation?

D. If there is a conflict of interests, who should be the principal beneficiary?

E. How would you rank-order the ethical issues and the ethical rules you have identified?

F. What are the possible consequences that result from utilizing different ethical rules?

G. When is it justified to shift the ethical decision obligations to another person (not the social worker)? To whom should it be shifted in this case? (p. 372).

You have been the administrator of a family service organization for approximately five years. With a staff of twenty-two people, including seven social workers and three psychologists, you have learned that your annual budget will be significantly reduced. As a result, you are forced to reduce the organization staff by at least three employees. How will you proceed with this unpleasant task? What are some of your retrenchment options?

Apply the described ethical decision-making process to the following exemplar. Imagine how you can best accomplish the necessary tasks while maintaining social work's principles and values.

According to Goodpaster (1997), two components of thinking ethically are rationality and respect. *Rationality* means being self-directed and motivated by ethical intentions. *Respect* is other-directed and involves seeing the situation as beyond one's self-interest. As might be expected, respect is crucial when working with diverse populations or unfamiliar communities.

In a multiethnic society, values are not culturally neutral. When values are presented as universal values within a system that articulates the world view of a dominant ethnic group they cannot provide the basis for fair and equitable treatment (Hugman & Smith, 1995).

EXERCISE 12.3

Macro social work practice often involves issues related to a number of people or particular groups. Consequently, solving problems usually reaches far beyond an individual. These complex situations frequently present social workers with an ethical dilemma. Please read the following exercise and use ethical decision making to tackle the problem solving.

You are the administrator of a social service program located in an urban housing project. You supervise a social worker named Jeanne, who is an excellent employee and lives near the project. Jeanne has been widowed for five years and supports her three children. Jeanne's health benefits are derived from her employment. Unfortunately, Jeanne has been diagnosed with lung cancer and needs considerable time off from work. She doesn't have the accumulated sick time that she requires. What would you do in this situation?

Table 12.2 Ethical Standards

The following ethical standards are relevant to the professional activities of all social workers. These standards concern (1) social workers' ethical responsibilities to clients, (2) social workers' ethical responsibilities to colleagues, (3) social workers' ethical responsibilities in practice settings, (4) social workers' ethical responsibilities as professionals, (5) social workers' ethical responsibilities to the social work profession, and (6) social workers' ethical responsibilities to the broader society.

Some of the standards that follow are enforceable guidelines for professional conduct, and some are aspirational. The extent to which each standard is enforceable is a matter of professional judgment to be exercised by those responsible for reviewing alleged violations of ethical standards.

1. **SOCIAL WORKERS' ETHICAL RESPONSIBILITIES TO CLIENTS**

   1.01 Commitment to Clients

   Social workers' primary responsibility is to promote the well-being of clients. In general, clients' interests are primary. However, social workers' responsibility to the larger society or specific legal obligations may on limited occasions supersede the loyalty owed clients, and clients should be so advised. (Examples include when a social worker is required by law to report that a client has abused a child or has threatened to harm self or others.)

   1.02 Self-Determination

   Social workers respect and promote the right of clients to self-determination and assist clients in their efforts to identify and clarify their goals. Social workers may limit clients' right to self-determination when, in the social workers' professional judgment, clients' actions or potential actions pose a serious, foreseeable, and imminent risk to themselves or others.

   1.03 Informed Consent

   (a) Social workers should provide services to clients only in the context of a professional relationship based, when appropriate, on valid informed consent. Social workers should use clear and understandable language to inform clients of the purpose of the services, risks related to the services, limits to services because of the requirements of a third-party payer, relevant costs, reasonable alternatives, clients' right to refuse or withdraw consent, and the time frame covered by the consent. Social workers should provide clients with an opportunity to ask questions.

   (b) In instances when clients are not literate or have difficulty understanding the primary language used in the practice setting, social workers should take steps to ensure clients' comprehension. This may include providing clients with a detailed verbal explanation or arranging for a qualified interpreter or translator whenever possible.

   (c) In instances when clients lack the capacity to provide informed consent, social workers should protect clients' interests by seeking permission from an appropriate third party, informing clients consistent with the clients' level of understanding. In such instances social workers should seek to ensure that the third party acts in a manner consistent with clients' wishes and interests. Social workers should take reasonable steps to enhance such clients' ability to give informed consent.

(d) In instances when clients are receiving services involuntarily, social workers should provide information about the nature and extent of services and about the extent of clients' right to refuse service.

(e) Social workers who provide services via electronic media (such as computer, telephone, radio, and television) should inform recipients of the limitations and risks associated with such services.

(f) Social workers should obtain clients' informed consent before audiotaping or videotaping clients or permitting observation of services to clients by a third party.

1.04 Competence

(a) Social workers should provide services and represent themselves as competent only within the boundaries of their education, training, license, certification, consultation received, supervised experience, or other relevant professional experience.

(b) Social workers should provide services in substantive areas or use intervention techniques or approaches that are new to them only after engaging in appropriate study, training, consultation, and supervision from people who are competent in those interventions or techniques.

(c) When generally recognized standards do not exist with respect to an emerging area of practice, social workers should exercise careful judgment and take responsible steps (including appropriate education, research, training, consultation, and supervision) to ensure the competence of their work and to protect clients from harm.

1.05 Cultural Competence and Social Diversity

(a) Social workers should understand culture and its function in human behavior and society, recognizing the strengths that exist in all cultures.

(b) Social workers should have a knowledge base of their clients' cultures and be able to demonstrate competence in the provision of services that are sensitive to clients' cultures and to differences among people and cultural groups.

(c) Social workers should obtain education about and seek to understand the nature of social diversity and oppression with respect to race, ethnicity, national origin, color, sex, sexual orientation, age, marital status, political belief, religion, and mental or physical disability.

1.06 Conflicts of Interest

(a) Social workers should be alert to and avoid conflicts of interest that interfere with the exercise of professional discretion and impartial judgment. Social workers should inform clients when a real or potential conflict of interest arises and take reasonable steps to resolve the issue in a manner that makes the clients' interests primary and protects clients' interests to the greatest extent possible. In some cases, protecting clients' interests may require termination of the professional relationship with proper referral of the client.

(b) Social workers should not take unfair advantage of any professional relationship or exploit others to further their personal, religious, political, or business interests.

(c) Social workers should not engage in dual or multiple relationships with clients or former clients in which there is a risk of exploitation or potential harm to the client. In instances when dual or multiple relationships are unavoidable, social workers should take steps to protect clients and are responsible for setting clear, appropriate, and culturally sensitive boundaries. (Dual or multiple relationships occur when social workers relate to clients in more than one relationship, whether professional,

(continued)

Table 12.2 (*continued*)

social, or business. Dual or multiple relationships can occur simultaneously or consecutively.)

(d) When social workers provide services to two or more people who have
a relationship with each other (for example, couples, family members),
social workers should clarify with all parties which individuals will be
considered clients and the nature of social workers' professional obligations to the various individuals who are receiving services. Social workers
who anticipate a conflict of interest among the individuals receiving
services or who anticipate having to perform in potentially conflicting
roles (for example, when a social worker is asked to testify in a child
custody dispute or divorce proceedings involving clients) should clarify
their role with the parties involved and take appropriate action to
minimize any conflict of interest.

1.07 Privacy and Confidentiality

(a) Social workers should respect clients' right to privacy. Social workers
should not solicit private information from clients unless it is essential to providing services or conducting social work evaluation or
research. Once private information is shared, standards of confidentiality apply.

(b) Social workers may disclose confidential information when appropriate
with valid consent from a client or a person legally authorized to consent
on behalf of a client.

(c) Social workers should protect the confidentiality of all information
obtained in the course of professional service, except for compelling
professional reasons. The general expectation that social workers will
keep information confidential does not apply when disclosure is necessary to prevent serious, foreseeable, and imminent harm to a client or
other identifiable person. In all instances, social workers should disclose
the least amount of confidential information necessary to achieve the
desired purpose; only information that is directly relevant to the purpose
for which the disclosure is made should be revealed.

(d) Social workers should inform clients, to the extent possible, about the
disclosure of confidential information and the potential consequences,
when feasible before the disclosure is made. This applies whether social
workers disclose confidential information on the basis of a legal
requirement or client consent.

(e) Social workers should discuss with clients and other interested parties
the nature of confidentiality and limitations of clients' right to confidentiality. Social workers should review with clients circumstances where
confidential information may be requested and where disclosure of
confidential information may be legally required. This discussion should
occur as soon as possible in the social worker–client relationship and as
needed throughout the course of the relationship.

(f) When social workers provide counseling services to families, couples,
or groups, social workers should seek agreement among the parties
involved concerning each individual's right to confidentiality and
obligation to preserve the confidentiality of information shared by
others. Social workers should inform participants in family, couples, or
group counseling that social workers cannot guarantee that all
participants will honor such agreements.

(g) Social workers should inform clients involved in family, couples, marital,
or group counseling of the social worker's, employer's, and agency's
policy concerning the social worker's disclosure of confidential information among the parties involved in the counseling.

(h) Social workers should not disclose confidential information to third-party
payers unless clients have authorized such disclosure.

(i) Social workers should not discuss confidential information in any setting unless privacy can be ensured. Social workers should not discuss confidential information in public or semipublic areas such as hallways, waiting rooms, elevators, and restaurants.

(j) Social workers should protect the confidentiality of clients during legal proceedings to the extent permitted by law. When a court of law or other legally authorized body orders social workers to disclose confidential or privileged information without a client's consent and such disclosure could cause harm to the client, social workers should request that the court withdraw the order or limit the order as narrowly as possible or maintain the records under seal, unavailable for public inspection.

(k) Social workers should protect the confidentiality of clients when responding to requests from members of the media.

(l) Social workers should protect the confidentiality of clients' written and electronic records and other sensitive information. Social workers should take reasonable steps to ensure that clients' records are stored in a secure location and that clients' records are not available to others who are not authorized to have access.

(m) Social workers should take precautions to ensure and maintain the confidentiality of information transmitted to other parties through the use of computers, electronic mail, facsimile machines, telephones and telephone answering machines, and other electronic or computer technology. Disclosure of identifying information should be avoided whenever possible.

(n) Social workers should transfer or dispose of clients' records in a manner that protects clients' confidentiality and is consistent with state statutes governing records and social work licensure.

(o) Social workers should take reasonable precautions to protect client confidentiality in the event of the social worker's termination of practice, incapacitation, or death.

(p) Social workers should not disclose identifying information when discussing clients for teaching or training purposes unless the client has consented to disclosure of confidential information.

(q) Social workers should not disclose identifying information when discussing clients with consultants unless the client has consented to disclosure of confidential information or there is a compelling need for such disclosure.

(r) Social workers should protect the confidentiality of deceased clients consistent with the preceding standards.

1.08 Access to Records

(a) Social workers should provide clients with reasonable access to records concerning the clients. Social workers who are concerned that clients' access to their records could cause serious misunderstanding or harm to the client should provide assistance in interpreting the records and consultation with the client regarding the records. Social workers should limit clients' access to their records, or portions of their records, only in exceptional circumstances when there is compelling evidence that such access would cause serious harm to the client. Both clients' requests and the rationale for withholding some or all of the record should be documented in clients' files.

(b) When providing clients with access to their records, social workers should take steps to protect the confidentiality of other individuals identified or discussed in such records.

1.09 Sexual Relationships

(a) Social workers should under no circumstances engage in sexual activities or sexual contact with current clients, whether such contact is consensual or forced.

(continued)

Table 12.2 (*continued*)

(b) Social workers should not engage in sexual activities or sexual contact with clients' relatives or other individuals with whom clients maintain a close personal relationship when there is a risk of exploitation or potential harm to the client. Sexual activity or sexual contact with clients' relatives or other individuals with whom clients maintain a personal relationship has the potential to be harmful to the client and may make it difficult for the social worker and client to maintain appropriate professional boundaries. Social workers—not their clients, their clients' relatives, or other individuals with whom the client maintains a personal relationship—assume the full burden for setting clear, appropriate, and culturally sensitive boundaries.

(c) Social workers should not engage in sexual activities or sexual contact with former clients because of the potential for harm to the client. If social workers engage in conduct contrary to this prohibition or claim that an exception to this prohibition is warranted because of extraordinary circumstances, it is social workers—not their clients—who assume the full burden of demonstrating that the former client has not been exploited, coerced, or manipulated, intentionally or unintentionally.

(d) Social workers should not provide clinical services to individuals with whom they have had a prior sexual relationship. Providing clinical services to a former sexual partner has the potential to be harmful to the individual and is likely to make it difficult for the social worker and individual to maintain appropriate professional boundaries.

1.10 Physical Contact

Social workers should not engage in physical contact with clients when there is a possibility of psychological harm to the client as a result of the contact (such as cradling or caressing clients). Social workers who engage in appropriate physical contact with clients are responsible for setting clear, appropriate, and culturally sensitive boundaries that govern such physical contact.

1.11 Sexual Harassment

Social workers should not sexually harass clients. Sexual harassment includes sexual advances, sexual solicitation, requests for sexual favors, and other verbal or physical conduct of a sexual nature.

1.12 Derogatory Language

Social workers should not use derogatory language in their written or verbal communications to or about clients. Social workers should use accurate and respectful language in all communications to and about clients.

1.13 Payment for Services

(a) When setting fees, social workers should ensure that the fees are fair, reasonable, and commensurate with the services performed. Consideration should be given to clients' ability to pay.

(b) Social workers should avoid accepting goods or services from clients as payment for professional services. Bartering arrangements, particularly involving services, create the potential for conflicts of interest, exploitation, and inappropriate boundaries in social workers' relationships with clients. Social workers should explore and may participate in bartering only in very limited circumstances when it can be demonstrated that such arrangements are an accepted practice among professionals in the local community, considered to be essential for the provision of services, negotiated without coercion, and entered into at the client's initiative and with the client's informed consent. Social workers who accept goods or services from clients as payment for professional services assume the full burden of demonstrating that this arrangement will not be detrimental to the client or the professional relationship.

(c) Social workers should not solicit a private fee or other remuneration for providing services to clients who are entitled to such available services through the social workers' employer or agency.

1.14 Clients Who Lack Decision-Making Capacity

When social workers act on behalf of clients who lack the capacity to make informed decisions, social workers should take reasonable steps to safeguard the interests and rights of those clients.

1.15 Interruption of Services

Social workers should make reasonable efforts to ensure continuity of services in the event that services are interrupted by factors such as unavailability, relocation, illness, disability, or death.

1.16 Termination of Services

(a) Social workers should terminate services to clients and professional relationships with them when such services and relationships are no longer required or no longer serve the clients' needs or interests.

(b) Social workers should take reasonable steps to avoid abandoning clients who are still in need of services. Social workers should withdraw services precipitously only under unusual circumstances, giving careful consideration to all factors in the situation and taking care to minimize possible adverse effects. Social workers should assist in making appropriate arrangements for continuation of services when necessary.

(c) Social workers in fee-for-service settings may terminate services to clients who are not paying an overdue balance if the financial contractual arrangements have been made clear to the client, if the client does not pose an imminent danger to self or others, and if the clinical and other consequences of the current nonpayment have been addressed and discussed with the client.

(d) Social workers should not terminate services to pursue a social, financial, or sexual relationship with a client.

(e) Social workers who anticipate the termination or interruption of services to clients should notify clients promptly and seek the transfer, referral, or continuation of services in relation to the clients' needs and preferences.

(f) Social workers who are leaving an employment setting should inform clients of appropriate options for the continuation of services and of the benefits and risks of the options.

2. SOCIAL WORKERS' ETHICAL RESPONSIBILITIES TO COLLEAGUES

2.01 Respect

(a) Social workers should treat colleagues with respect and should represent accurately and fairly the qualifications, views, and obligations of colleagues.

(b) Social workers should avoid unwarranted negative criticism of colleagues in communications with clients or with other professionals. Unwarranted negative criticism may include demeaning comments that refer to colleagues' level of competence or to individuals' attributes such as race, ethnicity, national origin, color, sex, sexual orientation, age, marital status, political belief, religion, and mental or physical disability.

(c) Social workers should cooperate with social work colleagues and with colleagues of other professions when such cooperation serves the well-being of clients.

2.02 Confidentiality

Social workers should respect confidential information shared by colleagues in the course of their professional relationships and transactions. Social workers

(continued)

Table 12.2 (*continued*)

should ensure that such colleagues understand social workers' obligation to respect confidentiality and any exceptions related to it.

2.03 Interdisciplinary Collaboration

(a) Social workers who are members of an interdisciplinary team should participate in and contribute to decisions that affect the well-being of clients by drawing on the perspectives, values, and experiences of the social work profession. Professional and ethical obligations of the interdisciplinary team as a whole and of its individual members should be clearly established.

(b) Social workers for whom a team decision raises ethical concerns should attempt to resolve the disagreement through appropriate channels. If the disagreement cannot be resolved, social workers should pursue other avenues to address their concerns consistent with client well-being.

2.04 Disputes Involving Colleagues

(a) Social workers should not take advantage of a dispute between a colleague and an employer to obtain a position or otherwise advance the social workers' own interests.

(b) Social workers should not exploit clients in disputes with colleagues or engage clients in any inappropriate discussion of conflicts between social workers and their colleagues.

2.05 Consultation

(a) Social workers should seek the advice and counsel of colleagues whenever such consultation is in the best interests of clients.

(b) Social workers should keep themselves informed about colleagues' areas of expertise and competencies. Social workers should seek consultation only from colleagues who have demonstrated knowledge, expertise, and competence related to the subject of the consultation.

(c) When consulting with colleagues about clients, social workers should disclose the least amount of information necessary to achieve the purposes of the consultation.

2.06 Referral for Services

(a) Social workers should refer clients to other professionals when the other professionals' specialized knowledge or expertise is needed to serve clients fully or when social workers believe that they are not being effective or making reasonable progress with clients and that additional service is required.

(b) Social workers who refer clients to other professionals should take appropriate steps to facilitate an orderly transfer of responsibility. Social workers who refer clients to other professionals should disclose, with clients' consent, all pertinent information to the new service providers.

(c) Social workers are prohibited from giving or receiving payment for a referral when no professional service is provided by the referring social worker.

2.07 Sexual Relationships

(a) Social workers who function as supervisors or educators should not engage in sexual activities or contact with supervisees, students, trainees, or other colleagues over whom they exercise professional authority.

(b) Social workers should avoid engaging in sexual relationships with colleagues when there is potential for a conflict of interest. Social workers who become involved in, or anticipate becoming involved in, a sexual relationship with a colleague have a duty to transfer professional responsibilities, when necessary, to avoid a conflict of interest.

2.08 Sexual Harassment

Social workers should not sexually harass supervisees, students, trainees, or colleagues. Sexual harassment includes sexual advances, sexual solicitation, requests for sexual favors, and other verbal or physical conduct of a sexual nature.

2.09 Impairment of Colleagues

(a) Social workers who have direct knowledge of a social work colleague's impairment that is due to personal problems, psychosocial distress, substance abuse, or mental health difficulties and that interferes with practice effectiveness should consult with that colleague when feasible and assist the colleague in taking remedial action.

(b) Social workers who believe that a social work colleague's impairment interferes with practice effectiveness and that the colleague has not taken adequate steps to address the impairment should take action through appropriate channels established by employers, agencies, NASW, licensing and regulatory bodies, and other professional organizations.

2.10 Incompetence of Colleagues

(a) Social workers who have direct knowledge of a social work colleague's incompetence should consult with that colleague when feasible and assist the colleague in taking remedial action.

(b) Social workers who believe that a social work colleague is incompetent and has not taken adequate steps to address the incompetence should take action through appropriate channels established by employers, agencies, NASW, licensing and regulatory bodies, and other professional organizations.

2.11 Unethical Conduct of Colleagues

(a) Social workers should take adequate measures to discourage, prevent, expose, and correct the unethical conduct of colleagues.

(b) Social workers should be knowledgeable about established policies and procedures for handling concerns about colleagues' unethical behavior. Social workers should be familiar with national, state, and local procedures for handling ethics complaints. These include policies and procedures created by NASW, licensing and regulatory bodies, employers, agencies, and other professional organizations.

(c) Social workers who believe that a colleague has acted unethically should seek resolution by discussing their concerns with the colleague when feasible and when such discussion is likely to be productive.

(d) When necessary, social workers who believe that a colleague has acted unethically should take action through appropriate formal channels (such as contacting a state licensing board or regulatory body, an NASW committee on inquiry, or other professional ethics committees).

(e) Social workers should defend and assist colleagues who are unjustly charged with unethical conduct.

3. **SOCIAL WORKERS' ETHICAL RESPONSIBILITIES IN PRACTICE SETTINGS**

3.01 Supervision and Consultation

(a) Social workers who provide supervision or consultation should have the necessary knowledge and skill to supervise or consult appropriately and should do so only within their areas of knowledge and competence.

(b) Social workers who provide supervision or consultation are responsible for setting clear, appropriate, and culturally sensitive boundaries.

(c) Social workers should not engage in any dual or multiple relationships with supervisees in which there is a risk of exploitation of or potential harm to the supervisee.

(continued)

Table 12.2 (*continued*)

(d) Social workers who provide supervision should evaluate supervisees' performance in a manner that is fair and respectful.

3.02 Education and Training

(a) Social workers who function as educators, field instructors for students, or trainers should provide instruction only within their areas of knowledge and competence and should provide instruction based on the most current information and knowledge available in the profession.

(b) Social workers who function as educators or field instructors for students should evaluate students' performance in a manner that is fair and respectful.

(c) Social workers who function as educators or field instructors for students should take reasonable steps to ensure that clients are routinely informed when services are being provided by students.

(d) Social workers who function as educators or field instructors for students should not engage in any dual or multiple relationships with students in which there is a risk of exploitation or potential harm to the student. Social work educators and field instructors are responsible for setting clear, appropriate, and culturally sensitive boundaries.

3.03 Performance Evaluation

Social workers who have responsibility for evaluating the performance of others should fulfill such responsibility in a fair and considerate manner and on the basis of clearly stated criteria.

3.04 Client Records

(a) Social workers should take reasonable steps to ensure that documentation in records is accurate and reflects the services provided.

(b) Social workers should include sufficient and timely documentation in records to facilitate the delivery of services and to ensure continuity of services provided to clients in the future.

(c) Social workers' documentation should protect clients' privacy to the extent that is possible and appropriate and should include only information that is directly relevant to the delivery of services.

(d) Social workers should store records following the termination of services to ensure reasonable future access. Records should be maintained for the number of years required by state statutes or relevant contracts.

3.05 Billing

Social workers should establish and maintain billing practices that accurately reflect the nature and extent of services provided and that identify who provided the service in the practice setting.

3.06 Client Transfer

(a) When an individual who is receiving services from another agency or colleague contacts a social worker for services, the social worker should carefully consider the client's needs before agreeing to provide services. To minimize possible confusion and conflict, social workers should discuss with potential clients the nature of the clients' current relationship with other service providers and the implications, including possible benefits or risks, of entering into a relationship with a new service provider.

(b) If a new client has been served by another agency or colleague, social workers should discuss with the client whether consultation with the previous service provider is in the client's best interest.

3.07 Administration

(a) Social work administrators should advocate within and outside their agencies for adequate resources to meet clients' needs.

(b) Social workers should advocate for resource allocation procedures that are open and fair. When not all clients' needs can be met, an allocation procedure should be developed that is nondiscriminatory and based on appropriate and consistently applied principles.

(c) Social workers who are administrators should take reasonable steps to ensure that adequate agency or organizational resources are available to provide appropriate staff supervision.

(d) Social work administrators should take reasonable steps to ensure that the working environment for which they are responsible is consistent with and encourages compliance with the NASW *Code of Ethics.* Social work administrators should take reasonable steps to eliminate any conditions in their organizations that violate, interfere with, or discourage compliance with the Code.

3.08 Continuing Education and Staff Development

Social work administrators and supervisors should take reasonable steps to provide or arrange for continuing education and staff development for all staff for whom they are responsible. Continuing education and staff development should address current knowledge and emerging developments related to social work practice and ethics.

3.09 Commitments to Employers

(a) Social workers generally should adhere to commitments made to employers and employing organizations.

(b) Social workers should work to improve employing agencies' policies and procedures and the efficiency and effectiveness of their services.

(c) Social workers should take reasonable steps to ensure that employers are aware of social workers' ethical obligations as set forth in the NASW *Code of Ethics* and of the implications of those obligations for social work practice.

(d) Social workers should not allow an employing organization's policies, procedures, regulations, or administrative orders to interfere with their ethical practice of social work. Social workers should take reasonable steps to ensure that their employing organizations' practices are consistent with the NASW *Code of Ethics.*

(e) Social workers should act to prevent and eliminate discrimination in the employing organization's work assignments and in its employment policies and practices.

(f) Social workers should accept employment or arrange student field placements only in organizations that exercise fair personnel practices.

(g) Social workers should be diligent stewards of the resources of their employing organizations, wisely conserving funds where appropriate and never misappropriating funds or using them for unintended purposes.

3.10 Labor–Management Disputes

(a) Social workers may engage in organized action, including the formation of and participation in labor unions, to improve services to clients and working conditions.

(b) The actions of social workers who are involved in labor-management disputes, job actions, or labor strikes should be guided by the profession's values, ethical principles, and ethical standards. Reasonable differences of opinion exist among social workers concerning their primary obligation as professionals during an actual or threatened labor strike or job action. Social workers should carefully examine relevant issues and their possible impact on clients before deciding on a course of action.

(continued)

Table 12.2 (*continued*)

4. **SOCIAL WORKERS' ETHICAL RESPONSIBILITIES AS PROFESSIONALS**

   4.01 Competence

      (a) Social workers should accept responsibility or employment only on the basis of existing competence or the intention to acquire the necessary competence.

      (b) Social workers should strive to become and remain proficient in professional practice and the performance of professional functions. Social workers should critically examine and keep current with emerging knowledge relevant to social work. Social workers should routinely review the professional literature and participate in continuing education relevant to social work practice and social work ethics.

      (c) Social workers should base practice on recognized knowledge, including empirically based knowledge, relevant to social work and social work ethics.

   4.02 Discrimination

     Social workers should not practice, condone, facilitate, or collaborate with any form of discrimination on the basis of race, ethnicity, national origin, color, sex, sexual orientation, age, marital status, political belief, religion, or mental or physical disability.

   4.03 Private Conduct

     Social workers should not permit their private conduct to interfere with their ability to fulfill their professional responsibilities.

   4.04 Dishonesty, Fraud, and Deception

     Social workers should not participate in, condone, or be associated with dishonesty, fraud, or deception.

   4.05 Impairment

      (a) Social workers should not allow their own personal problems, psycho-social distress, legal problems, substance abuse, or mental health difficulties to interfere with their professional judgment and performance or to jeopardize the best interests of people for whom they have a professional responsibility.

      (b) Social workers whose personal problems, psychosocial distress, legal problems, substance abuse, or mental health difficulties interfere with their professional judgment and performance should immediately seek consultation and take appropriate remedial action by seeking professional help, making adjustments in workload, terminating practice, or taking any other steps necessary to protect clients and others.

   4.06 Misrepresentation

      (a) Social workers should make clear distinctions between statements made and actions engaged in as a private individual and as a representative of the social work profession, a professional social work organization, or the social worker's employing agency.

      (b) Social workers who speak on behalf of professional social work organizations should accurately represent the official and authorized positions of the organizations.

      (c) Social workers should ensure that their representations to clients, agencies, and the public of professional qualifications, credentials, education, competence, affiliations, services provided, or results to be achieved are accurate. Social workers should claim only those relevant professional credentials they actually possess and take steps to correct any inaccuracies or misrepresentations of their credentials by others.

4.07 Solicitations

(a) Social workers should not engage in uninvited solicitation of potential clients who, because of their circumstances, are vulnerable to undue influence, manipulation, or coercion.

(b) Social workers should not engage in solicitation of testimonial endorsements (including solicitation of consent to use a client's prior statement as a testimonial endorsement) from current clients or from other people who, because of their particular circumstances, are vulnerable to undue influence.

4.08 Acknowledging Credit

(a) Social workers should take responsibility and credit, including authorship credit, only for work they have actually performed and to which they have contributed.

(b) Social workers should honestly acknowledge the work of and the contributions made by others.

5. SOCIAL WORKERS' ETHICAL RESPONSIBILITIES TO THE SOCIAL WORK PROFESSION

5.01 Integrity of the Profession

(a) Social workers should work toward the maintenance and promotion of high standards of practice.

(b) Social workers should uphold and advance the values, ethics, knowledge, and mission of the profession. Social workers should protect, enhance, and improve the integrity of the profession through appropriate study and research, active discussion, and responsible criticism of the profession.

(c) Social workers should contribute time and professional expertise to activities that promote respect for the value, integrity, and competence of the social work profession. These activities may include teaching, research, consultation, service, legislative testimony, presentations in the community, and participation in their professional organizations.

(d) Social workers should contribute to the knowledge base of social work and share with colleagues their knowledge related to practice, research, and ethics. Social workers should seek to contribute to the profession's literature and to share their knowledge at professional meetings and conferences.

(e) Social workers should act to prevent the unauthorized and unqualified practice of social work.

5.02 Evaluation and Research

(a) Social workers should monitor and evaluate policies, the implementation of programs, and practice interventions.

(b) Social workers should promote and facilitate evaluation and research to contribute to the development of knowledge.

(c) Social workers should critically examine and keep current with emerging knowledge relevant to social work and fully use evaluation and research evidence in their professional practice.

(d) Social workers engaged in evaluation or research should carefully consider possible consequences and should follow guidelines developed for the protection of evaluation and research participants. Appropriate institutional review boards should be consulted.

(e) Social workers engaged in evaluation or research should obtain voluntary and written informed consent from participants, when appropriate, without any implied or actual deprivation or penalty for refusal to participate; without undue inducement to participate; and

(*continued*)

Table 12.2 (*continued*)

with due regard for participants' well-being, privacy, and dignity. Informed consent should include information about the nature, extent, and duration of the participation requested and disclosure of the risks and benefits of participation in the research.

(f) When evaluation or research participants are incapable of giving informed consent, social workers should provide an appropriate explanation to the participants, obtain the participants' assent to the extent they are able, and obtain written consent from an appropriate proxy.

(g) Social workers should never design or conduct evaluation or research that does not use consent procedures, such as certain forms of naturalistic observation and archival research, unless rigorous and responsible review of the research has found it to be justified because of its prospective scientific, educational, or applied value and unless equally effective alternative procedures that do not involve waiver of consent are not feasible.

(h) Social workers should inform participants of their right to withdraw from evaluation and research at any time without penalty.

(i) Social workers should take appropriate steps to ensure that participants in evaluation and research have access to appropriate supportive services.

(j) Social workers engaged in evaluation or research should protect participants from unwarranted physical or mental distress, harm, danger, or deprivation.

(k) Social workers engaged in the evaluation of services should discuss collected information only for professional purposes and only with people professionally concerned with this information.

(l) Social workers engaged in evaluation or research should ensure the anonymity or confidentiality of participants and of the data obtained from them. Social workers should inform participants of any limits of confidentiality, the measures that will be taken to ensure confidentiality, and when any records containing research data will be destroyed.

(m) Social workers who report evaluation and research results should protect participants' confidentiality by omitting identifying information unless proper consent has been obtained authorizing disclosure.

(n) Social workers should report evaluation and research findings accurately. They should not fabricate or falsify results and should take steps to correct any errors later found in published data using standard publication methods.

(o) Social workers engaged in evaluation or research should be alert to and avoid conflicts of interest and dual relationships with participants, should inform participants when a real or potential conflict of interest arises, and should take steps to resolve the issue in a manner that makes participants' interests primary.

(p) Social workers should educate themselves, their students, and their colleagues about responsible research practices.

6. **SOCIAL WORKERS' ETHICAL RESPONSIBILITIES TO THE BROADER SOCIETY**

   6.01 Social Welfare

   Social workers should promote the general welfare of society, from local to global levels, and the development of people, their communities, and their environments. Social workers should advocate for living conditions conducive to the fulfillment of basic human needs and should promote social, economic, political, and cultural values and institutions that are compatible with the realization of social justice.

6.02 Public Participation

Social workers should facilitate informed participation by the public in shaping social policies and institutions.

6.03 Public Emergencies

Social workers should provide appropriate professional services in public emergencies to the greatest extent possible.

6.04 Social and Political Action

(a) Social workers should engage in social and political action that seeks to ensure that all people have equal access to the resources, employment, services, and opportunities they require to meet their basic human needs and to develop fully. Social workers should be aware of the impact of the political arena on practice and should advocate for changes in policy and legislation to improve social conditions in order to meet basic human needs and promote social justice.

(b) Social workers should act to expand choice and opportunity for all people, with special regard for vulnerable, disadvantaged, oppressed, and exploited people and groups.

(c) Social workers should promote conditions that encourage respect for cultural and social diversity within the United States and globally. Social workers should promote policies and practices that demonstrate respect for difference, support the expansion of cultural knowledge and resources, advocate for programs and institutions that demonstrate cultural competence, and promote policies that safeguard the rights of and confirm equity and social justice for all people.

(d) Social workers should act to prevent and eliminate domination of, exploitation of, and discrimination against any person, group, or class on the basis of race, ethnicity, national origin, color, sex, sexual orientation, age, marital status, political belief, religion, or mental or physical disability.

SOURCE: Adapted with permission from *Code of Ethics* (1996), pp. 7–27. Copyright 1996, National Association of Social Workers, Inc., NASW *Code of Ethics.*

SOCIAL JUSTICE

Of the social work values presented, social justice is particularly crucial to macro practice from a strengths perspective. Chapter 5 explores this topic, but it seems important enough to consider social justice as it relates to professional values and ethics. In this discussion, social justice should be considered as both a goal and a process.

Justice is defined as "fairness in relationships between people as these relate to the possession and/or acquisition of resources" (Beverly & McSweeney, 1987, p. 6). Because social workers traditionally work with consumers who have limited access to resources and are faced with prejudice and discrimination the challenge is to replace injustice with justice. Therefore, the goal of **social justice** is full and equal participation in society that is equitable whereby all members feel physically and psychology secure.

Historically, the most common criteria for distributing limited resources have been the principles of equality, need, contribution, and compensation. These principles at times have been interpreted to mean actual equality, with all recipients acquiring equal shares of the distributed resources, such as a social worker's time or public funds. In some instances the principle of equality has been interpreted to mean merely equality of opportunity—for example, that resources or services are made available to all on a first-come, first-served basis.

Although some philosophers have argued that the principles of equality should guide the distribution of limited resources, others believe that the extent of one's current need should be the primary determinant or that there is an obligation to distribute resources based on the extent of one past's contributions. Controversy about which criteria should be used to distribute scarce resources properly has persisted for centuries. Although it is unlikely that this controversy will be settled easily, if at all, it is important for social workers to be sensitive to it.

Principles of social justice in social work practice reflect philosophical frameworks. For example, Walz and Ritchie (2000) suggest that Mahatma Gandhi's theory of nonviolent social change and the pursuit of social justice complement social work practice. Gandhi's methods of social service and social action combine micro and macro practice, "something social work has struggled to synthesize. Gandhi achieved this integration by reducing his ethical theory to two primary foci: service to insure social justice" (pp. 213–214).

Gandhian theory highlights social justice as fairness to people, with a particular focus on those people who are disadvantaged. In a similar manner Rawls, in his seminal work, *A Theory of Justice,* argues that we can best construct our moral vision of a good or a just society by trying to imagine its internal arrangement from behind a "veil of ignorance," which obscures our own current status (such as income) or personal access to opportunities (Rawls, 1971, p. 85). Rawls concludes that if people are aware of their current status they are likely to want to maintain the same societal structure even if it means that inequalities will continue (Jansson, 1998, p. 37). Building on the work of Rawls, it can be said that the process of social justice involves using the professional self as an instrument to challenge inequalities and support social reform as part of our professional role.

Embedded in this discussion of social justice is the concept of **professional power.** People depend on professional services to help them gain control over their lives during times of trouble and distress. The power to intervene carries with it unique responsibilities to society that are not connected to other kinds of work. The ethics of professional practice are directly related to the use and abuse of power. According to Manning (1997), every decision and action taken by social workers communicates a message to society about what social work values and, indirectly, what society values. The social work pioneer, Charlotte Towle (1969) discussed the moral function of social work as social conscience—a sense of what is right or good. Thus, Towle conceptualized the profession as the "conscience of the community . . . using head, heart, and hand" to do social work (1969, p. 14).

Similarly, Jennings, Callahan, and Wolf (1987) argue that social work as a profession has a public duty to make the invisible visible—to show the underside of a system that seems to work adequately. The foundation of this endeavor is the values and purpose of the profession that direct ethical issues.

C. Wright Mills (1956) suggested that there are **power elites** who control the needed resources in societies. Further, these power elites play instrumental

© Thomson Higher Education/Heinle Image Bank.

roles in three primary institutions: the government, the military, and corporations. Wright (1956) claims that these hierarchies of power are the key to understanding modern industrial societies. The sheer power accumulated by the power elites dictates not only that their interests will be served over the good of society but also that interests of the elites become the interests of common people. For example, if the power elite concludes that tax reductions will be of benefit to them, taxes will be reduced even at the cost of increased national debt. Mills states that it is common experiences and role expectations that produce people of similar character and values.

According to Mills, power in U.S. society is found at two levels. The vast majority of people are at the bottom of society's hierarchy. As might be expected, people at this level are largely economically dependent and often economically and politically exploited. For instance, they are employed in positions with little chance of advancement and have few opportunities to gain economic ground even with a lifetime of diligent work. In other words, this group of people holds little power.

Between the masses and the power elite Mills describes a middle level of power comprising local leaders and special-interest groups (1956). Though vocal, these groups have minimal impact on the real source of society's power. The nation's politicians and elected officials fall into this group, according to

Mills (1956). The U.S. Congress and political parties are a reflection of this middle-level power. Issues are debated and policies are approved, but the power elites maintain their control. As a result, it should not be surprising that many people have lost their faith in the political system to the point that they do not vote or follow political events. For all practical purposes, they are disenfranchised from the American system of governance.

To apply Mills's theory to current events, take some time to read a newspaper article that describes a policy debate or social issue. Assess who you think are the power elite, the politicians, and the general public. Then consider the following questions:

- How is the balance of power maintained?
- What could be done to shift the power base?
- What would be the intended consequences?
- What might be the unintended consequences?

OUTLOOK FOR MACRO PRACTICE

Social justice is important because many of the issues that confront our consumers, including poverty, unemployment, homelessness, hunger, inadequate health care, and unequal and inadequate education, exist due to injustices in the social, political, and economic systems (Segal, Gerdes, & Steiner, 2004, p. 99). Social workers engaged in macro practice, such as administration, policy analysis, and program development, who want to ensure social justice have sought to serve as advocates and to create and sustain empowering policies, programs, and services. By combining social work values and ethics in support of social justice, social work practices create a reinforcing environment that will:

- Identify the valued outcome for consumers in the public policy that directs and supports the program.
- Identify the values outcomes for consumers as described in the program design.
- Identify other values important to producing the desired consumer outcomes.
- Identify worker-directed values required to maintain staff morale and produce consumer outcomes.
- Anticipate value conflicts and assist staff to make decisions in light of these conflicts.
- Use as many vehicles as possible to communicate these values to consumers, staff, and other constituents (Rapp & Poertner, 1992, p. 178).

Use the following situation to consider change that extends beyond an individual or group of consumers. As you think about the change effort, list the policies, organizations, systems that will be affected by the change. What

Table 12.3 Characteristics of the Strengths Perspective in the Context of Social Justice

- Organizations and communities can learn and retain information.
- The role of the social worker is to transfer knowledge and skills useful to organizations and communities.
- Organizations and communities are the experts on their own experiences.
- Social workers facilitate the competencies of organizations and communities by transferring advocacy, mediation, and political skills.
- Intervention strategies help communities and organization perceive their conditions in a broader societal context and help connect individual matters to the environmental conditions.
- Organizations and communities gain from consciousness-raising activities associated with political power and economic growth and development.
- All organizations and communities deserve respect and acceptance for their strengths, including resilience.
- Collaboration, cooperation, and egalitarian partnerships strengthen the fiber of organizations and communities.
- Networks are crucial to the health of organizations and communities.
- Communities and organizations should emphasize cooperative and interdependent activities for the accomplishment of goals related to social justice.

SOURCE: Adapted with permission from Cox, E. O., & Parsons, R. J. (1994). *Empowerment-oriented social work practice with the elderly*. Pacific Grove, CA: Brooks/Cole Publishing, pp. 39, 94, 100–101.

interventions will you use to initiate the change effort? How does your work reflect the values and ethics of social work? What are the social justice issues involved?

You are the director of a social work department in a rural community hospital. As part of your work, you review the reason for admissions to the hospital. It has come to your attention that there is an increasing number of alcohol-related injuries and accidents associated with teens and people well over the age of sixty-five years. There are no substance abuse programs in the tri-county region. However, approximately 110 miles from your hospital there is a prosperous city with a drug and alcohol treatment unit.

An environment that nurtures social justice will find social workers simultaneously involved in the personal, interpersonal, and political aspects of leadership and development (Gutierrez, Parsons, & Cox, 1998). In this way, macro practice entails public education as an integral element of interventions with strategies tailored to (1) political decision makers, (2) decision makers of foundations,

(3) other potential private funding sources, (4) the public at large, (5) consumer-supported action groups, and (6) ongoing staff and consumer education (Gutierrez et al., 1998, p. 176). Problem solving in this context is viewed as part of a sociopolitical movement. For instance, the director of a homeless shelter who is committed to social justice connects the problems of consumers to the larger political aspects of the nation's housing stock. Table 12.3 on page 275 defines other characteristics of practice that combines a strengths perspective with a social justice orientation. As is apparent, these characteristics require long-term communication, diligence, and education with consumers, staff, volunteers, and the general public.

A vital step for social workers is developing their own power on the personal level. This requires recognizing the power they already have. As individuals working in organizations and communities, social workers need to analyze their power in the workplace and strategize how to use any such power to rally around issues of social justice. A third step involves identifying allies in the organization or community and finding how social workers can work with these allies to meet common goals of the community and social change.

SUMMARY

Creating opportunities for practice that supports the values and ethics of social work and enhances social justice requires reflection and thought. How can social workers use their knowledge, power, and skills in working with consumers to effect change? It also requires optimism regarding human and social potential. As stated by Simon (1994), "only practitioners who believed deeply that people can change and that environments can be transformed have been able to work from an empowerment perspective in a sustained fashion" (p. 3). Social workers must maintain a positive focus not only on the strengths and possibilities that exist out in the world, but also on the strengths and possibilities of their profession.

Much of what was presented in this chapter addresses moral citizenship, the awareness, critical thinking, and social action that achieve social justice through the values and ethics of macro practice. In the words of Towle (1969; Manning, 1997) social workers must have the "courage to be as oneself" and to be relentless in their attempt to shape society and the distribution of resources according to the social consciousness of the profession.

A FEW KEY TERMS

values	social justice	power elites
ethics	professional power	

USING INFOTRAC®
COLLEGE EDITION AND INFOWRITE

InfoTrac College Edition

Every day, social workers make ethical decisions. Often these decisions are made quickly and with little consideration. Chapter 12 suggests that it is essential that social workers assess their values to ensure that their decision making reflects the core of social work: respect for the dignity and uniqueness of individuals and for consumer self-determination. Consider the following exercise as a method for doing just that:

1. Go to InfoTrac College Edition.

2. Under the Keyword Search, search for "social work ethics."

3. Select an article that describes the concept of a social work ethics audit.

4. Read the article.

5. Using InfoTrac College Edition's online resources and other articles linked to this subject, read about a current example of a social worker who acted in accordance with social work ethics. Then answer the following questions:

   a. What was the outcome of the social worker's actions?

   b. How would you have responded in the situation?

   c. Did the social work *Code of Ethics* provide you with a clear course of action? Why or why not?

   d. What was the relationship between the outcome and sense of social justice?

InfoWrite

Social work education curricula contain coursework on multiculturalism. For the most part, such material is treated as an area of knowledge and competence rather than a guiding belief or value. Let's examine your thoughts on this pertinent issue to practice.

1. Go to InfoTrac College Edition.

2. Under the Keyword Search, search for "social work ethics."

3. Select an article, such as the one by Robert Walker and Michele Staton, "Multiculturalism in Social Work Ethics," *Journal of Social Work Education, 36*(3), 449–462.

4. Read the article.

5. Go to InfoWrite.

6. Scroll to Critical Thinking.

7. Read under the bullet "Recognizing Ethnocentrism and Stereotypes."

8. Write a statement that argues for or against the repositioning of multiculturalism in the Code as a principle of ethical practice rather than a knowledge area.

CASE EXAMPLE: The Hiring of Paraprofessionals

Susan Milan is a social work supervisor in a child protection unit at the county cabinet for children and family services. She has eight social workers and four social work assistants under her authority. As caseloads have swelled, the agency has decided to hire additional protective service workers. The cabinet is currently experiencing a fiscal crunch, as the county has not passed new monies for services to children in five years. As a result, county administrators have approved the hiring of three new social work assistants in Susan's unit, but no additional social workers.

Susan, other professional social work administrators, and the agency's consumer council firmly believe that the new hires should be professional social workers. Asking paraprofessionals to assume professional positions and perform professional duties is inappropriate, irresponsible, a possible violation of state law, and arguably unethical. Susan and others fear the harmful consequences of such action for consumers. Susan worries that she will be held responsible for any incompetent actions of people under her supervision.

Susan has quickly entered into discussions with members of the consumer council, other supervisors, the unit social workers, members of her local chapter of the NASW, empathetic administrators at the agency, and a variety of others to assess and strategize about her personal power as well as the power of consumers and professionals. To date, most agree that the hiring of new paraprofessionals presents a huge liability issue for Susan, the organization, the county, and public officials.

THINKING CRITICALLY
ABOUT THE CASE EXAMPLE

1. Identify ways in which the misuse of paraprofessionals as substitutes for professionals is detrimental to consumers, the agency, and professionals. How could consumers and professionals work together to document and provide information to substantiate harmful consequences?

2. It is imperative to cite and validate information sources when posing ethical dilemmas involving social justice. For example, "caseloads have swelled" at Susan's agency. What does this mean with respect to the actual number of cases and the severity of issues in the people being served? What types of information would be important in documenting the need for additional professionals? Remember, this is a child protection agency.

3. This is a good case example for illustrating the role of power in decision making. Although administrators at the agency appear sympathetic concerning the staffing situation, it is crucial to identify who has the power to rectify the situation. Is there a "power elite" in the county that dictates decisions? How can the strengths of consumers, professionals, and concerned others be utilized to influence key decision makers? Given those in power, what types of information would be compelling?

REFLECTION EXERCISES

1. After a thorough reading and review of the NASW *Code of Ethics,* create in large print a succinct list of the principal values that you wish to uphold in macro-level social work practice. Post these tenets in an area within view of your workspace.

2. Identify a mechanism through which you can explore on a regular basis ethical and value-oriented questions and issues. This might be a subset of local NASW members or an interdisciplinary group of professionals at your organization. Consider holding brown-bag lunches or sponsoring monthly speakers as means of organizing forums. Examine the participation of consumers.

3. How are the NASW and your identity as a professional sources of strength in macro social work practice? Given the current political climate, identify three ways (e.g., information, support, guidance) in which the NASW can strengthen your practice.

SUGGESTED READINGS

Conrad, A. P. (1989). Developing an ethics review process in a social service agency. *Social Thought, 15* (3/4), 102–115.

Joseph, M. V. (1989). Social work ethics: Historical and contemporary perspectives. *Social Thought, 15*(3/4), 4–17.

Levy, C. S. (1972). The context of social work ethics. *Social Work, 17*(2), 95–101.

Reamer, F. G. (1998). The evaluation of social work ethics, *Social Work, 43*(6), 488–506.

REFERENCES

Abramson, M. (1984). Ethical issues in social work practice with dying persons. In L. H. Suszchi & M. Abramson (Eds.), *Social work and terminal care.* New York: Praeger.

Beverly, D. P., & McSweeney, E. A. (1987). *Social welfare and social justice.* Englewood Cliffs, NJ: Prentice Hall.

Brueggemann, W. G. (1996). *The practice of macro social work.* Chicago: Nelson-Hall.

Butrym, Z. (1976). *The nature of social work.* London: Macmillan.

Compton, B. R., & Galaway, B. (1979). *Social work processes.* Homewood, IL: Dorsey.

Cox, E. O., & Parsons, R. J. (1994). *Empowerment-oriented social work practice with the elderly.* Pacific Grove, CA: Brooks/Cole.

Croxton, T., & Jayaratne, S. (1999). The code of ethics and the future. *Journal of Social Work Education, 35*(1), 2–4.

Croxton-Smith, C. (1965). Professional ethics—III. *The Account, 153*(4731), 240–247.

Elliott, L. J. (1931). *Social work ethics.* New York: American Association of Social Workers.

Goodpaster, K. (1997). The concept of corporate responsibility. *Journal of Business Ethics, 2,* 1–22.

Gutierrez, L. M., Parsons, R. J., & Cox, E. O. (1998). *Empowerment in social work practice: A sourcebook.* Pacific Grove, CA: Brooks/Cole.

Hepworth, D. H., & Larsen, J. A. (1982). *Direct social work practice: Theory and skills.* Homewood, IL: Dorsey.

Hugman, R., & Smith, D. (1995). *Ethical issues in social work.* London: Routledge.

Jansson, B. S. (1998). *Becoming an effective policy advocate.* Pacific Grove, CA: Brooks/Cole.

Jennings, P., Callahan, D.. & Wolf, S. (1987). The public duties of the profession. *Hastings Center Report, 17*(Suppl.), 1–20.

Johnson, A. (1955). Educating professional social workers for ethical practice. *Social Work Review, 29*(2), 125–136.

Levy, C. (1993*). Social work ethics on the line.* New York: Haworth Press.

Lewis, H. (1984). Ethical assessment. In *Social Casework,* pp. 203–211.

Lewis, J. A., Lewis, M. D., Packard, T., & Soufflée, F. (2001). *Management of human service programs* (3rd ed.). Belmont, CA: Wadsworth.

Loewenberg, F. M., & Dolgoff, R. (1992). *Ethical decisions for social work practice* (4th ed.). Itasca, IL: F. E. Peacock.

———. (1995). Guides to ethical decisions. In J. Tropman, J. Erlich, & J. Rothman (Eds.), *Tactics and techniques of community intervention* (3rd ed.). Itasca, IL: F. E. Peacock.

Manning, S. S. (1997). The social worker as moral citizen: Ethics in action. *Social Work, 42*(3), 223–230.

Mills, C. W. (1956). *The power elite.* New York: Oxford University Press.

National Association of Social Workers. (1996). *Code of ethics.* Washington, DC: NASW Press.

Perlman, H. H. (1976). Self-determination: Reality or illusion? *Social Service Review, 39,* 41–22.

Pilsecker, C. (1978). Values: A problem for everyone. *Social Work* (January), 54–57.

Rapp, C. A., & Poertner, C. A. (1992). *Social administration: A client-centered approach.* New York: Longman.

Rawls, J. (1971). *A theory of justice.* Cambridge, MA: Harvard University Press.

Reamer, F. G. (1983). Ethical dilemmas in social work practice. *Social Work,* January–February, pp. 31–35.

———. (1990). *Ethical decisions in social work practice: A guide for social workers* (2nd ed.). New York: Columbia University Press.

———. (1998). The evaluation of social work ethics. *Social Work, 42*(6), 488–500.

Reid, P. N., & Popple, P. R. (1992). *The moral purposes of social work.* Chicago: Nelson-Hall.

Segal, E. A., Gerdes, K. E., & Steiner, S. (2004). *Social work: An introduction to the profession.* Pacific Grove, CA: Brooks/Cole.

Simon, B. L. (1994). *The empowerment tradition in American social work.* New York: Columbia University Press.

Towle, C. (1969). Social work: Cause and function. In H. Perlman (Ed.), *Helping: Charlotte Towle on social work and social case work.* Chicago: University of Chicago Press.

Walz, T., & Ritchie, H. (2000). Gandhian principles in social work practice: Ethics revisited. *Social Work, 45*(3), 213–222.

Index